MEMOIRS OF

A GREAT DETECTIVE

Photograph by *George Prince, Washington*

JOHN WILSON MURRAY

MEMOIRS OF A GREAT DETECTIVE

INCIDENTS IN THE LIFE OF

John Wilson Murray

A TOTEM BOOK
TORONTO

First published 1904 by William Heinemann Ltd.
London, England
Revised edition published 1977 by Collins Publishers
100 Lesmill Road, Don Mills, Ontario.

This edition published 1979
by TOTEM BOOKS
a division of Collins Publishers

Canadian Cataloguing in Publication Data

Murray, John Wilson, 1840-1906.
Memoirs of a great detective

Originally published 1904. First Canadian ed.
published 1977 under title: Memoirs of a great
Canadian detective.

ISBN 0-00-216168-0 pa.

1. Murray, John Wilson, 1840-1906. 2. Detectives
— Ontario — Biography. I. Title.

HV7914.M9 1979   364.12′092′4   C78-001634-5

Printed in the U.S.A.

ACKNOWLEDGEMENTS

Our thanks to Rex Williams and Gerry Davis for bringing this book to our attention; to Mr. A. Salam, Head, Social Sciences Department, Metropolitan Toronto Library for loaning us their copy of the original edition; and to the Community Services Branch, Ontario Provincial Police for providing reference material from their files.

Special thanks to William Heinemann Ltd., London, England for permission to reproduce the text of their original 1904 edition.

CONTENTS

Continued

Continued

INTRODUCTION

John Wilson Murray was appointed Detective of the Department of Justice of the Province of Ontario in April of 1875. From that time until shortly before his death over thirty years later, he was the most famous policeman in Canada.

A tireless investigator who never gave up on a case, Murray was far ahead of his time in scientific criminal detection. He was one of the first detectives in the world to realize the importance of footprints; to regularly have an autopsy performed on murder victims; and to regularly have clothing and murder weapons chemically tested for signs of blood or hair or any other clue they might contain. He spent hours reconstructing the crime, and in checking and cross-checking alibis and motives. These procedures, common now, were a revelation in their day.

In an era in which fingerprints were unknown, when the photograph was a rare and imperfect tool, when much of the population could neither read nor write, and when one man had to cover the entire province of Ontario, the hundreds of cases solved by Murray easily qualify him for the title of The Great Canadian Detective.

His death, in 1906, was front page news. On June 13, 1906, the old *Toronto Globe* included these words in its long obituary. They are perhaps the most concise tribute to a pioneer criminologist.

> John Wilson Murray, for 31 years a detective in the employ of the Ontario Government, was one of the most widely known of men. His fame was international, thousands of people knew him by sight, many hundreds prized the pleasure of his acquaintance. In his time he travelled through most

> every known country, and he frequently attained success in his objective when others had given up in despair, declaring the task beyond the bounds of human achievement. He was proud, but not boastfully so, of his work, and to the very day he was stricken his physical and mental energy and capacity warranted the belief that he would continue for many years in harness, a terror to the evildoer, a delightful companion to those worthy of his companionship. His knowledge of the criminal classes was amazing, even for a man who had been so long a detective as he had – and he was of that profession long before coming to Canada. He not only knew by sight many leading criminals besides those he had himself arrested, but he kept himself well informed as to the noted criminal men in many countries. "You never can tell," he used to say; "they might drift to Canada at any time."

Born in Scotland on June 25, 1840, Murray moved with his family to New York when he was five years old. He enlisted in the United States Navy in 1857 and, as a sailor during the Civil War, he had his first experience of the mystery and fascination of detective work. In 1862 he successfully uncovered a complicated Confederate plot to free 4,000 Confederate prisoners from an island in Lake Erie, capture the USS *Michigan* and shell Detroit, Cleveland, and Buffalo. That experience convinced him that his future lay in the pursuit of criminals rather than at sea.

After the war, he spent two years working as a special agent for the Navy Department before joining the Erie Police Force in 1868. He left Erie to become Head of Detectives of the private police force of the Canadian Southern Railway and established his headquarters in St. Thomas, Ontario.

His success in the railway police brought Murray to the attention of Sir Oliver Mowat, then Attorney General of Ontario, who asked for his help in breaking up a gang of counterfeiters operating out of Owen Sound.

In 1874, after repeated attempts by Mowat to secure his

services, Murray finally agreed to accept the position of Provincial Detective of Ontario. He spent the rest of his life solving crimes committed in the pioneer settlements of Ontario. His jurisdiction was the entire province.

In the 1870's and 1880's Canada was still a world where men and women faced a lifetime of back breaking effort to wrest a living from the land. The remoteness and loneliness of many of the pioneer settlements made them perfect victims for crime. Their physical isolation in the wilderness was compounded by the difficulty of transportation and communication, and the general lack of education. This was an era when people locked and barred their door at sundown and depended on their own guns as the first, and often the only, line of defense.

Most of the crime Murray saw was personal and brutal. In that largely unregulated age, what is now called whitecollar crime was either legal or, because of the local cash and barter economy, impossible. With travel beyond the reach of most settlers, criminals were usually found in the immediate area.

Murray's most famous case was undoubtedly the Birchall murder in 1893. This case, involving the practice of English younger sons being sent out to the colonies, received attention throughout Canada, England and the United States.

Other cases, however, present a fascinating look at the problems of life in pioneer Ontario only a century ago. This was a world in which men were hung when clearly insane (the case of Almeda Chattelle, The Hairy Man); where the poverty of the poor was unrelieved by the state; and where murder was done for amazingly small sums of money. In the case of The Driverless Team On The Caledonia Road, premeditated murder was committed for $35. And disease raged virtually unchecked. In two cases, The Whitesides of Ballinafad, and George Alger's Graveyard Policy, consumption, the common killer of the 19th century, plays a role.

The attitude toward children during these years, although only a short time ago, had advanced little from Dicken's day. An 18 year old murderer arrested by Murray (the case of The Crime of Charlie King) was brought to Canada by a charitable organization called The Fagan Home, which "imports English waifs to Canada and places them in honest lines of work."

While far ahead of his time in the scientific investigation of crime, Murray's attitude toward the criminals his society produced was typical of the time. He believed that the criminal was a bad type, likely unrepentant and probably unsalvageable. Crime was genetic and ran in families, and criminals were the clear enemy of society. The detective's job, clear and simple, was to catch the criminals and prove their guilt so that the court could hand out a suitable punishment. As Murray himself put it:

> Crime is a disease. It is hereditary, just as consumption is hereditary. It may skip a generation or even two or three generations. But it is an inherent, inherited weakness. I am satisfied of this . . . Crime also is contagious. Constant contact with criminals often leads others to become criminals. It is the old story of "evil associations".
>
> Once dishonest, always dishonest. That is the general rule. I believe in it absolutely. Reformation is the exception. The degree of dishonesty may vary, but the fact of dishonesty does not alter. I made up my mind slowly on this point, and I reached my decision with reluctance. But I have seen it over and over again.

But, as the case of The Tookes Revel in Riches shows, the Victorian age also had its settled and happy side in which the danger of too many people passing a high school examination could be reason enough to call Murray into the fastest and muddiest chase of his career.

Despite all the crime he had seen, Murray believed that society had little to fear from criminals so long as the laws were strictly enforced. At the end of his long career, spent largely in the company of criminals and amongst the roughest elements of the Canadian wilderness, he thought the world a "grand place".

> I suppose I should take the view that this world is a wicked, dangerous place, infested with masked

murderers or desperate workers in the darkness. But I hold no such opinion.

This world is a grand place, life is a glorious thing. Crime increases, but not out of proportion to the increase in population of our countries and of the whole world. Where men and women are, there will be found good and bad. But the bad are a hopeless minority. Our prisons do not hold the bulk of the majority of our population, and yet a fair share of those who ought to be in prison eventually get there.

Murray's homelife, during his last years, was in distinct contrast to the relentless and fearless officer who pursued criminals across Canada and around the world. He spent his last years in a world of settled peace.

He lives alone, with a trusted housekeeper and discreet servants. His pleasure, apart from his work is in outdoor life, with his dogs and gun, his fishing tackle, or, above all, a boat on the open sea. Beside his desk in the library of his house, are his favourite books on a separate shelf – the poems of Robert Burns, the works of Scott, the essays of Emerson, the Count of Monte Cristo, Gulliver's Travels, and the Bible. He is an omnivorous reader, but these are his favourites. On the wall, side by side, are pictures of Queen Victoria and Abraham Lincoln. His den is filled with reminders of his life's work. There are rusty bullets that have come from the brains of murdered men; there are bludgeons, knives, revolvers, sandbags, pieces of pipe, jemmies, kits of burglars, outfits of counterfeiters, symbols of the crucial clues that fastened on criminals the guilt of their crimes. Each has its history, and in the story of his life all have their place.

The first edition of the *Memoirs* of John Wilson Murray was published in London, England, in 1904. The editor, Mr. Victor

Speer, has inserted his own voice throughout the text, and it is probable that he had a large hand in turning Murray's memoirs into a coherent narrative.

It is Speer's presence, as a sort of Dr. Watson, recording the Great Detective's deeds, that is responsible for the repeated use of "Murray said" and "Murray did" throughout the text.

The original edition of the *Memoirs*, now extremely rare, is almost twice the length of the present book. The intention in selecting the cases that appear here has been to include those that give the most interesting picture of Murray and the society that flourished in Ontario only a century ago.

Readers interested in the original edition of *THE MEMOIRS OF A GREAT DETECTIVE* can find a copy in the Metropolitan Toronto Public Library and in the Library of the University of Western Ontario.

Michael Worek
Port Hope 1977

MURRAY

IN a tangled swamp on a farm near Galt, in the county of Waterloo, Province of Ontario, Canada, in August 1897, searchers were hunting for the body of a farmer's wife. She had disappeared, and blood by the wood pile and near the house told of a crime and the hiding of the body. One of the party beating the swamp came upon a half-dug grave. He kept silence as to his discovery, and, when night fell, he secreted himself in the thick brush near the grave and waited, in the faint hope that the murderer would return and finish his task, perchance bringing the body with him.

It was bright moonlight overhead. In the thicket of the swamp all was gloom, save for a broken filtering of pale light where the underbrush and tall briar had been thinned out. It was a lonely, dismal place. An owl's wailing and the swamp-frog's croaking were the only sounds. The hours passed. Midnight came and went. Not even a lizard appeared by the grave. The watcher was about to creep closer and ease his limbs, when a rustle sounded in the brush, a noise like the wind swishing a bush. It ceased, then came again, then all was still. Suddenly, on the side of the grave farthest from the watcher, a figure crept swiftly out of the thicket and stood erect.

The moon shone full upon him. He was tall and broad-shouldered, with a pose like that in the old-fashioned prints of heroic figures of the ancient wars. He wore knee-boots, with a long, loose coat reaching to their tops, and buttoned to the chin. A slouch hat, pulled well down on the forehead, shaded his face. In his left hand he held a spade. He paused by the grave, thrust his spade into the earth, and left it upright like a headstone, then shoved back the hat, and knelt on all fours, with his face close to the ground, for all the world like a bloodhood sniffing for a scent. On hands and knees he crept around and around the grave. Finally, from a pocket of the long coat, he produced a tiny lamp, and turning its light full upon the ground, he resumed his circling of the grave, his face not five inches from the earth, his eyes searching every foot of ground.

For half an hour this creeping around the grave continued. Then the figure squatted by the mound of earth and sat motionless. Suddenly he arose, seized the spade, and swiftly tossed away the mound of earth dug from the grave. All was done so noiselessly, so deftly, that it seemed unreal, phantom-like, the antics of a ghost. As he neared the bottom of the pile of earth his care redoubled. At length, he began to dig around the remnant of the pile as if making a second grave, beside the first. He had left about four inches of the earth from the first grave lying undisturbed on the site of the second grave. It was thick, sticky soil, that held together firmly, being less watery than elsewhere in the swamp, yet being full of heaviness and moisture.

He dug cautiously, sinking the spade about four inches in the soil, then driving it under, as would a man in cutting sod. When he thus had cut under the entire remnant of earth from the first grave he cleared a space on the ground beside it, and as one would turn a pancake on the griddle, he flipped the earth out and turned it on to the cleared space, so that the remnant of soil from the first grave was underneath. He then painstakingly lifted away the upper layer, and thus exposed to view the soil from the first grave, precisely as it had formed the surface or top of the earth before the digging of the grave began. He knelt over this earth as a mother over her child. He turned the light of the little lamp full upon it. Then he grunted, a subdued, deep, satisfied grunt. With the spade he carefully cut out a piece of the earth about a foot long and half as wide. He produced a measuring rule, and for half an hour worked over the piece of earth. Then he took the earth in his arms as tenderly as if it were a babe, picked up the spade, and vanished in the thicket.

Like a flash it dawned on the watcher that this mysterious figure had been searching for footprints. He had found no clear footprint around the grave. The marks there had been trampled by those of the watcher. But on the surface of the earth, where the grave had been dug, the footprints of the digger were certain to appear. So the figure in the long coat had reclaimed this surface undisturbed, and, judging from the one sound he made, the grunt of joy, he had found what he sought.

The watcher trailed after him, ignorant of who he was or whence he came. The grey dawn was creeping into the sky as he entered his hotel at Galt. A sleepy porter was lolling on a table. Footsteps sounded in the hall, and past the office door on his way upstairs went the figure of the long coat. The coat was in his arms, borne carefully, for it concealed the precious piece of earth.

"Who is that?" asked the watcher.

"That!" said the porter, with a yawn. "That's Old Never-let-go."

"Who?" asked the watcher.

"Old Never-let-go," answered the porter. "Murray, John Murray, Old Never-let-go, the greatest genuine detective that this here or any other bloomin' country can produce. He's snoopin' around now a gettin' ready to fix a hangin' for whoever killed Mrs. Orr."

The figure of the long coat was in his room before the porter finished. He had laid the piece of earth on a table and turned the light full on it. A footprint showed, distinct in every detail of the shoe's outline. He remeasured it carefully, noting the measurements on a slip of paper. When he finished he compared this slip with another slip. Then he went to a closet, and drew forth an old shoe, earth-stained and worn. He gently lowered this shoe into the imprint on the piece of earth. It matched. The clue held true.

After locking the piece of earth in an iron box, he went straight to the gaol or lockup, where a suspect was under guard. He entered the cell, and slammed the door. An hour later he returned to his room at the hotel, glanced longingly at the bed, then at his watch, shook his head, and five minutes later was in a cold bath. When he appeared in the hotel office shortly after, the newspaper men and others including the watcher in the swamp, crowded around him.

"Any news?" they asked eagerly.

"The murderer's locked up," was the reply.

"Who is he?"

"Jim Allison, the chore boy. He'll confess before he's hanged."

Allison was tried and convicted, and he confessed before he was hanged. At the trial there was no inkling of the all-night labours in the swamp or of the fatal footprint. The case was complete, without a revelation of the methods of the man who ran down the necessary evidence. If it had been necessary, the piece of earth with the tell-tale tread, a plaster cast of it to make it still plainer, would have been in evidence at the trial. It was not needed, and hence it did not appear. In a somewhat similar case a few years before, proof of footprints was needed, and it did appear.

"You're sure Allison did it?" asked the newspaper men at the Galt hotel.

"Sure," said Murray, and he went to breakfast.

It was the writer's first experience with John Wilson Murray, Inspector of the Department of Criminal Investigation of the Department of Justice, with head offices in the Parliament Building at Toronto, Canada. For almost thirty years he has been inspector, and, in that time, murders by the dozen, burglaries by the score, crimes of all kinds, totalling thousands, have been solved by him, and the perpetrators apprehended. His career is a record of events outrivalling the detective tales of fiction; for fact, in its fullest scope, is stranger far than fiction. He has followed men over two continents; he has pursued them over land and sea, from country to country, from hemisphere to hemisphere, from New World to Old World and back again. He has travelled over 30,000 miles in the chase of a single man. He has shot and has been shot. He has been worsted in desperate struggles when help came in the nick of time, and he has fought grim battles single-handed when defeat would have meant death. His prisoners have ranged from men of high estate to creatures of the lowest depths. The cases he has solved range through every variety of crime known to the police records of the world. He has run down counterfeiters of $1,000,000 and more; he has unravelled the mysteries of murder where life was taken for eighty cents. He has the counterfeiting plates, valued at $40,000, as a trophy of the one chase, and he has a rusty iron pipe as a souvenir of the other.

He lives in Toronto, in a comfortable brick house in Brunswick Avenue. As he comes and goes, a stranger seeing him would regard him as a prosperous business man, of placid life and uneventful career. His home life is the antithesis of his official life. He lives alone, with a trusted housekeeper and discreet servants. His pleasure, apart from his work, is in outdoor life, with his dogs and gun, his fishing tackle, or, above all, a boat on the open sea. Beside his desk in the library of his house, are his favourite books on a separate shelf—the poems of Robert Burns, the works of Scott, the essays of Emerson, the Count of Monte Cristo, Gulliver's Travels, and the Bible. He is an omnivorous reader, but these are his favourites. On the wall, side by side, are pictures of Queen Victoria and Abraham Lincoln. His den is filled with reminders of his life's work. There are rusty bullets that have come from the brains of murdered men; there are bludgeons, knives, revolvers, sandbags, pieces of pipe, jemmies, kits of burglars, outfits of counterfeiters, symbols of the crucial clues that fastened on criminals the guilt of their crimes. Each has its history, and in the story of his life all have their place.

In a gold frame on the top of his desk, in old English lettering on heavy paper, is the following:—

> They talk about a woman's sphere
>   As though it had a limit:
> There's not a place in earth or heaven,
> There's not a task to mankind given,
> There's not a blessing or a woe,
> There's not a whisper, yes or no,
> There's not a life, or death, or birth
> That has a featherweight of worth,
>   Without a woman in it.

Murray smiles when a visitor reads it.

2

FROM BABYHOOD TO BATTLESHIP

EVEN the early years of the life of John Wilson Murray were eventful. He was born in the city of Edinburgh, Scotland, on June 25th, 1840. He is sixty-five years old, and looks little past fifty. He came of a sturdy family of sea-faring men, who had been sailing the globe for generations before him. His father was Daniel Duncan Murray, a sea captain, and his grandfather was Hector Murray, a sea captain of some note, who owned a number of coasting vessels off the north of Scotland and in the German Ocean, and who was a rich man until a storm at sea swept many of his ships away.

Murray's mother was Jeanette Wilson, daughter of Dr. Alex. Wilson, of Belfast, County Antrim, in the north of Ireland. Her father and mother died when she was quite young, and the lass was raised in Scotland at the home of a relative of Murray's godmother, named MacDonald, an Edinburgh merchant's wife. There Daniel Duncan Murray met her, a winsome maid, whose picture is a gem, and married her in 1834. He sailed the seas, returning to Edinburgh for short visits after long voyages to all parts of the earth. There were two children who survived infancy. One was John Wilson Murray, the other was his sister, Mary, five years older, who died some years ago.

When young Murray was five years old the family moved to New York. Captain Daniel Duncan Murray sailed ships out of New York for a number of years. Among them were the *Benjamin Adams*, the *Flying Cloud*, and the *Ocean Wave*, in its day a fast clipper. Young Murray was sent to school in New York, but in 1851, when he was eleven years old, his mother's health failed, and she returned to Scotland, taking him with her, but leaving his sister, Mary, attending school in Hartford, Conn. The mother, on her arrival in Edinburgh, placed her son at the old Royal High School on the east end of Princess or Regent Street. A few months later she heard that her daughter in Hartford had been thrown from a horse, and that her arm had been broken. She immediately started for New York, leaving young John Wilson Murray at school in Edinburgh. The son soon showed the family love for roving, a trait dominant in his father and his father's father. He became dissatisfied; he disliked his teacher. The dissatisfaction and dislike grew when he heard his father was due a month later in Liverpool.

In 1853 this boy of thirteen ran away from school, shipped on a coaster and made his way to Liverpool. He travelled the Liverpool docks a night and a day before he found his father's ship.

"I'll tack you back to Edinburgh on the morrow," said Captain Daniel Duncan Murray.

"Gin you do, I'll be off again on the next morrow," replied his thirteen-year-old son.

Captain Murray laughed mightily at this, and when his ship sailed for New York he took his son with him and turned him over to his mother again. Mrs. Murray took him to Washington and sent him to the Georgetown Academy. He stayed there until 1855, when the spirit of adventure seized him and he ran away a second time. With him went another lad of the school, who now is a prominent man in the business affairs of the United States.

The two boys went to Baltimore. They tried to ship aboard a whaler. At the first shipping office they entered, the man in charge eyed them suspiciously as they glibly told of an imaginary career, since infancy, at sea.

"Hold out your hands," he said suddenly.

The astonished lads obeyed.

"Bah!" he roared, as he spat on the white unmarked palms. "Out of here, or I'll have you both arrested. Go back to your mas and your milk, ye pair of unweaned liars. Ye're dressed for a party."

Thereupon he spanked them both soundly, and sat them down with a thud. They fled, not alone from the office, but from Baltimore, going to Philadelphia. They prowled around the water-front of the Quaker City looking for a whaler. After their Baltimore experience they had decided to steer clear of all shipping offices. After a week of unavailing search for a whaler that would carry them to the far north, where they expected to bag whales by the score and seals by the thousand, young Murray met a fruiter. She was a brig. They wanted a boy, but did not want two boys. Murray's companion in adventure found a berth on a Liverpool ship, and the lads separated, not to meet again for thirty years,

The fruiter on which Murray shipped was the *Sequence*. She went to the West Indies, Murray receiving the princely wage of $7 a month. The *Sequence* stopped at the Barbadoes. Trinidad, and St. Kitts, then sailed for Boston. The boy, who had stepped aboard in velvet knickerbockers at Philadelphia, stepped ashore in duck togs at Boston. He sailed on the *Sequence* four months; then returned to Philadelphia and shipped again, this time on the *Dauntless*, a full-rigged ship bound around the Horn. He left Philadelphia early in October 1855, going out for guano on the islands off Lima on the west coast of South America. She struck appalling weather off the Horn, and limped into Callao badly battered. In this hurricane young Murray was sea-sick for the first and last time in his life. On his return from the guano islands, he shipped on the brig *Tortoise*, for a short trip to San Domingo after logwood. He was out two months, and when he landed in Philadelphia he heard of a grand new vessel on the great lakes, and straightway started for Buffalo, and shipped on the *Great West*, at that time (1856) the biggest vessel on the lakes. Captain John Bampton, a giant in bulk and heart and voice, was her master, and Toppy McGee, of Oswego, was mate. She was a full-rigged ship, the only one on the lakes at that time.

Murray sailed on the *Great West* between Buffalo and Chicago, and had made several trips when, one morning at the docks in Buffalo, Captain Daniel Duncan Murray appeared and led his runaway offspring back to New York.

"This time you go to school and you stay at school," said the captain. "'Tis a profession I intend you should follow.

From the cut of your jib you'll make a fine preacher-person; or, at the worst, I'll turn you out a doctor-man."

"I may go, but I will not stay," said young Murray.

The captain placed him in school. Young Murray languished through the winter months, and when spring came, the spirit of unrest stirred within him, and away he went, back to the sea. In the late spring he returned to the Great Lakes, and on June 5th, 1857, he enlisted in the United States Navy, joining the U.S.S. *Michigan*, then in Chicago, although her headquarters were in Erie, Pa. He stayed aboard the *Michigan* until the Civil War broke out in 1861. He was twenty-one years old then, and the opportunity came for him to realise the ambition of his early years. There was a shortage of officers in the regular service, and Murray was picked as one of the likely young fellows to be sent on to the training-school at Washington. He worked and studied faithfully then, and when the examinations were held he passed, and received a commission in the United States Navy.

Murray served through the Civil War in the Navy. He was in the Mississippi or Gulf Squadron a part of the time, under Commander Jewett, and he fought under Farragut, and was in a number of engagements, including the fight at Mobile.

"The first time I saw Farragut was aboard the *Hartford*, and I can see him now, over forty years after, as distinctly in memory as I saw him then in reality," says Murray, in speaking of the great naval genius of the war. "Once seen, never forgotten."

From service in the Mississippi and the Gulf, Murray was ordered to the Great Lakes aboard the *Michigan*. He continued aboard her until after the close of the war, and in December 1866 he left the *Michigan* and the service.

Thus, at the age of twenty-five, Murray had sailed the south seas and around the Horn, had stood the gruelling of a six months' trip to the guano fields, had been through the pounding life aboard the West Indies fruiters, had fought through the Civil War, and stood, a powerful, self-reliant young giant on the look-out for his calling in life.

One of those who knew Murray in these days, and who is a banker in Ohio now, says of him:

"He was strong as a bull, quick as a cat, rather a silent fellow, slow to anger, and plenteous in vengeance once he was aroused. He feared neither man, gun, nor belaying pin. He was a faithful friend and a relentless foe. He was the last to pick a quarrel, but once it was picked he was the last to drop it. His associates liked him. He was a silent, sturdy, self-contained man, with a remarkable gift for gaining the confidence of other men."

The war left its indelible imprint on the life of Murray, as it did on the life of many another man. It tended to mould his ambitions and direct them along the line of what later became his occupation. In Murray's mind it is a settled belief that if he had not served in the Navy during the Civil War he would have been a sailor until he died, following in the way of his ancestors, and traversing all the seas to all parts of the world as master of his own ship. His career was not cast ashore by any dread of hardship afloat, or by any dislike of service at sea. It was influenced by an event that is one of the important, yet little-known, episodes of the Civil War. It sufficed to decide finally the future work of Murray. He holds it, therefore, a bit apart from other excitements of his career, for in it the hand of fate pointed the way of his destiny.

THE FIRST CASE: CONFEDERATE COLE'S COUP

It is a wonderful story, this narrative of the attempt of the Confederates, in 1864, to capture the U.S.S. *Michigan*, to take Johnson Island in Sandusky Bay in Lake Erie, release 4,000 Confederates imprisoned there, burn the island, if possible, destroy Detroit, Cleveland, and Buffalo by fire, and strike terror to the heart of the North. The man who discovered the plot was Murray, and it was he who unearthed the identity of the picturesque leader and was instrumental in frustrating the schemes so cunningly devised.

The war was at it zenith, says Murray, in telling the story. It was the year 1864. Commander J. C. Carter of the United States Navy sent for Murray and detailed him to special duty. There had been talk of a Confederate plot to blow up Johnson Island and liberate all Confederate prisoners and land them safely in Canada across Lake Erie.

"'Try to get to the bottom of the conspiracy, if there is one,' said Commander Carter to me, in the latter part of May 1864," says Murray. "Carter added: 'Go to any place and every place; you have an unlimited commission. Report to me from time to time.'"

Murray went first to Detroit and conferred with Colonel Hill, who gave him what information he had. It was meagre. At that time, Vallandingham, a member of Congress from Ohio, was in exile in Windsor, Ontario, across the river from Detroit. Vallandingham was a Southern sympathiser. Murray—in the garb of a civilian, of course—crossed to Windsor, and settled down to learn, first of all, the ways of Vallandingham and any other Confederate sympathisers gathered there. He observed closely all who called on Vallandingham. Among them he noted a dapper, energetic, little fellow, who came and went at Vallandingham's headquarters. Murray, unsuspected, learned his name was L. C. Cole, and that he was reputed to be a Confederate agent. Cole was about thirty-eight years old, five feet seven inches tall, weighed a hundred and thirty-five pounds, with red hair and long mustachios, and grey eyes, so small and sharp and bright, that Murray says the first thing he noticed about Cole was his eyes. Murray finally çaught a scrap of conversation between Cole and Vallandingham that convinced him Cole was an important and dangerous figure. He communicated with Commander Carter and made ready to follow Cole, if it led to the ends of the earth.

Cole left Windsor, with Murray on his trail. He went first to Toronto and stopped at the Queen's Hotel, where he was joined by a number of other rebel sympathisers. Murray says a dozen or more gathered instantly to greet him, all being strangers. Cole clearly was the chief among them, as they deferred to him. After long conferences, Cole went to Montreal. Murray went on the same train.

Thus the chase began. Murray was a young fellow of twenty-four, inexperienced as a detective, untrained in shadowing a man or in running down a clue or solving a mystery. Cole, on the contrary, was an experienced and trained agent, schooled in all the tricks of that branch of war in which he was engaged. The difficult task, however, seemed simple to Murray ; he adjusted himself to it from the outset. It serves to indicate his natural bent toward the work of a detective. A coincidence of his career is that his first visit to Toronto, where later he established his headquarters in his life work, was as a detective, trailing his man.

"I learned then the simple rule for following a man," says Murray. "Keep him in your sight as much as possible, and keep yourself out of his sight as much as possible."

When Cole alighted from the train in Montreal, Murray was a car length behind him. Cole went to the St. Lawrence Hall Hotel and Murray followed. There Cole was joined by a woman.

"She was an elegant-looking lady," says Murray. "She was big and stately, a magnificent blonde, with clothes that were a marvel to me. I did not know her then, but later she turned out to be the celebrated Irish Lize. The contrast between her and Cole was striking. She was big, stout, and fine-looking; he was a little, sandy, red-haired fellow, but smart as lightning."

From Montreal, Cole and Irish Lize went to Albany. The impulse was strong on Murray to seize them and notify Commander Carter. He debated it with himself. He had evidence that they were Confederate sympathisers, but he had not the desired evidence as to a plot or their plans. He decided to follow them, half expecting they would go far South before returning to execute any desperate plans in the North. They stopped over night in Albany, then went to New York and then on to Philadelphia and thence to Washington. Murray trailed them from city to city, from hotel to hotel. Cole and Irish Lize met one, or sometimes two or three strangers in each city, evidently by previous appointment, as in every instance they were waiting Cole's arrival. From Washington, Cole and Irish Lize went to Harrisburg, Pennsylvania, and from Harrisburg to Buffalo, New York, and thence to Cleveland, Ohio. In Cleveland they were joined by a young man, whom they had seen in Philadelphia. He was Charles Robinson, son of a former judge. They stayed in Cleveland two days and then went to Sandusky, Ohio, where Cole and Irish Lize stopped at the West House, and Robinson at a private boarding-house. They arrived at Sandusky about June 20th, 1864. Murray arrived on the same train.

"I learned for myself on that trip," says Murray, "the various ways to ascertain a man's destination before he boards his train. Sometimes he states it at the hotel when paying his bill, sometimes it can be learned when he buys his ticket, sometimes the conductor is obliging, and sometimes, when the worst comes to the worst, you can sit in another car, or at the other end of the same car, and keep an eye on the stations. All this has changed greatly in recent years. Co-operation among the police forces of all cities and of hotel, railroad, and other detectives has simplified this task of trailing a traveller."

Cole posed at Sandusky as an oil prince. Irish Lize passed as his wife. Soon after their arrival an assistant joined Cole. He was known as G. C. Beal. One week to the day after Cole arrived at the West House, a young man registered as John U. Wilson of New Orleans. In the course of a few days he met Cole casually, as guests staying for long at the same hotel are apt to meet. They drank together, and seemed to become well acquainted. Cole bought fast horses and finally chartered a yacht. He made the acquaintance of the officers of the U.S.S. *Michigan*, then lying off Sandusky, and also of Colonel Hill (not the Colonel Hill whom Murray had seen in Detroit) and the U.S. Army officers in charge of Johnson Island. Cole appeared a jolly good fellow, who spent money like water, and was too busy having a merry time to give heed to the affairs of war. He became a great favourite with both the Naval officers aboard the *Michigan* and the Army officers on the Island. He sent baskets of wine and boxes of cigars aboard the vessel and over to the Island.

Murray, meanwhile, had reported to Commander Carter. About the middle of July 1864 Cole arranged a party to the Seven Mile House, seven miles out of Sandusky. He invited all the officers of the Island and the ship. A number of them were making preparations to go. Young Wilson, of New Orleans, was Cole's assistant in planning the details of the outing. Early that morning Cole received a telegram from Detroit:

"I send you sixteen shares per messenger.—B.D."

On this particular morning, on the steamer *Philo Parsons*, plying between Sandusky and Detroit on daily trips, with a stop at Windsor, Ontario, ten men got aboard at Windsor, and eight more got aboard at Amherstburg, in Canada, at the mouth of the Detroit River. They had their luggage with them. They were the sixteen shares sent by two messengers to the merry Mr. Cole at Sandusky. After the steamer *Parsons* got well out into Lake Erie, these eighteen men opened their luggage boxes, took therefrom braces of revolvers and captured the *Parsons*, making her captain a prisoner. Then they steamed on to Kelly's Island, off Sandusky, where the steamer *Island Queen* was lying. They sent some of their men aboard the *Queen*, caught the few of her crew aboard unawares, gave orders to Engineer Richardson, and when he refused to obey, shot him dead. They then took the *Island Queen* out into the lake and ran her on to Gull Island and abandoned her there. Then they headed for Sandusky in the *Parsons*, which was due at 6 o'clock in the evening.

While this was occurring on Lake Erie, Cole was in Sandusky with his plans all made for the party that would call practically all the officers on the *Michigan* and on Johnson Island to the Seven Mile House, well away from their posts of duty. They were to start from Sandusky in the afternoon. Cole and young Wilson waited, and finally Cole, becoming impatient, said to Wilson :

" It's strange these officers are not ashore before this. You go off and see them."

"They would not come for me," said Wilson. You'd better go."

Cole, who usually dressed in black or dark clothes, was dressed on this day in a suit of grey. He discussed the matter of going over for the officers with Wilson, who walked down to the dock with him and said :

" Here's a boat belonging to the ship now. Go off in her and get them. I'll go with you."

Cole handed a $10 bill to the coxswain of the boat's crew and told him to take the boys up for a drink. All went except the boat-keeper, who waited with Cole and Wilson, and James Hunter, an officer of the *Michigan*, who was ashore. When the crew returned they willingly pulled off to the U.S.S. *Michigan*, lying three miles off Sandusky. About half way out, Cole, who seemed to have a presentiment of trouble, decided to turn back.

"The pennant of the ship is flying," remarked young Wilson to the coxswain.

"Yes, we'll have to go on and I'll bring you back as soon as I've reported," said the coxswain.

They went on to the *Michigan*. The officers aboard greeted Cole cordially and invited him to have a glass of wine, telling him they were sorry to disarrange his plans or delay his party. Young Wilson called on Carter in his cabin.

"I have the man," he said as he entered.

"The right man?"

"Not a shadow of doubt," said Wilson.

"Bring him up," said Carter.

Young Wilson turned to the orderly. "Tell Mr. Cole Captain Carter wishes to see him," he said.

Cole appeared, smiling and merry. Young Wilson met him on deck.

"The captain wants to see you," said young Wilson.

At the tone of his voice Cole stopped short and looked at him, his eyes like gimlets boring for what it all meant. Then he laughed and went to see Carter. He entered with Wilson.

"Captain Carter, this is Mr. Cole, a rebel spy," said Wilson.

"Murray, arrest him," said Carter to young Wilson.

"I am not a spy; I am a Confederate officer," said Cole, who had straightened and stiffened.

Carter smiled. Cole thrust a hand in his grey coat and drew forth his commission, signed by Jeff Davis, showing him to be a major in the Confederate army. Murray took it and read it.

"Take him and search him, Murray," said Carter.

Cole, accompanied by his former friend, Wilson of New Orleans, now Murray of the *Michigan*, went to a cabin, and a sentry was placed at the door. Murray searched him and found $600 in currency, some letters and papers, and ten certified cheques for $5,000 each, on the Bank of Montreal, Canada, payable to bearer. Murray laid them all out. Cole eyed him and laughed.

"You served me well, Murray Wilson, or Wilson Murray, or whatever the deuce your name may be," he said.

"I served the best I could," said Murray.

"Sit down," said Cole.

Murray and Cole sat down.

"'Now, you're a pretty smart young fellow,' said Cole to me," said Murray, in telling of what occurred. "'We got along very well, didn't we? You wouldn't like to see me hung, would you?'

" I said : ' I wouldn't like to see anybody get hung.'

" ' Well, that's what you're trying to do with me,' said Cole.

" I said : ' It's a very unfortunate thing, and I hope I am not responsible.'

" Cole was very cool. He had the best nerve of any man I ever saw. He made no fuss, his voice never changed, his face never lost its jolly, careless expression for a minute. ' I suppose I ought to shoot you,' he said, ' and, if I had a gun and could get away, I'd probably do it, for business is business, Wilson, and war is hellish business. There is $50,000 in gold in those cheques. They are as good this minute as the gold in the Bank of Montreal. You can keep them. No one aboard here knows I have them. You can cash them when you wish. All I ask is that you won't know enough to get the rope around my neck and that, if the chance comes, you'll do me a friendly turn to get away. Once I'm out, you can give me $500 or enough to get South, or you needn't give me five cents. It's a fair bargain, isn't it, Wilson? My young friend, you'll never get such a chance again in your life."

" I saw the possibilities of it in a flash. It was a fortune in my grasp, yet if I took those cheques, the merry little Mr. Cole could have sent for Carter and said : ' Let me suggest you search your man, Murray, or Wilson. I think he's the one of us who should be under arrest.' Or, if Cole saw that to play me false would mean his own death, there still was the idea of selling out your country ; and I wouldn't have done that for as many millions. I was a young fellow and $50,000 was more then than $500,000 would look now, but I thank the everlasting God that I had the sense to say : ' That may be, Mr. Cole. I may never get such a chance again. I'll do what I can consistent with my duty, but I cannot well make you any promises.'

" ' Wilson, you're a fool,' he said.

" ' Mr. Cole, would you sell out the Confederacy ? ' I asked, for I was vexed over the turn of affairs with him.

" His manner changed. He put out his hand and shook mine.

" ' No, Mr. Wilson, I wouldn't,' he said. ' I understand you now.'

"We chatted pleasantly. He asked me where I first saw him. I told him the whole story of my trailing him, giving him even the numbers of the rooms in the hotels at which he had stopped.

"'You're right,' he said, 'but I could swear, on a stack of Bibles as high as this ship, that I never saw you before I saw you in Sandusky.'

"As I left him, a prisoner, he shook hands and said: 'You won't reconsider about the cheques?' I shook my head and left him smiling in the little cabin with the sentry at the door."

Carter alone had been in the secret of Murray's masquerade as Wilson. Officer James Hunter, of the *Michigan*, rendered valued assistance on the day of the arrest. Murray had arranged for the boat's crew to be waiting at the landing to take Cole to the ship, and Murray had intercepted telegrams to Cole and thus had learned of the telegram about the "sixteen shares."

"My own common sense told me the sixteen shares meant sixteen men," said Murray. "The way they would come would be on the *Parsons*."

With Cole a prisoner aboard the *Michigan*, Carter made ready to capture the men on the *Parsons*. Neither Murray nor Carter knew at that time that Cole had arranged for the *Parsons* to stay outside until he should go out with his yacht and give them a signal to come in. He was to slip away from his guests at the Seven Mile House, drive swiftly to Sandusky, and go out to meet the *Parsons* while the officers were enjoying themselves seven miles away.

"They had all their plans made," says Murray, "to meet Cole, and go in small boats to the *Michigan*, capture the ship, and then run over to Johnson Island and release the four thousand Confederate prisoners, chiefly officers, imprisoned there. They planned to land them at Point Pelee in Canada, right across the lake. They were to approach the *Michigan*, and when asked who came there Cole would answer. He was well known to all, and relied on no one to suspect him. Once aboard, he believed he could carry the hatches with a rush. The *Michigan* had fourteen cannon aboard her, six parrot rifles, six twenty-four pound howitzers, two light howitzers, and over a hundred tons of ammunition. They had no other heavily armed craft to fear on the lake. They believed they could not only liberate their four thousand men on Johnson Island and land them in Canada, but also could sail the lake without fear of superior vessel until they had bombarded and burned Detroit, Cleveland, and Buffalo. Some of the captured papers corroborated details of this plot."

But the *Parsons* did not go in at Sandusky. Her Confederate crew waited in vain for the signal from Cole. They became alarmed, scented disaster, went back to the Detroit River under cover of darkness, scuttled the *Parsons*, and landed in Amherstburg, Canada. The *Michigan*, after watching all night for the *Parsons*, went searching for her the next morning, and found her scuttled.

"The rumour of the plot had spread with the arrest of Cole," says Murray; "and when the *Michigan* returned to Sandusky all guns were trained on her until it was learned that the Confederates had not captured her. Some of her officers went off her, and were recognised, so that she would not be fired on.

"That night, another officer went with me, and we arrested Robinson at his boarding-house in Sandusky. He had twenty revolvers in a trunk. A family of Southern Hebrews, named Rosenthal, also found themselves in trouble. Quite a little colony of Southern sympathisers were clustered in Sandusky at that time. I next went to Irish Lize. She was infuriated. When I searched her trunk she seized me, and when I shook her off she wanted to shoot me. In one of her trunks were dozens of pairs of gloves. She informed me gratuitously that she never wore a pair of gloves a second time. I told her that, if she had not tried to shoot me, I would have believed her a perfect lady, even if I knew nothing about the gloves.

"There was quite a how-de-do over the entire affair. Major-General Hancock and Major-General Heinzelman were sent on to investigate. I was sent to Cleveland to meet them, and accompanied them to Sandusky. They talked at first of trying Cole by a military commission. I told them what I knew of the matter, and what sort of chap Cole was. After hearing all the facts they returned to Washington.

"Cole was transferred from the *Michigan* to Johnson Island, and thence to Fort Lafayette at New York, and from there to Fort Warren, in Boston, where he was held until after Lincoln's proclamation. I had sold his horses for him, and closed up his business affairs at Sandusky, and turned over the proceeds to him. The Rosenthals were liberated. Beal disappeared. Robinson was held until after Lincoln's proclamation. Cole never was tried. He came to see me after his release.

"'Murray,' he said, 'you were a —— fool.'

"I thought of Irish Lize, and concluded that while Cole was a little fellow he was a bigger fool than I."

4

A WORD BY THE WAY

WHEN the war was over and Murray left the Service he went to Washington. It was the day before Christmas in 1866. He called at the Navy Department. There were officials there who remembered his work in the Cole case, and before New Year arrangements had been made for Murray to become identified with the United States Service on special duty.

"Wood was chief of the Secret Service in those days," says Murray. "I became, so to speak, a special agent in the Navy Department. For about two years I engaged in this work. It took me all over the country, particularly through the South. I was in New Orleans, Mobile, Charleston, Pensacola, and other Southern cities, and was on duty in New York for some time. My experience here settled finally my determination to make the detective business my life work. I realised that to make a success of it I would have to go to work to perfect myself in it, just as does a man fitting himself for any other business, and advancing himself after he engages in it.

"The detective business is the higher branch of the police business. A man may be an excellent policeman, and yet be an utter failure as a detective; and I have seen many a clever detective, who was out of his element in the simpler lines of police duty. There is no magic about the detective business. A detective walking along the street does not suddenly hear a mysterious voice whisper: 'Banker John Jones has just been robbed of $1,000,000.' He does not turn the corner and come upon a perfect stranger, and then, because the stranger has a twisted cigar in his mouth, suddenly pounce upon him and exclaim: 'Aha, villain that you are! give back to Banker Jones the $1,000,000 you stole ten minutes ago!' The detective business is of no such foolish and impossible character. Detectives are not clairvoyants, or infallible prophets, or supernatural seers. They possess no uncanny powers and no mantle of mysterious wonder-working. I remember a few years ago I was subpœnaed before a grand jury in the city of New York to testify on a matter pertaining to a prisoner, whose record I knew here in Canada. The foreman of that jury was a man prominent in New York's business life. When I was called he looked at me and suddenly said:

"'Inspector Murray, what crimes have been committed within the past hour in New York, and who committed them?'

"'I have not the slightest idea,' I replied.

"'Oh, ho! So you cannot go out and put your hands on every man who has committed a crime? You are a detective, yet cannot do that?' he said.

"'I am not that kind of detective,' I replied. 'When I get a guilty man it usually is by hard work or good luck, and often by both.'

"'Thank the Lord we've found a detective who is not greater than God,' he said.

"As a matter of fact the detective business is a plain, ordinary business, just like a lawyer's business, a doctor's business, a railway manager's business. It has its own peculiarities because it deals with crime, with the distorted, imperfect, diseased members of the social body, just as a surgeon's business deals with the distorted, imperfect, diseased members of the physical body. But it is not an abnormal or phenomenal or incomprehensible business. There is nothing done in it, nothing accomplished by any detective, that is not the result of conscientious work, the exercise of human intelligence, an efficient system of organisation and inter-communication and good luck. A good detective must be quick to think, keen to analyse, persistent, resourceful, and courageous. But the best detective in the world is a human being, neither half-devil nor half-god, but just a man with the attributes or associates that make him successful in his occupation.

"A wide acquaintance is one of the most valuable assets

of a detective. The more crooks he knows the better. I have seen detectives visit a prison, and walk through it, recognising man after man—hundreds of them. I have seen detectives stand before photograph cases, and name and describe criminal after criminal, even to the minute eccentricities of each one. A good memory is a great help; in fact, it is essential to the equipment of a clever detective. A wide acquaintance of the proper sort is invaluable. Personal friendship, among detectives and police departments of different cities and different countries, is one of the greatest aids to efficient detective work. Detectives and police departments can help one another, for by their co-operation they create a detective system that covers the world. If a criminal escapes in one city he is apt to be captured in another, and times without number the perpetrators of crime in one community are arrested by the police of another, and held until called for by the police of the place where they are wanted. From the outset of my career I have made it a point to increase steadily and systematically my acquaintance among detectives, among criminals, among bankers, lawyers, business men, professional men, people of all sorts and conditions. Hundreds of times I have had occasion to be glad I did this. By knowing a man in the right way personally, you will find he will do things for you in a pinch, that he never would do for you otherwise, under any circumstances.

"Personal knowledge of crooks is valuable, for many reasons. Often you may recognise the perpetrator of a crime from a witness's description of a person seen in the vicinity. You may recognise a certain kind of burglary as the work of a certain gang. In an emergency you may gather information from crooks that will enable you to lay your hands on the very man you are after.

"Much has been written about crooks by students of the social problem and by scientists. At least all writers agree that they are a queer lot, a class by themselves, with a life of their own and a point of view that is peculiarly their own. They have the characteristic of gratitude in perhaps a greater degree than some other classes of humanity. Of course, there are exceptions. But crooks as a whole have a code of honour, or rather a code of dishonour, that is always paradoxical, yet they adhere to it. If you do one of them a favour—that is, a turn that he, not you, regards as a favour to him—he will not forget it. More opportunities than are imagined present themselves where, in no way inconsistent with his duty, a detective may gain the favour instead of the disfavour of a crook. The best crooks make the least trouble personally to a detective. They are the hardest to catch, next to unknown crooks who are on the road for the first time, but once they are caught they realise that the part of wisdom is to acquiesce.

"Crime is a disease. It is hereditary, just as consumption is hereditary. It may skip a generation or even two or three generations. But it is an inherent, inherited weakness. I am satisfied of this. I have seen instances where the identical kind of crime has appeared in generation after generation, great-grandfather down through grandfather, father, son, and grandson. I have known men whose grandfathers were horse thieves or counterfeiters, and whose fathers were honest, to become horse thieves or counterfeiters and do nothing else dishonest. In the oldest records of crime we find inherited crime traced through three hundred years, and even longer. The conditions of the criminal may be bettered, just as the conditions of the consumptive may be bettered. The disease may be checked: in some instances it may be averted, but the crime-germ, if I may use the word, is there, lurking in the life of the victim. You have read of people living immaculate lives for many years and suddenly succumbing to crime. The disease was ever present, but was not manifest. Crime also is contagious. Constant contact with criminals often leads others to become criminals. It is the old story of 'evil associations.'

"Once dishonest, always dishonest. That is the general rule. I believe in it absolutely. Reformation is the exception. The degree of dishonesty may vary, but the fact of dishonesty does not alter. I made up my mind slowly on this point, and I reached my decision with reluctance. But I have seen it over and over again. It is observed more clearly about professional dishonesty than amateur dishonesty, if I may draw such a distinction. The crook who goes to prison once is apt to turn up again in the hands of the police. The mark of professionalism in dishonesty is acquaintance, as a prisoner, with the police. There is many an amateur who belongs to the professional class; and there are those in the professional class who belong to the amateurs. That is one of the vexations of the detective business.

"The business is full of vexations. There are times when you know to a certainty the doer of a deed, yet arrest must wait until the evidence is in hand. Sometimes the evidence never comes, and you see the years go by, with a guilty man enjoying the liberty denied to another, no more guilty, who had not the good fortune to lose some links in the chain of evidence that surrounded him. It is the law of chance.

"I believe in circumstantial evidence. I have found it surer than direct evidence in many, many cases. Where circumstantial evidence and direct evidence unite, of course, the result is most satisfactory. There are those who say that circumstances may combine in a false conclusion. This is far less apt to occur than the falsity of direct evidence given by a witness who lies point blank, and who cannot be contradicted save by a judgment of his falsity through the manner of his lying. Few people are good liars. Many of them make their lies too probable; they outdo truth itself. To detect a liar is a great gift. It is a greater gift to detect the lie. I have known instances where, by good fortune, I detected the liar and then the lie, and learned the whole truth simply by listening to the lie, and thereby judging the truth. There is no hard and fast rule for this detection. The ability to do it rests with the man. It is largely a matter of instinct.

"The best detective, therefore, is a man who instinctively detects the truth, lost though it may be in a maze of lies. By instinct he is a detective. He is born to it; his business is his natural bent. It would be a platitude to say the best detectives are born, not made. They are both born and made for the business. The man who, by temperament and make-up, is an ideal detective, must go through the hard years of steady work, must apply himself, and study and toil in making himself what he is born to be. Sandow was born to be a strong man, but, if he had not developed himself by hard work, he would not have become the strongest man of his time. As a detective advances in his business he will find that the more he studies and works, the stronger his powers of intuition, of divination, of analysis, become. A very simple broad illustration will prove this. If a detective is chasing a criminal from country to country, and has learned, by study of the extradition treaties, that a certain country offers a better haven than another, he may save himself many a weary mile by going to the country where his common sense tells him his man is more likely to be. A mechanical knowledge of the use of tools, a knowledge of the effects of poisons, a knowledge of the ways of banking, of the habits of life of the various classes in various callings, a knowledge of crooks, and, above all, a knowledge of human nature, in whatsoever way manifest, are invaluable elements of the equipment of a good detective.

"In a vague way I held these opinions away back in 1866, when, as a young fellow of twenty-six, I left the Service in the Navy after the war, and for about two years served as a special agent in the employ of the United States Government. I made acquaintances all over the country in those days, many of them being young fellows like myself, who were in the police business then, and later became heads of detective or police departments. I obtained my first experience then in the secrets of counterfeiting, in the arts of burglars, in the ways of the classes of thieves busy in those days in all parts of the United States, and more or less bothersome at times to the Government. It was precisely the experience and training I needed at that time.

"In 1868 I was persuaded to go to Erie, Pennsylvania, where I had made friends during my early days on the lakes, including prominent railroad men, and joined the police force there. In the four or five years I remained there I had plenty to do, and it fitted me further for the work I had outlined for myself. I became a detective on the force in Erie. Tom Crowley, a man I loved and respected, was chief at that time.

"Sometimes, when the wind howls and the world is full of gusts and gales, and I am caught where the man next me has a pipe as old as Methuselah, and tobacco as strong as Samson, my mind turns back to Crowley, and there flit through my memory, like ghosts of long ago, episodes of the old days in Erie when I was a sleuth from Sleuthville, and mighty proud of it, too."

HOW A FEUD ALMOST BURNED ERIE

A FEUD broke out in the Fire Department in Erie in 1869. Crowley, Murray, and the police were busy on other matters, and paid no attention to it at the outset. It began with a contest for the position of chief of the Fire Department. Before the struggle was over, Erie was threatened with destruction by fire, and the underwriters refused to issue insurance.

"There were two bodies of the City Council," says Murray. "The Common Council discharged the old fire chief, and the Select Council would not sanction the appointment of the new chief. The Fire Department also promptly took sides. Part of it stood with the old chief and part of it stood with the new chief. Feeling ran high and there was much bitterness.

"When the fight first started, various fires occurred. Old houses and old barns in out-of-the-way places caught fire in mysterious ways, and the rival factions in the Department were kept busy. Each endeavoured to get to a fire first and thereby obtain an opportunity to jeer at the other. At length the fires began to get rather numerous. The crop of old houses and old barns became pretty well thinned out. All the rickety buildings in Erie went up in sparks and smoke. Then the fires seized upon buildings a grade better than those destroyed in the first blazes. Thousands of dollars' worth of property was damaged. Property owners became alarmed, and finally sent for outside aid, and detectives were brought to Erie from New York and Chicago.

"Their presence quickly became known. It enraged the firemen. They called indignation meetings in the Fire Department, and arranged to put themselves on guard against them. Then the fires began to blaze up in bigger buildings, and, despite the presence of the outside detectives, they burned factories. At length the underwriters refused to issue insurance, and Erie was at the mercy of the Fire Department feud.

"They were so devilish sly about the fires that it was next to impossible to catch them. Neither side would agree to a compromise on the chiefship, and the fires nightly reddened the sky.

"One night there was a fireman's ball at Uncle Sam's Garden. I was there, of course, and so were other police. I was full of hope that before the night was over, during the dancing and the drinking, I might get some stray hint that would lead to evidence sufficent to catch some of the firebugs. Finally I went out in what they called the wine garden and lay down under a bench and pretended to be asleep. Soon two firemen came out. The bench was in a secluded corner of the garden. If there was to be any talking done that night it would be done in such a place. They came over to the bench.

"'Hello,' said one of them, 'John has his collar full.'

"'Let him sleep,' said the other.

"They whispered a moment and then chuckled softly. I listened intently but could hear nothing save their subdued laughter. Then suddenly I was sprinkled, deliberately and thoroughly, from shoulders to shins, and those two firemen did it without calling the engines. My first impulse was to spring up and wallop them. But the damage had been done, so I sprawled out motionless and took it. In that interval I vowed ten thousand times that, if the chance ever came, I would get even. After tiring of the sport of saturating me, they sat down on the bench.

"'A great night for a blaze,' said one.

"'Yes,' said the other, 'and there's the nigger's barn on Parade Street.'

"They were confident I was dead to the world. They talked over their plot, planning to slip away from the dance. I, under the bench, supposed to be in a stupor, heard all that was said. When they walked away I got up, shook myself and called my partner, who was in the dance hall.

"'What's happened, John?' he called, as he caught sight of me. 'Did you fall into the creek?"

"'No,' said I, 'the Fire Department has been practising on me.'

"Then I told him what had occurred and what I had heard in the wine garden. I knew both the young fellows and they came of respectable families. It was a dark night, black as soot. We knew the two firemen had started for their firehouse or the old barn, and we took a short cut across a cemetery, cutting off about a mile. On the way we lost track of the pair of firemen, but we knew their firehouse and we knew the barn and we skipped on as fast as we could go. They had quite a start of us, but we got to the firehouse just in time to see one of them come out with a can of oil and a bunch of shavings wrapped up in paper. He darted over to the old barn on Parade Street. I followed. He set the shavings and sprinkled the oil over them and touched a match and away she went.

"The fire-engine was there in a jiffy. In fact, the flames hardly seemed to have begun to leap when the engine arrived. The old barn burned like a tinder-box, and nothing was left but a pile of ashes. When the engine from the other faction in the department came up, there was a lot of jeering because it had not arrived first.

"After the fire I went to the young fellow. I knew him well, and was a family friend. His name was Ed, and he was about twenty years old.

"'Come on, Ed; I want you,' I said.

"'What for?' said he.

"'You know,' said I. 'Come on, without a fuss.'

"'I thought you were asleep, John, or I'd never have disturbed you,' he said.'

"'It's not that,' said I.

"Then I told him what I had heard and seen. We walked quite a distance. He sat down and began to cry. I advised him to tell me the whole story. He did so; telling me all who were in the feud and all about it. I told him to go home to bed and report at police headquarters at nine o'clock in the morning. He did so. Crowley was so tickled he chuckled off and on for a week. Whether it was at my getting it under the bench, or my getting the firebug at the darkey's barn, I never could tell.

"As a result of the information obtained, we arrested five firebugs, and all were convicted and sent to the penitentiary.

"It simply was a rivalry of factions. I saw a young fellow, who set fire to a factory, hang on the eaves on a winter's night until the water froze to an ice-coating on his clothes, putting out the fire he had set. They had no desire to destroy property. What they wanted was an opportunity to gain glory for their faction and outdo the rival faction. The great trouble was the opportunities were too costly. When I think, even at this late day, of what the eaves-dropping cost me, I am moved to retire to a Turkish bath and sojourn in the steam-room for a fortnight, at least. Yet a fortnight in a Turkish bath is better than a year in the penitentiary, and he laughs best who laughs last."

6

A KING, A LUNATIC, AND A BURGLAR—THREE IN ONE, AND NONE AT ALL

MURRAY had his full share of exciting experiences during his service in Erie. One episode in particular he laughs over, for in it he was mistaken for a king, a lunatic, and a burglar, all in a single night.

"In November 1872 a Miss Julia Oliver, sister of a prominent man in Erie, became demented," says Murray. "Her family were English people. She imagined they had large estates in England, and one of her delusions was that her brother was trying to beat her out of them. At times she had brief lucid intervals, but gradually she became worse, and they decided to send her to the Dixmont Asylum, up on the mountain near Pittsburg. I was acquainted with her, and her family, and they suggested that I would be the proper person to take her to the asylum. All the plans were made. We intended to start in the morning, but she locked and barred her bedroom door and windows, and we could not get into the room until after the morning train had gone. Fearing to have her at home another night, lest she should do some overt act or kill herself, the family decided I should take her on the afternoon train. It was an hour or two late. Miss Oliver and I arrived at the small asylum station long after dark. I remember it was a bright, cold, moonlit night in the latter part of November. The train steamed away, leaving this crazy woman and myself alone on the platform of the little station. There was not a soul around, no agent, no one from the asylum, not even a station lounger. It was as deserted as the North Pole, and almost as cold. The asylum was a mile or so up on the mountain from the station. There was a terraced walk for a part of the distance. The wind was howling, and everything was frozen tight. I looked far up the mountain, where I could see the asylum lights shining out in the night. The crazy woman passively waited.

"'Come, Miss Oliver,' said I. 'We will have to walk. I am very sorry, but there is no other way.'

"She looked at me with big, innocent, reproachful eyes. She had a very sweet, child-like voice. She made no move.

"'I know you are going to kill me,' she said so sorrowfully, and with such sweet simplicity and directness, that I started guiltily at the very candour of the accusation. 'Do kill me here,' she continued. 'Do not kill me on the mountain side, and let me roll down the hill. The one thing I dread after death is to have to roll down long hills.'

"There was no use to argue. She was insane. Yet she was so self-possessed, so gentle a lady, so frank, that if I had not known positively she was crazy, I would have believed her as sane as any other person I knew.

"'If you will not walk with me I must carry you,' I said.

"'I weigh over one hundred and forty pounds,' she said solemnly. 'I will not resist, although I prefer to be killed here rather than on the mountain side. Please kill me here.'

"No one likes to be regarded seriously as a murderer, even by insane folk. So, without further ado, I picked up Miss Oliver in my arms and started up the mountain. She certainly had stated her minimum weight! She lay in my arms like a sack of salt. The wind raged about us. Step by step I made my way up the mountain, heading for the lights of Dixmont. Despite the bitter cold I sat her down and threw off my overcoat, then picked her up and laboured on. It was weary, toilsome work. I stumbled and staggered, but ever nearer shone the lights. The insane girl begged piteously to be killed.

"'Kill me; why don't you kill me?' she kept crying. 'Oh, think how far I must roll after I am killed!'

"It was useless to be angry. I trudged on. Then she began to resist. She kicked and screamed and clawed. I was compelled to put her down and sit on her while I threw off my undercoat. Then up the mountain we went, in a perambulating wrestling match. She fought valiantly. Once she tripped me, and we rolled far down the path before I could stop. She shrieked with delight as we rolled. Then slowly, laboriously I worked our way back over the lost ground. All the asylum lights went out while we were on our way, except the few that burned all night. Finally I got her up to the door and rang the bell. As I rang, she wrenched away. I grabbed her, and she began to shriek so piercingly that it seemed as if her family away back in Erie must hear it. We were in a tangle on the ground when the door opened, and a flood of light poured out on us.

"There I stood—hatless, coatless, dishevelled, wet—with a wild woman wailing piteously, struggling, and crying to be freed from a monster. They well might have wondered which of us was insane. I carried her inside, and the doors were closed. I knew Dr. Reed, the Superintendent, but he was away. They roused the assistant superintendent out of bed. He was none too pleased at being disturbed. I had my commitment papers in my shirt, and I drew them forth. They were as wet as if they had fallen into a basin of water. Miss Oliver was a pay patient, of course, and her bed was ready. She looked serenely around the reception room, noting the paintings and the furnishings.

"'What do you think of my castle, King George?' she said to me. 'Is it not beautiful, your majesty? Pray make yourself at home, your majesty.'

"There never was a King George who looked as I looked just then. Small wonder a nurse sniggered. They took Miss Oliver to her quarters, and I returned to the office. I could hear the wind whistling around the corners outside. I asked if I could stay all night. They said no, it was against the rules.

"'If Dr. Reed was here I could stay all night,' I retorted.

"'Dr. Reed is not here,' was the icy reply, matching the zero weather outdoors.

"They showed me the door. I went out, hatless, coatless, into the night. I stumbled down the mountain, and hunted for my undercoat. I found it, and then found my overcoat. But my hat was nowhere around. The wind must have blown it away. I made my way down to the station. I was getting cold, and my damp clothes were stiffening on me. I tried to find warmth or shelter at the station, but there was none. I shivered and stamped to and fro, endeavouring to keep warm. There was no hotel around, none within a couple of miles. The only house near was a gashouse, where they made gas for the asylum. It was across from the station. I saw a light in it, and I went over and stepped in. A lone man was sitting by the fire, watching the drafts. He turned as the door slammed, and seeing me hatless, with scratched face, he groaned and jumped over to the other side of the room.

"'Get out! get out!' he shouted, waving his arms. 'You cannot stop here! Get out; I'm closing up now!'

"'You poor fool,' said I. 'I want to get warm, that's all. Nobody will hurt you. Sit down.'

"'Go back to the asylum if you want to get warm!' he yelled, as if I were a deaf lunatic. I don't warm crazy men here.'

"The fellow was beside himself with terror. He thought I was an escaped madman from Dixmont, and I did not blame him. I certainly must have looked the part. Suddenly his manner changed.

"'If you're really cold, my friend, I'll show you the new tavern that has been built right down the road,' said he.

"I thanked him heartily. He put on his hat and overcoat, and we started out of the door. As I stepped outside he slammed the heavy door behind me, and locked it from within. It simply was a ruse to get me out. I saw it was useless to try to get into the gashouse again, so I started on a brisk walk down the road, looking for a tavern or boarding house, or place of shelter for a half-frozen man. I walked over two miles before I came to what appeared to be a boarding-house. I banged on the door. There was no answer. I shook the door by its handle. Suddenly an upstairs window was raised, and a hoarse voice shouted: 'Who's there?' I answered that I was an officer who had come from the asylum and desired a bed for the night.

"'Get out of there!' roared the voice.

"'Come down and open this door!' I shouted in reply.

"The answer was the bang of a shot gun, and a charge of buckshot bored into the woodwork about a yard from where I stood. I scooted around the corner of the house as the second barrel followed the first. I crawled along behind fences until I struck a bend in the road, and then crossed to the railroad track, and started on a fast walk back toward the gashouse. On my way I met the gasman. When he saw me he let out a shriek of terror and fled across the fields. I walked fully three miles, past the gashouse, which was locked, before I came to a tavern. Profiting by my former experience I knocked, and when I heard a window raised upstairs I got around to the other side of the house.

"'Vat you vant?' asked a heavy German voice.

"'I want to get in,' said I.

"'Go away!' said the voice.

"'I want to get in!' I shouted.

"Bang! bang! went a gun. But I was around the corner of the house. I waited a few minutes, then thumped again on the door. Three times I thumped, and every time the old German roared. Finally I crossed the road and got behind a tree.

"'Hello, there!' I shouted. 'You'll kill some one if you don't stop.'

"'Vell, vat you tink I am shootin' for, eh?'

"I began a long palaver with him.

"'I want to get a bed for the night,' I said in conclusion.

"'So? Why ain't you say so first?' said he.

"I could hear him talking to his wife. They went away from the window. I waited fifteen minutes, and kicked again on the door. Presently a light appeared in the hall. Through the glass alongside the old-fashioned door I could see them coming down the stairs. The wife was ahead carrying a lighted candle. The husband was behind carrying the shot-gun.

"'Hello, out there!' he shouted, as they neared the door.

"'Hello!' I answered.

"'Who are you?' he asked.

"I told him.

"'How do I know you are who you say you are?' he demanded.

"I recited a long list of people I knew.

"'How do I know you know them?' he asked.

"I pondered. The only way to convince him was to hit upon some man he would be sure to know well. I saw a whisky sign by the door.

"'Do you know Fred Applebaum, of Pittsburg, the singer and whisky man?' said I.

"'Freddie Applebaum? Do I know him?' he said, and I could hear the bolt shot back.

"I fairly leaped inside. The old German kept pointing the shot-gun at me. He said there had been many burglaries in the vicinity, some of the robberies having been committed by men who called late at night and said they wanted lodgings. His wife brought me whisky, and I took a big drink. The old German meanwhile held the shot-gun full upon me. I sat close to the fire, and after thawing out I went to bed. The old German followed me with the shot-gun and a candle. He sat down in a corner of the room with the candle on the window sill and the shot-gun pointed at the bed. I fell asleep. It was daylight when I awoke. There sat the old German sound asleep in his chair, with the shot-gun across his knees and the candle down in the socket. I coughed, and he awoke with a snort. When I came to pay my bill he said, 'Fifty cents for bed, fifty cents for breakfast, and fifty cents for extra.'

"'What's the extra for?' I asked.

"'For keeping watch on you,' said he. 'How do I know you ain't a burglar?'

"'Would you take in a burglar?' said I.

"'If he was half froze,' said he.

"I took the first train for Erie, after buying a hat in Pittsburg, and patching my scratched face with court plaster. It was the only night of my life in which I had been invited to a palace as a king, locked out of a gashouse as a lunatic, shot at as a burglar, and put to bed with a shot-gun pointed at my head."

7

THE BOX-CAR BATTLE OF SWEETMAN, AND THE THRASHERS WITH THE WHEAT

IN addition to his regular work on the Erie police force Murray was gradually drawn into the service of the men at the head of the Pennsylvania Central Railroad. His success in the cases he undertook attracted their attention to such a degree that they finally urged him to sever his connection with the Erie Police and devote himself exclusively to railroad detective work. William L. Scott, the railroad magnate, whose home was in Erie, and for whom Murray had done considerable difficult railroad detective work, was particularly desirous of obtaining Murray's undivided services.

Mr. Scott, Milton Cartwright, who built the Dismal Swamp canal, and was interested in the building of the Elevated Railway system in New York, James Casey, George Ham of Boston, and others, united in the building of the Canada Southern Railroad, now the Michigan Central, between Buffalo and Detroit, with its route in Canada from Fort Erie, opposite Buffalo, through St. Thomas to Windsor, opposite Detroit. They had difficulties in Canada. Station houses were burned. Trains were derailed. Bridges were fired. The trouble primarily grew out of the right of way. Some of the country folk seemed to think the railroad should make them all rich. The officers of the company knew Murray, and they held a conference and urged him to leave Erie and straighten matters out in the Canada Southern's troubles. Their offer to Murray was so flattering that he agreed to go for three months, with the right to return at the end of that time if he did not find matters satisfactory.

In May 1873 Murray left Erie and went to Canada as head of detectives of the Canada Southern Railroad of which William L. Scott was president and F. N. Finney was general superintendent. He established headquarters in St. Thomas and travelled between Buffalo and Detroit, and frequently Chicago.

"The bridge-burning stopped first," says Murray. "I began a systematic watch of the bridge that was the scene of the most trouble. Night after night I lay in a clump of brush by the railroad track. They were hard to catch, but eventually the bridge-burning stopped, along with the firing of stations, for I gave chase in earnest and caught some of the incendiaries and they were sent to the penitentiary.

"Soon after the bridge-burning was broken up, L. D. Rucker, of the Canada Southern, called my attention to complaints of wholesale robbery of cars. Goods consigned from Boston and New York to the west were found to be missing on the arrival of the cars at their destination. The various roads over which the cars passed had to pay *pro rata* the loss to the shippers."

The selection of Murray to run down this wholesale train robbing, affecting various railroads, indicates the reputation he had earned at that time as a clever detective. It was a hard case.

"I went to Boston and started over the route of the goods," says Murray. "I saw the cars go through unbroken to Black Rock at Buffalo, where customs officers and sealers inspected and resealed the cars, after which they went on west through Canada. After following the route of goods several times I became convinced that the robberies were perpetrated at Black Rock, and that car sealers and railroad employees were in collusion. They, alone, could have the necessary knowledge or opportunity.

"Mose Mills was Customs Officer at the International Bridge at that time. I put up a job with Mills. We made a fake manifest showing boots, shoes, silks, and clothing, making a fat car. We gave the number of the car and sent the manifest out as usual, and then had the car placed at the old Bathurst Street yards at Black Rock. I got Police Captain Dixon, of old No. 5 station in Buffalo, and two of his men, Joe Henderson and Andy Dayton, a brother of Mayor Dayton. A fence ran along by the tracks. We got outside the fence and lay in wait.

"I remember the night well. It was the night of July 12th, 1874. It was blazing hot, breezeless, suffocating. We crouched alongside the fence for several hours. About 1.30 o'clock in the morning we saw two lanterns dodging in and out among the trucks. Three fellows slipped along silently, looking for the car numbered in the fake manifest.

"'Here it is,' said one of them.

"They broke the seal, slid the door, climbed in and began to open the boxes. When they were well along with their work we made a break for the car. Two of the three ran, with Dixon, Henderson, and Dayton after them. I grabbed the third fellow, a powerful giant in a cotton shirt and overalls. We grappled in the car and fell among the boxes. It was stifling hot in the box car and the water began to pour off us. Neither spoke a word. It was a silent struggle in the darkness. I recognised the fellow as one of our road's employees named Sweetman, counted one of the huskiest men in the business. He tried to strangle me to death, tried it so deliberately I had to admire his coolness. I broke his hold and, when he tried to jam me behind the boxes where he could shove a big packing case on me and crush me, I forced him over by the car door. There we heaved and strained amid the big boxes.

"I had stripped him naked in the first grapples of the fight. His cotton shirt and overalls had come off like the peeling of a banana. In his fury he tore my clothes off me and as we lurched toward the car door we fell out to the track below, two naked men, drenched with perspiration as if a tub of water had been emptied on us. We fell in a bunch and over we went on to the cinders and ballast and ties. There was no let up. Whichever man got the chance banged the other's head on the rails, jammed his face in the cinders or thumped his bare body on the ballast and ties. A free hand meant a stunning blow. We fought under the car and out on to the other tracks. All the while we were silent as two mutes. It was a case of which or t'other on top. He was worrying me. I was busy as I could be and I could not yell, and my gun was gone.

"We came to a full stop on the track between the rails beyond the car where our fight began. Neither of us was on top. We were a tangled bunch. As we lay straining, gasping, we heard a creaking and crunching. Instinctively both of us looked down the track. An engine had backed some cars in and they were bearing slowly, steadily down upon us. Sweetman was a game man, he never flinched. 'You first!' he gasped, as he strove to roll me nearest the approaching cars. My answer was a heave that turned him prone between the rails and there I held him, panting and desperate, not daring to relax my hold. Nearer and nearer came the cars. We could hear the grind of the flange. Sweetman writhed and strove to drag me down and force me over.

"'Give up?' I gasped.

"Sweetman shook his head and butted me full between the eyes. Together we reeled back on the track. The trucks of the nearest car were not thirty feet away, when Joe Henderson came running down the track, from the chase after the other two men, and dragged us back and snapped the handcuffs on Sweetman. Henderson had captured his man and the third escaped. I was somewhat disfigured and had to borrow some clothes, but I was mightily relieved when I saw the grim trucks of the freight cars go by and felt my bones safe beyond their reach. Sweetman was a partner of Slip Lewis. He was locked up, and later his attorney made a fight on some technicality.

"But this stopped the car burglaries. The railroads thanked me, and thereafter goods went west and arrived at their destination unmolested."

When Murray returned to St. Thomas, after breaking up the car burglaries, he found complaints of train tapping and quickly located it at the west end of the road in the vicinity of Amherstburg, on the Canadian side of the mouth of the Detroit River. Cars laden with grain would lose bushels in transit, in some unknown way. The cars were weighed at Detroit to make sure of their cargo and when weighed later by the railroad they were many bushels lighter. Murray by a plan of frequent weighing of the cars, narrowed the territory, where the thefts were committed, to the vicinity of Amherstburg.

"The method employed by the train tappers," says Murray, "was to crawl under a grain car at night, bore holes in the floor of the car with an auger, fill as many bags with grain as they could cart away, and then plug up the auger holes, and the car would bear no visible outward sign of having been robbed. Hundreds of bushels of grain would be stolen in this way. One night a single train was rifled of enough grain to make two waggon loads of filled bags. The quantity stolen in such a short time satisfied me that a gang of six or or seven did the job, and that it was not the work of only one or two. So I nosed around looking for sixes or sevens who would be apt to engage in train-tapping. I was puzzled to learn what became of the grain, if the thieves were people in the vicinity, for I could find no trace of any sales of grain apart from the usual barter in crops by farmers.

"I arranged for a string of grain cars to be laid out on a siding, and the first night I spotted a figure sneak under some of the cars and bore holes and put in plugs. No attempt was made that night to steal any of the grain, and evidently the cars were being prepared for the next night's raid. I decided to follow the fellow to his home on the first night, and I did so. The trail led to the home of the five Thrashers, a father, mother, and three sons, whose constant companions were two fellows named Johnson and Mike Fox.

"I went back and got two constables, and told them to meet me at a point in the yards, where I would have a freight engine. I got a switch engine, but the constables failed to appear, so I went alone with the engineer, John Savina by name, and the fireman. The engine stopped opposite the Thrashers, and I went out to the house to arrest the five people. I told the engineer and fireman to be prepared to come in a jiffy. I knocked at the door, and no one answered. I knocked again, and when no response came I shoved against the door and walked in. No one was in sight. I passed through the kitchen, and was about to enter a room opening off it when a tremendous screech came from the room. I stood and listened. It was like the high, quavering note of a calliope or steam piano. Without further ado I shoved open the door and entered. All I could see was a big, old-fashioned bed, surmounted by a mosquito net. Sitting upright in this bed was one of the ugliest women I ever saw in my life. She would glance at me, and then throw back her head and screech just as a coyote howls when he serenades the moon. She was Mrs. Thrasher. I bade her get up. She answered with a series of ear-splitting screeches. I spent about ten minutes trying to persuade her to get out of bed. When words were of no avail I laid hold of the mosquito netting and pulled it out of the way.

"'I am palsied!' shrieked Mrs. Thrasher. 'I am paralysed, and cannot be moved!'

"I approached the bed, and she dealt me such a thump on the head with her clenched hand as no paralytic ever was able to do. I sought to take her out of bed, but she buried herself in the bed clothes. So I simply took the tick, and pulled it off the bed, and was preparing to take the bed apart with her in it, when she sprang out and fled through the kitchen. I knew I could get her later, and the tick had seemed very heavy in my hands. I slit it open, and found it filled with new boots and shoes. While I was emptying them out I heard a stealthy step behind me, and whirled around just in time to see Mrs. Thrasher swing an axe and aim it at me. I dodged, and laid violent hands on Mrs. Thrasher's ankles, and landed her on the floor with a thud. Before she could regain the axe I just rolled her into the emptied tick, and fastened her by one of the tall bedposts, where she kicked and screeched, and probably well-nigh suffocated while I was searching the house.

"They had a number of bed ticks all filled with wheat. They also had a big chimney that was unused. They had stuffed this chimney full of bags of wheat. Old man Thrasher came out of a closet, and I arrested him. The engine hands helped me take the plunder away. I went to the place of Mike Fox near by, and arrested him after finding more of the stolen stuff on his premises. I also arrested Johnson, and took the whole batch before Magistrate George Gott, who also was Canadian customs officer, and he committed them to

Sandwich gaol for trial before Judge Horne, who sent them to Kingston Penitentiary for four years each.

"That broke up train-tapping. Mrs. Thrasher averred that after she was bagged in the tick she experienced a sensation similar to that caused by smiting the outside of the tick with the open hand. I suggested to her that perhaps she had wriggled and kicked so much as to bump herself against the bedpost. But she seemed to cling to the idea that she had been spanked soundly, not beaten or bruised, but simply spanked strenuously. What could a woman named Thrasher expect?"

8

THE COURSE OF A CAREER

AFTER Murray had been with the Canada Southern Railroad for about a year, the Canadian Government began to inquire if he was restricted exclusively to railroad detective work. His line of work had brought him under the constant and direct notice of the Department of Justice.

He received requests from the Department of Justice to aid them, first in matters in his territory as head of the Canada Southern's Detective Department, and finally to take up a baffling case for the Crown and work it out. In the fall of 1874 Murray received this telegram:

"JOHN W. MURRAY.—Come to Toronto.—O. MOWAT."

The signer was Sir Oliver Mowat, at that time Attorney-General and head of the Department of Justice. Murray turned the telegram over to the railroad people. They told Murray to go to Toronto and see what was wanted, as they desired to keep on good terms with the Government. Thus Murray, as chief of detectives of the Canada Southern, went to Toronto in 1874 to see Attorney-General Mowat. The Attorney-General asked Murray to become connected with the department. Murray declined, saying he had come, in response to a telegram, to aid the Government in any particular matter it had in hand.

"The matter was stated by the Attorney-General and his deputy, J. G. Scott," says Murray. "For a number of years counterfeiters had been at work in Owen Sound and vicinity. Some of them had dealt in counterfeit money for a long time, and had grown very wealthy and had influential connections. In fact, their relationships made it a doubly difficult matter. The Government was annoyed greatly by their actions, and the conditions finally had become such as to make it necessary to break up the gang, regardless of their influential connections. Once more I was thankful for my early training in the counterfeiting line. I went direct to the vicinity stated by the Attorney-General, and it was not long before I was in the confidence of the men who were handling the queer. The families of some were among the most respectable in that part of the country. I went ahead and obeyed my instructions. The members of the gang were arrested and convicted, and sent to the penitentiary.

"One of the gang had disappeared. He forged bonds and mortgages on various farmers, including a $1,500 mortgage on a farmer named Laycock, in the township of St. Vincent, County of Grey. He sold the forged paper in Toronto to Blakely & Alexander and fled the country, leaving no trace of his whereabouts. His name was John C. Bond, of Owen Sound.

"I returned to St. Thomas, after breaking up the gang and putting a stop to the counterfeiting, and resumed my duties with the Canada Southern. At intervals I received communications from the Department of Justice relative to securing my services permanently. Sir Oliver Mowat was Attorney-General then, and J. G. Scott, now Master of Titles, was Deputy Attorney-General. In the spring of 1875 came a formal tender of appointment as Detective of the Department of Justice. I conferred with my friends in St. Thomas. They advised me to accept. Mr. Finney, however, urged me to remain with him; and later, when he went west and built the Wisconsin Central, he endeavoured to get me to go with him.

"In April 1875 I was appointed by the Canadian Government. When I received the notice of appointment, I wrote at once saying it would be impossible for me to get away for at least three months. They replied that this was satisfactory. I finished the work I had then in hand, and in July 1875 I reported for duty in Toronto as Detective for the Provincial Government. I was the only regular officer, and I succeeded a man named Smith. My territory was all the Province of Ontario, and also I was to follow criminals to any place and run them down. I took charge of the detective work in the Department of Justice, of which the Attorney-General was the head."

Murray was thirty-five years old at this time. He found himself in charge of the detective work in a field extending practically from Montreal on the east to Rat Portage on the west; from the United States on the south to the wastes of snow and ice above Georgian Bay on the north. Its total area was 101,733 square miles, and its division was into eighty-four counties. It was girdled by the Ottawa River, the Upper St. Lawrence and Lakes Ontario, Erie, Huron, and Superior. From south-east to north-west it stretched 750 miles, and from north-east to south-west it was 500 miles.

In this field to which he was called, Murray found that the Department of Justice, otherwise the Attorney-General's Department, had charge of all the criminal business of the Province. For the expense of the administration of criminal justice there is an appropriation made by the Legislature, or Parliament, every year. A certain proportion of this appropriation is charged up to the various counties for work done therein. Each county has a County Crown Attorney, equivalent to a District Attorney in the United States. The County Crown Attorney is under the direction of, and is paid by, the Department of Justice. The counties have their local constables appointed by the County Judge of each county, but any criminal matter of importance is reported immediately to the Department of Justice. If the Department deems the case of sufficient importance, Murray takes it up either in person or supervises the investigation, the constables and others being subordinate to him in the matter.

"It is an excellent system, and the splendid record of the Department of Justice for many years indicates how efficient it is and how well it works," says Murray.

Murray thus entered upon the full course of his career over twenty-eight years ago. He brought to his work a rich experience and rare training. His dangerous and exacting duties during the Civil War were followed by busy years with the United States in special service and hard years, filled with all sorts of experiences, on the police force at Erie. He learned all the details of the lower forms of police work and gradually broadened his field of activity until he was graduated from the detective work at Erie to the duties of head of the Canada Southern Railroad's detective department. He had learned what it meant to come in contact with desperate criminals. He had improved the opportunities to study the ways of the keenest crooks. He had schooled himself in the details of information of every class of crime. The severity with which his skill and knowledge and ability were tested in the years to follow is shown again and again in the tales of the crimes whose mysteries he solved and whose perpetrators he ran to earth.

His new field included cities, towns, and villages, thickly populated places, and vast stretches of country unsettled and wild. In the flock of this new shepherd were the keen city thieves, the riff-raff of towns, the roughs of the country, and the outlaws of the wilds. The people of the province varied as much as did its physical geography. There were strong French settlements, strong German settlements, strong English settlements, strong Irish settlements. Each had its distinguishing characteristics. They were clannish in their ways. Entire counties were known as German counties, or French counties, or English counties. Scattered among the honest, peaceful folk were desperate and lawless men. In addition to those who had sought the country from the old world as a haven wherein to hide, or who had grown up to disregard the law in the liberty which the land afforded, were those who fled from the United States and buried themselves in out-of-the-way places. There were endless opportunities for the perpetration of all kinds of crime. In the outlying villages or sparsely settled country, ruffians were able to outrage law and order, and escape to other remote parts of the Province.

Burglaries, murders, assaults, forgeries, counterfeitings, all classes of crime and all classes of criminals were known to the Province at that time, as they have been known to it since. But the criminals soon were to learn the grip of a new master. They were to feel the iron hand of a man who feared none of them ; they were to hear the tread of footsteps in pursuit, that never ceased until the pursued was dead or behind prison bars; they were to behold a new face and listen to a new voice, and realise that the old order of things had passed away, that a new figure had risen among them and ruled in absolute sway.

Murray in 1875 was a broad-shouldered, powerful giant, sandy haired, sandy moustached, blue-eyed. His voice, then, as now, was remarkable for its wide range, and particularly for its power to change from gentle, tender tones to ones so deep, so rough, so harsh, that at times the guilty, on hearing it in thunderous accusation, have burst into tears and confessed. In all the years that have passed since he began his work in Canada, Murray has changed little in appearance. Age has dealt kindly with him. The broad shoulders and powerful frame are giving their meed of deference to the fateful years that have gone, but the blue eyes look out upon the world, as of old, bright and unafraid.

SANCTIMONIOUS BOND

ONE of Murray's first acts after becoming identified with the Department of Justice at Toronto, was to turn back to the case of John C. Bond, of the Owen Sound gang, who disappeared the year before when Murray, at Sir Oliver Mowat's request, broke up the gang, and sent all but Bond to prison. Bond had sold a $1,500 forged mortgage in Toronto, and vanished. Murray saw at the outset it was important he should impress upon the mind of all the criminal classes in Canada that, once he set out after them, he would land them, no matter where they went or how snugly they hid. So he undertook to find Bond. The man had over a year's start of Murray. He had gone, no one knew where. He had money to aid him, and friends to protect him. He might be in China or Labrador, in Australia or Russia. He might be dead.

"The first thing I did was to bill him," says Murray. "I prepared bills or hand posters giving his description, his habits, his crime, and any other information of use in identifying him. I sent these all over the world—to Scotland Yard, to Paris, to Berlin, to Rome, to New York, to Chicago, and all the chief police departments in the United States, and elsewhere. This is called billing a man. Sometimes I do not bill them, for I prefer a still hunt, and I conduct it through personal letters to my personal friends in all these police departments. In the course of my life I have had occasion to make friends with able men in practically all the detective bureaus of all the great police departments. But I desired to take no advantage of Bond. It was to be a fair chase, with fair warning, his wits against mine. No tidings came from billing him. So I took the next step in hunting a man. I located his nearest kin.

"Bond had a brother, who was chief clerk in the post office in Lindsay, Ontario. That year a new postmaster was appointed. I went to Lindsay with a letter of introduction to the postmaster. I had obtained specimens of Bond's handwriting for purposes of comparison, and the next day, after my arrival, there was a new assistant clerk in the Lindsay post office, who opened the bags of incoming mails, and ran over the letters. Soon two letters came. I got a glimpse of one, but not sufficient for my purposes. The brother was quick and wary, and scooped the letters over. The second letter I saw, for the simple reason that some candy I offered to the brother caused him to rush out very frequently. He looked for a letter every other Thursday, and it was on a Thursday I gave him the candy, and he was called out about the time the mail arrived. The letter was postmarked Evanston, Ill. The handwriting was unlike that of Bond, except for a kink in the B. I remembered his skill as a forger, and did not worry. When the brother re-entered the office his letters lay in the bunch, without a sign of having been touched.

"I quietly got my warrant for Bond's arrest, and slipped away to Chicago. Bill McGrogle was chief in Chicago in those days. Later, he foolishly hurried over into Canada for a sojourn when, as I understand, there was no necessity for it. From Bill I received a letter of introduction to the chief of police in Evanston, Ill., whose name was Carney, and who was a deputy sheriff, and several other officials, as well as chief of police. Carney was away when I first arrived.

"I had a good description of Bond, although I never had seen him, as he skipped out of Owen Sound the year before, when I went there to break up the gang. I also had a blurred photograph, but as I have said before, a good description is worth more than a dozen photographs. It gives you an accuracy in idea of how your man looks and acts, that no photograph can do. I began to walk the streets of Evanston, not much of a town in those days, on the look-out for a man answering the description of Bond. I was smoking a big, black cigar, and was blowing the smoke skyward with great gusto. In fact, I stopped at a street corner and became absorbed in blowing smoke rings and watching them float away, expanding and fading as they went. Suddenly I heard a voice beside me, one of those smooth, flat, oily voices, that causes you to think its owner soaks it every night in a vat of tincture of hypocrisy.

"'My friend,' the voice was saying, 'are you not aware that smoking is a filthy and wasteful habit?'

"'It depends on the point of view,' I remarked mildly, for I was a stranger in a strange land, and desired to make friends not foes just then, to aid me in my hunt for Bond.

"As I spoke I eyed him, and, while his hair decorations were different, he answered to a dot my description of Bond. If I could see him walk I would be sure. Bond had no limp, but my description was particularly good as to his general appearance and manner when walking. He was revelling in a tirade against smoking, and finally took up the theme of the evil of intemperance. I said just enough to keep him going, and when he began to pace to and fro I stepped back about fifteen feet and watched him. I saw him clasp his hands behind his back. Bond did the same thing, according to my description. I saw him clasp his hands in front of him. Bond did the same. Bond also interlaced his fingers, and I vowed that if this sanctimonious, hypocritical haranguer interlaced his fingers, I would seize him on the spot. Lo and behold! he did so. I stepped forward, seized his right hand, and shook it heartily.

"'Why, Bond, old fellow, I didn't recognise you at first,' I said, and continued to shake his hand with increased fervour.

"He stopped short in his sermonising on smoking.

"'You are mistaken,' he said, endeavouring to draw away his hand which, by that time, I was shaking violently.

"'No,' said I, seizing both hands, and shaking them so that his teeth chattered. 'I met you in Hamilton, where you were in the sewing-machine business.'

"'Oh, yes,' he chattered, for I had his head bobbing by my hand-shaking. 'What name?'

"'MacDonald,' said I, and I shook his hands until I warrant his arms almost fell out of their sockets.

"This hand-shaking a man until he almost falls apart is not

an accepted form of arresting a man, and I never had done it before, but I actually was glad to see Bond, and also, I was very fond of tobacco then, although I do not use it now, and I resented his interfering with my morning smoke, particularly when the rings were floating so beautifully. Also I hoped to shake an acknowledgment of his identity out of him, if he was Bond. So I simply stood there and shook him. I shook his hands until his hat fell off. I shook his hands until he was red in the face and was gasping for breath. The few people who saw us grinned understandingly, as if witnessing the reunion of two long-lost brothers. I shook his hands relentlessly, furiously for several minutes. Then I stopped and looked at him.

"'Bond, I am glad to see you,' I said, and I made as if to shake hands again.

"'No,' no,' said Bond, hastily clasping his hands behind him.

'"Will you have a drink, Bond?' I said.

"The sanctimonious expression settled down over his face again, like a putty mask. I respect a sincere temperate man, but a hypocrite makes me feel as if I had mosquitoes down my back.

"'This is a temperance town, and I neither smoke nor drink,' said Bond.

"'Well, I tell you, Bond,' said I; 'you may not smoke or drink, but I arrest you just the same. It's not because you neither smoke nor drink, but because you are wanted over in Canada for a little business you did over there.'

"I arrested him then and there. All I had was the Canada warrant, and it alone was not worth the paper it was written on in Illinois. But the chief of police, Carney, had come home, and I handed over my letter of introduction, and after he read it I locked Bond up, and took him to Chicago by the next train. He was in the piano business, and was a temperance lecturer and organiser.

"'Where am I wanted?' asked Bond, on his way from Evanston to Chicago.

"I knew Bond relied on his ability to escape conviction in Owen Sound, for in those days it was a mighty difficult task to convict a man in Owen Sound, who had money and friends there. So I answered: 'Owen Sound.' Bond smiled outwardly; so did I smile, inwardly.

"Bond had a brother in Chicago who was a member of the Board of Trade. When we arrived there the brothers talked it over, and were satisfied Bond should return, they thinking it was the aftermath of the troubles of the Owen Sound gang. Bond came with me, and when I arrived in Canada I informed him we were going to Toronto, instead of to Owen Sound. He was one of the maddest hypocrites I ever saw. He was so hot that, despite his not using tobacco, he almost blew rings of smoke. I landed him in Toronto on October 16th, 1875. He was sent to the penitentiary for seven years. I brought him back over a year after he disappeared, and a little over three months after I became a Government official.

"Bond was a hypocrite. He posed as a saint, and in fact he was a crook. A change of countries did not work a change of character. To look at him as he sermonised on the street of Evanston, one might mistake him for a minister, but a second glance would tell the difference. However, the countenance does not always betray the crook. I have read often about the most accomplished crooks having the most clerical faces. That does not exist, as a rule, at all. Crime leaves its traces just as consumption leaves its traces. Yet I have known desperate criminals who looked like ignorant bumpkins or scholarly ministers. The eye is the great betrayer. Some crooks have a hard, steady eye; others have a small, restless eye; others a large, placid eye. It is not so much the size or kind of eye, as it is the sudden gleam or flicker, or waver or droop, the barest flash of guilt, oft-times merely fractional or intangible, yet as ample as the flare of a beacon light to locate the danger and reveal the true character. Often you instinctively know your man. It is as if some mysterious transmission of intelligence told you certainly: 'There he is,' or 'He is lying.'

"Bond was one of the immaculate sort, so far as countenance was concerned. But I will venture that never again in all his life has he approached a stranger, who was enjoying a quiet smoke, and poured forth upon him a street corner tirade against the evils of tobacco. Evanston lost a thrifty piano dealer and loquacious temperance lecturer, but Kingston Penitentiary gained a sanctimonious prisoner."

THE DRIVERLESS TEAM ON CALEDONIA ROAD

A LONG road of many turnings leads out of the town of Caledonia, fifty-five miles beyond Toronto, and winds its way through the county of Haldimand. In parts it is broad and open, and in parts it is narrow and shaded. One evening, in December 1875, a waggon drawn by two horses, moved out this road. No driver was visible. The horses jogged along of their own accord, the reins hanging loose from the seat and flapping as the horses went their way. Some cows passed, and the horses turned out to give them part of the road. Then on they went as if a driver handled the reins Night fell, and in the darkness the waggon rumbled on. Lights flashed out in farmhouses along the way and voices were heard in the darkness. The driverless team plodded on until they came to a broad pathway of light shining out across the highway through the open door of a farmhouse, standing close by the road.

The team stopped in this light. A dog rushed out, sniffed at the horses, then at the waggon, and fell to barking furiously. A farmer appeared in the doorway, and shouted to the dog to be silent. He saw the team standing in the light, and called out a cheery good-night. There was no answer. The dog whined, and ran to and fro, and darted out to the waggon, and began barking again, more excitedly than before. The farmer, standing in the doorway, shaded his eyes with his hand and peered out into the night.

"Anything wrong?" he called toward the waggon.

No answer came. He called again. When no one answered he walked down to the waggon, looked it over, saw no one, then stepped up on the hub of a wheel, and looked in to see what load it carried. All he saw was a big, black bundle lying in the bed of the waggon beneath the seat. He called to those in the house, and they took a lantern to him. He held it over the waggon bed, and the bundle took the form of a man, doubled over. The farmer clambered into the waggon, set the lantern beside the figure, undoubled it, and took the man's head in his hands. An ugly wound was slashed across the head. The body had a faint warmth, but the eyes were dimming fast, and, as the farmer held the injured head, the eyes glazed, the jaw set, and death came.

The dead man was a stranger to the farmer. He carried the body into his house, and sent for doctors, who came and found the unknown dead. The team and waggon were not recognised by any one who looked at them. The dead man was past fifty years of age, evidently a well-to-do farmer of the better type. There was nothing in his belongings to identify him. A strange team had come jogging out of the darkness with a dying stranger, halted in the light, and waited for death to overtake him.

Murray, who had been busy on the evidence in the Findlay and Pettit cases, as well as travelling from one end to another of the province on various other matters, was notified through the Department of Justice by telegraph, and straightway went to the place where the stranger lay dead.

"To learn who he was, of course, was the first thing," says Murray. "The country folk gathered rapidly for miles around, and soon there were several who knew him. He was Abel McDonald, a prosperous farmer, who lived in the township of Walpole, about eighteen miles away. There were some bags in the waggon, and the team had been travelling on the road leading out of Caledonia. A tour of the town of Caledonia resulted in learning that the old man had driven into town on the day of his death, with a load of wheat, had sold it, and started home at twilight. He had about $35 with him when he last was seen in Caledonia. No money was found on him or in his waggon. An inquest was held, but no evidence of value had developed.

"The fact that Caledonia was a little place, where everybody knew everybody, aided me. I set out to account for the whereabouts of almost everybody in or around Caledonia about the time of the murder. I went from house to house, talking to every one. Finally I learned that John Young and William James Young, his nephew, two farmers with none too good a reputation, who lived in the township of Ancaster, over the mountain five or six miles from Hamilton, were among the people seen on this road on the day of the murder. John Young was about thirty-five years old, a big, burly, powerful fellow, and William James Young, his nephew, was about twenty-two years old, and a well-built, good-looking young fellow. I found a man who knew them, who had seen them going out the road before McDonald started home, and I found other witnesses who had seen them later coming back along this road, walking.

"The two Youngs went with two Barber girls in Caledonia, and were at their house after they were seen coming back on the Walpole road. It was slim evidence on which to arrest them, but it was wiser to get them into gaol, so they were arrested. When arraigned before Magistrate John Scott they laughed and scoffed at the evidence. In truth, we had barely enough evidence to commit them for trial. But we had enough, although none to spare, and they were held. I saw I had an uphill job. The Barber girls were prepared to swear that the Youngs were with them, and could not have been near the scene of the murder. I went over the road foot by foot. I found the club used to kill McDonald. It was hid under a fence. I found also the sapling from which it had been cut. In fact, it was a young tree about two inches in diameter, and I had both the roots of the tree and the club itself in court at the trial. I had the road surveyed, and the scene of the murder located exactly. This was all very good, but it was not enough to convict the Youngs beyond any doubt in a jury's mind.

"So I sent over to Buffalo in New York State, and brought over a friend of mine, Hugh Massey, a former member of the Buffalo police force. I got Massey before Major Hugh Stewart, then warden of the county and justice of the peace, and had him committed to gaol for sixty days. He was locked up in a cell near the Youngs, and in due time he ingratiated himself into their confidence. I had studied the Youngs, and had come to the conclusion that a clever man, if unsuspected, could draw their story from them. I was right. Massey got the whole story out of them. They told him how they had been in Caledonia, and had seen the old man with his money, how they went out the road ahead of him, how John cut the club, with the knife found on him when he was arrested, how they waited about two and a-half miles from the town, how they jumped on McDonald's waggon when he drove along, how John struck him over the head with the club, how they robbed him, left him in the bottom of the waggon, started the horses, jumped out, and returned to Caledonia. I had Mr. Lawrence, governor of the gaol, and the turnkey to hear the story.

"The trial occurred in March 1876, before Judge Adam Wilson, at Cayuga. John Idington, now County Crown Attorney of Stratford, prosecuted, and Attorney Duff, of Hamilton, defended. It was a long, tedious case. They sought to prove an alibi by the Barber girls, just as I expected. The Crown swore over eighty witnesses, and we disproved the alibi. Massey, on the stand, told his story in such a straightforward way that, not only the jury, but every one who heard him, believed him. Late on the night of March 27th, 1876, the jury brought in a verdict of guilty. Both Youngs were sentenced to be hanged. John Young was a desperate man, and after the sentence the governor of the gaol was instructed to put a special guard over the two men, to make sure they would not escape. The governor was a well-meaning and honourable old fellow, but he had an idea he knew his business better than any one could tell him. Sure enough, the Youngs broke gaol and got away. The question was, who was responsible? I was instructed to investigate, in connection with the inspector of prisons. Governor Lawrence was removed. In those days the sheriff had the appointment of gaolers, but now the Government appoints them.

"The Youngs made their way by night to some remote place, beyond reach of those who tried to find them. I immediately thought of the Barber girls, and sent word to watch them. They were seen going to a thick wood some distance from Caledonia. They went to meet the Youngs, who had secreted themselves in an old barn in the woods This barn was filled to the top with hay. The Hamilton police were notified, and they went out to the barn, and, after a stubborn revolver fight, captured the Youngs, and they were taken back to Cayuga gaol."

In September, 1876, Murray went to Philadelphia, for a month at the Centennial, where James Tilley, of New York, was chief of the detective department at the Exposition. Tilley was a fast friend of Murray, and had been endeavouring to have him join the corps of detectives, culled from all over the country, and stay during the entire Centennial, but Murray was so busy in Canada that the Government spared him for only one month, September.

"While I was in Philadelphia, on September 21st, 1876, John Young was hanged at Cayuga," says Murray, "and James Young's sentence was commuted to imprisonment for life. Sixteen years later I was in Caledonia one pleasant afternoon on a matter, and had to wait an hour for a train. I strolled over the big bridge across the grand river, while waiting for the train. In the middle of the bridge stood a man, gazing into the water flowing beneath. I got just a side glance of him as he turned his head away, but I said to myself: 'If James Young was not in the Penitentiary that would be he.' I turned back and looked at him. He walked away. I went back to my hotel, and said to the landlord, 'If I did not know James Young was in the Penitentiary I would swear I saw him on the bridge.'

"'Yes,' said the landlord, 'he's pardoned, and is around looking at the old familiar places for the first time in many years.'

"'I am sorry not to have talked to him,' said I, and if my train had not been almost due I would have gone back and had a chat with him, for he seemed lonely."

11

THE WHITESIDES OF BALLINAFAD

MURRAY'S first year with the Canada Government won for him the praise of those in authority. He had convicted the guilty, despite powerful influences exerted to acquit them; he had established throughout the Province the understanding that a man who committed a crime and fled, would be followed and brought back and punished. He had failed in no case; he had solved every mystery arising; and perpetrators of crimes had been brought to justice.

"There were many more cases than those I have mentioned," says Murray. "I was busy day in and day out; ever on the go; always working. I remember in August 1876, just after my first year had been rounded out, I sat down to look over again my records for the year, when a telegram told of the Ballinafad murder."

Ballinafad was a mite of a hamlet in the Township of Esquesing, County of Halton, near Georgetown, about forty miles from Toronto. On the finest timber-tract in that part of the country lived John Whiteside, an old man in his sixty-eighth year. He was regarded as a miser. Instead of gold, land was his god. All that he could rake or scrape or get together went to buy land. He worshipped his timber. He would walk through his woods, rubbing his hands and chuckling. He would sit by the base of a big tree, his cheek pressed affectionately against its trunk. He would fall prone upon the earth with limbs outstretched and murmur: "Mine, mine, mine."

"Sometimes he would pause and pat a tree as if it were a little child," says Murray. "A broken bough caused him as much distress as if a child had broken a limb. His forest was his family, and his trees were his little ones. He loved them. Sometimes in the night, when the wind was moaning in the tree-tops, or the forest was swaying in the song of the gale, the old man would steal out of the house, bare-headed, and listen as if the wind-music were a lullaby.

"He had a wife, and sons and daughters. He seemed to be so engrossed in his timber and his land that he gave little heed to his family. A number of his children went away, leaving his wife and second son, Harry, and a daughter at home. It was alleged that the old man barely permitted them to have the actual necessaries of life. He had his house in a little clearing, with his timber towering all around.

"One night he stepped outside, as he had done so often. It was a black night. He did not return. A neighbour, passing in the dim dawn, hailed the house, and when the family opened the door they saw the old man lying near by, dead. His head had been chopped open with a single blow, followed by others, in the dark. The axe was found near by, with some of his grey hairs on it.

"The son Harry was arrested, and I also arrested the wife, Harry's mother. At the inquest they gave evidence that the dogs barked in the night, the old man went out and did not come back, and that was all they knew about it. The magistrate remanded them from time to time, and they were held in Milton gaol for a considerable period.

"It was a difficult case, and there was not sufficient evidence for conviction then. I called from time to time to see them. On one of my visits, as I approached in the corridor I heard a hacking cough.

"'Who is that?' I asked.

"'Harry Whiteside,' was the reply.

"I looked him over more carefully than on previous visits. His eyes were bright, and in each cheek a pink spot glowed. I saw the mother, and her eyes and cheeks were like those of her son. Nothing more was done towards convicting them. They were released. Quietly I made regular trips to the vicinity of their place. I could hear from quite a distance the coughing—dry, hard, and hacking—of the son. I used to stand a moment and listen, then softly go away. One day I went and waited, and heard nothing. I drove to the cemetery, and he was there—asleep for ever.

"The mother lived on. I had gathered together what evidence I had been able to find, and I held it pending a series of occasional visits to where she was living. I never annoyed her by my presence. I could stand off some distance and listen and learn all that I desired to know. Occasionally I would get a glimpse of her as she appeared, very white and feeble, by the door in a big chair, to get the sunlight. She went very slowly, far more deliberately than her son. He had galloped from the gaol to the grave; she plodded along a weary way. But at last she, too, ceased coughing, and was borne away.

"Consumption had killed both of them. The Crown had done its full duty, in so far as the evidence warranted. The malady was hereditary in the family, and seized violently upon both mother and son soon after the old man was murdered. I visited the vicinity, to make sure there was no shamming, and to ascertain whether, on the eve of the arrival of death, any farewell word was to be uttered. I remember vividly the occasions on which I stood in the background listening while mother and son coughed their lives away."

12

THE SIX-FOOT NEEDHAMS: FATHER AND SON

WHILE Murray was trailing the cutter in the Monaghan case he passed on the road near London a swarthy giant who waved to him as he vanished in the woods. He was a man of colossal build, over six feet tall, with a massive frame and huge head and shoulders. His skin was copper, and his tread, despite his great size, was light and panther-like. His hair was jet-black, coarse and glossy. When Murray waved in response the man's voice called back a cheery welcome, followed by a perfect imitation of the barking of a fox.

"He was young Needham," says Murray, "and thereby hangs a tale that recurs to me every time I see an Indian who is fearless, or a bully that is beaten. The Needhams, father and son, were Indians. Both of them were giants in build and strength. Either one of them could pick up a two hundred pound man, and toss him over the fence as if he were a bag of buckwheat. They lived in an out-of-the-way place in the county of Elgin, but roamed all over that part of Canada. One interesting feature of their appearance was they looked so much alike that many people mistook them for one another and could not tell them apart. In fact, they looked more like twin brothers than like father and son. Both were superb specimens of physical manhood, and their constant trudging about the country kept their muscles hard as steel.

"The father was called Doc Needham. He was not a regular practitioner, but was an Indian herb doctor. A great many people believed in his medicines, and there were tales of marvellous cures he had wrought. One legend was that with three drops of the essence of a certain root he had restored to life a man who was about to be buried. The son helped the father. He dug roots and gathered herbs, and kept the medicine pot boiling, and accompanied his father on some of his trips around the country, particularly to county fairs. They came to be a feature at these fairs and their fame spread far and wide. Sometimes they drew crowds for their medicine-sellings, by short exhibitions, in which the father and son both displayed, in small degree, the great strength they possessed. They were a peaceable pair and never sought trouble.

"At the township fair in Wallace, county of Elgin, in 1874, the Needhams were present with their supply of herbs. Crowds gathered to see their exhibition and to buy their medicines. Among those at the fair was Harry Fitzsimmons, a big fellow, built like a bull, with thick neck and deep chest and heavy head. He claimed to be a fighter, and prided himself he could lick any man in the county. He had a boon companion with him that day, George Lipsey. Lipsey was something of a fighter himself, but deferred to Fitzsimmons as the king of the county when it came to a fight. Fitz was bent on trouble. He thrashed that day two or three husky country fellows who had thought they could fight. Then, flushed with his easy victories and a stranger to defeat, he came upon the Needhams, father and son, busy with their medicines. Fitz's brow clouded. He had heard of the Needhams and their feats of strength until he was sick of the tales of their prowess. He would show the countryside that Fitzsimmons was master. He tried to pick a fight. The Needhams ignored him. Fitz and Lipsey grew boisterous and the Needhams moved away. They followed. Young Needham could be seen speaking earnestly to his father, who shook his head sternly. Fitz and Lipsey persisted in annoying the pair, and at last Doc Needham nodded to his son. Young Needham doffed his coat and slipped over to within ten feet of Fitz and Lipsey. Fitz spied him and bore down upon him with a rush. The crowd fell back and the strong arm of Doc Needham drew Lipsey back as if he were a child, and kept him out of the fray. It was a fight for gods and men. Young Needham, light-footed and graceful, played around the bull-like Fitz, dodging his blows, evading his rushes, until with sudden swoop of arms and stiffening of body he seized Fitz, banged him upon the earth with terrific thud, then heaved him upward and tossed him, literally threw him, full fifteen feet, as a man would hurl a heavy hammer. As he struck the earth young Needham was on him like a panther, and he dug a hole in the Wallace Fair grounds, using the face and head of Fitz as a spade. When he finished, he picked him up again and slammed him down, and the mighty Fitz lay still, with a zigzag gash on his cheek.

"Doc Needham released Lipsey, who cared for his beaten crony, fanning his face, resuscitating him, and leading him away. The Needhams, amid the plaudits of the crowd, resumed their medicine vending. They were not molested again, but in the evening Fitz limped over to their stand with Lipsey and shook his fist at young Needham.

"'I'll get even with you,' he said. 'I'll break every bone in your body.'

"Young Needham leaped at him, the whole savage in his being aroused, but the giant arms of Doc Needham closed on his boy and held him as a mother could clutch her child, and those who saw it beheld, for the first and last time, which of the two Needhams was the mightier man.

"'Go away or I'll loose him,' said Doc Needham, and Fitz and Lipsey limped away.

"But for Doc Needham there would have been murder at the Wallace Fair that day.

"Some time after the vanquishing of Fitz, Doc Needham and his son were in St. Thomas. They had their own team. They took a little firewater before they started home. They stopped, on their way home, at the tavern by Kittlecreek Bridge, on the outskirts of St. Thomas. Young Needham alighted before reaching the tavern and started off to see a man on business. Doc Needham drove up to the tavern and stopped. In a bag in his waggon he had an axe-head and some pork, both of which he had bought in St. Thomas. When he drove away from the tavern, Fitz and Lipsey jumped into the waggon, grabbed the bag containing the pork and axe-head, and while one tried to hold Doc Needham the other beat him over the head with the bag and killed him. They mistook him for his son and thought they were beating young Needham.

"They escaped in the darkness and got out of the country. This had occurred before I began to work for the Government, but I took up the case. Doc Needham was popular throughout the entire country round about. I sent circulars all over Canada and the United States describing Fitz and Lipsey. Young Needham had marked Fitz for identification in the fight at the Wallace Fair. Through a stray letter I got track of Fitz out near Red Wing in Minnesota. I went after him, taking Governor John King of the St. Thomas gaol with me to identify him. Governor King knew Fitz well, as Fitz had worked for him at one time. King and I arrived in Red Wing late at night. We had a double-bedded room. It was late in November. King snored like a hippopotamus and I could not sleep, so I arose at the first sign of dawn and went out to find a barber's shop. I walked the silent streets of Red Wing for about an hour, when a barber's shop opened and I started for it. As I crossed the street an enormous fellow came slouching along and entered the shop. He had a full beard and long hair. I followed him into the shop. I waited while the barber was cutting his hair. He sat with his eyes shut, and as I studied him in the mirror, the description I had of Fitz seemed to fit, bit by bit, to the bearded giant in the chair.

"I recalled the zigzag scar on the cheek, and waited while the barber's shears snipped, snipped, snipped at the hair. The man fell asleep in the chair. He must have been up all night. He snored and the barber smiled. A voice outside began shouting: 'Joe! Joe!' The barber answered by going to the door and calling: 'Yes, in a minute.' The man outside yelled again, and, with a glance at his sleeping customer, the barber laid down his shears and stepped out. I waited. If I only knew whether there was a zigzag scar on the sleeper's cheek. I tiptoed to the door and looked out. The barber was talking busily to a man in a waggon. I tiptoed back to where the sleeper snored in the chair. His head was on one side. The scissors were within easy reach. He snored. I seized the scissors, moved them close to his cheek, snipped and quickly laid them down and resumed my seat. He snored on. I stood up, and there, where the hair had been cut away, I saw the outline of a zigzag scar. I arose and walked out of the shop. The barber called to me as I passed him.

"'I'll be back presently,' said I.

"I simply located the gaol accurately and returned to the barber's shop. The giant was just getting out of the chair, and was raging at the barber for slashing his beard so close on the cheeks.

"'I said to trim it on the chin, not the cheeks,' he growled.

"I walked out with him. He growled to me about the barber, and said I did right to leave without a shave.

"'What might your name be, friend?' I finally asked him.

"'Church,' he said; 'and I'm bound down the river instanter.'

"It was a desperate situation. I was sure he was Fitz. Yet I might be mistaken. I must find some way to hold him until I could get Governor King to look him over. The giant refused an invitation to drink or breakfast. He was angry and determined to get out of town at once. An idea struck me.

"'Well, Church,' said I; 'I am sorry, but I want you.'

"'Want me? What for?' he roared.

"'You stole a canoe and a coil of rope down river last night,' said I.

"'You're a —— liar,' said he, in a rage.

"'It's not what I say, it's what a fellow over here says,' said I.

"'Over where?' growled the giant. 'Show him to me.'

"'Come on,' said I. 'Face him, and make him face you.'

"The ugly bully side of the man was aroused. For once in his life, whoever he was, he had been accused wrongfully and was innocent. He would wreak his vengeance on his accuser.

"The court house and gaol were in the centre of a square. A man stood in the doorway. We approached, I walking ahead, and I quickly said to him: 'I want the sheriff.'

"'He's just getting up,' was the reply.

"'Well, he'd better be quick about it,' rumbled my companion, who had not heard my question, and who thought I had asked for the man who had made the charge of stealing against him.

"The man in the doorway was the turnkey. Without a word he opened the door and we entered, and the door clanged shut behind us.

"'Wait here,' I told my huge friend, and I went in and saw the sheriff.

"Chandler was his name. He was a bachelor, a fine man, and was serving his third term as sheriff. I told him my whole story: that I was an officer from Canada, and that I had a man charged with murder. The sheriff was very nice. He called Church in, told him to step into the next room, and when he did so, locked him in. I hurried back to the hotel and awakened Governor King.

"'I've got Fitz.' said I.

"'Nonsense,' said he. 'You don't even know him when you see him.'

"'Come to the gaol,' said I.

"Governor King dressed in a jiffy. On the way to the gaol I told him the story. I reminded him that, if it was not Fitz, all he needed to say was that he was not the man who stole the canoe and rope. If it was Fitz, he should give him a nice talk about the folks at home, and how the people felt, and jolly him along, as we could not take him back, under the circumstances, unless he was willing to go. We entered the gaol. We could hear a thunderous roaring. It was my friend Church, bellowing in rage over being locked in. King went to the door. Church spied him.

"'Hello, Harry,' said Governor King.

"'Hello, governor,' said Fitz, meek as a lamb, and no longer roaring.

"They shook hands and talked for an hour. I breakfasted with the sheriff. Fitz consented to return to Canada, after talking with King. We started that night. The news of a murderer being arrested spread like wildfire. When we left the gaol over two thousand people were waiting to see the murderer from Canada. The crowd grew rapidly, until the entire town and many from round about followed us to the train. A number boarded the train and rode to the next station. We rode in the smoker that night, and in the morning a fellow-passenger told me that a lawyer from Milwaukee had heard of the matter and would try to make trouble for me with my prisoner. Fitz and King and I still were riding in the smoker at that time.

"'Harry,' said I to Fitz, 'a shyster is coming in here soon to make trouble for you. Give him a short answer.'

"Presently in came the Milwaukee lawyer, with a high hat and lofty air.

"'Where is this prisoner charged with murder they are going to take to Canada?' he demanded in a loud voice.

"No one answered. He spotted Harry.

"'My man,' he said to Fitz, 'don't you know you have a right in this country, and only the President can have you taken out? What are you charged with?'

"'Kissing a mule's tail. Ain't you glad you found out?' said Fitz, at the top of his voice.

"Everybody in the car laughed. The lawyer from Milwaukee grew red as a beet.

"'You *ought* to be hung!' he snorted, and everybody laughed again.

"As our train near home crossed Kittlecreek Bridge, Fitz pointed out the tavern and started to tell me about the murder. I told him not to tell me. He was convicted of manslaughter, and was sentenced to ten years in the Penitentiary.

"All four men who were figures in the fight at the Wallace Fair came to tragic ends. Doc Needham was murdered; Fitzsimmons died in the Penitentiary; Lipsey was killed in a circus row in a Western State; young Needham was killed in 1902, up near Spring Bank, not far from London. Spring Bank was a picnic place near the Indian Reserve at Muncietown. Young Needham, no longer young, was there with numerous Indians on a holiday, in August 1902. He was drinking at the pump. Big McCarter, of London, was there, and he ordered Needham away from the pump. Needham refused to go. It was about ten o'clock at night. McCarter said he would make him go. Needham stood off to meet him. Everybody fell back to make room for the fight.

They were fighting, when suddenly Needham, who had been untouched, fell like a log. McCarter kicked him savagely as he lay, and when they picked young Needham up, he was beyond need of aid.

"McCarter was arrested. An autopsy was held. It showed several of Needham's ribs had been kicked in; but it showed also, according to the testimony of those who performed the autopsy, that the direct cause of death was heart failure. Big McCarter was tried at the Fall Assizes in 1902 and acquitted. The autopsy saved him. It also saved young Needham's record, and sent him to his grave unbeaten."

13

PRETTY MARY WARD OF THE GOVERNMENT GARDENS

A WINDOW of Murray's office in the Department of Justice in the old time Government building in Toronto, looked out on the flower gardens, the gravel walks and close-cropped lawns and luxuriant shade trees of the Government grounds. Daily, the old gardener, and his wife might be seen working in the grounds. Early in 1876 a new face appeared in the gardens, amid the flowers. It was a face so winsome and sweet that it seemed to have caught the fragrant beauty of the flowers, with roses blooming in the cheeks and violets nestling in the big dark eyes. She came and went with her uncle and aunt, and gradually became a familiar figure as she delved in the flower beds or gathered bunches of blooms.

The girl had come out from England in the early part of the year. She came to make her home in the New World with her aunt and uncle, who kept the Government gardens. Aboard ship, on the way out, she met Ebenezer Ward. Ward was a big, handsome, well-to-do cattleman, about thirty-four years old. He owned a fine farm in the township of Caledon, in the county of Peel, about thirty miles from Toronto, and his family was highly respected in that part of the country. They were prosperous farmers and came of very nice English people. Ebenezer was a bachelor. He was shrewd and industrious. He bought and sold cattle and also was a butcher. He visited England in the fall of 1875, and was on his way home when he met the pretty English lass on her way to Toronto.

From his window Murray could see, of an occasional bright afternoon, the pretty girl of the flower gardens walking in the shady paths with a large handsome fellow, and at times their happy laughter rang out, and once, amid the flowers, the big man took her in his arms and lifted her up and kissed her. Soon after, she went away, and Murray saw her no more. The old woman said she had married Ward, and they were living happily on his farm in the county of Peel. The old woman delighted to tell of her niece Mary's fine home and farm. She would dwell on the beauties of the large log house, with a cellar the entire length, with a good barn and all the desired outbuildings, even to a fine modern dairy; but above all was the house, with the cellar its entire length, and the grandest of new furniture, including a big, new Gurney range, bought in Toronto and sent to the farm. Moreover, Mary had her own maid, a girl named Jennie Morrison, the fifteen-year-old daughter of a neighbouring farmer. Mary wrote frequently to her aunt, telling of how devoted her husband was, how he spent much of his time with her, and how happy she was in her new home and new life. One day the old woman, brimful of joy, called cheerily up to Murray's window that Mary Ward was coming to visit her that day. The day passed, but Mary Ward did not come.

About one o'clock that night a red glow lighted the skies in the township of Caledon. It grew and deepened as the great tongues of flame leaped up from the home of Ebenezer Ward and licked the night. A naked figure burst through the doorway and fled across the fields a half mile to his father's house. It was Ebenezer Ward. He rolled over at intervals as he ran and his body was marked with many burns.

"My house is on fire!" he shouted, as he fell exhausted in his father's house.

"Where is Mary?" they asked.

"The last I saw of her, she was at the door, going out," he said, and burst into tears.

They roused the countryside. The house was burning furiously. In his cellar Ward kept barrels of tallow and the heavy logs fell into the cellar one by one. The heat was intense. Mary Ward was nowhere to be found.

"I was notified," says Murray, "and I went to the Ward farm. The place took a long time to burn. It was still burning when I arrived. The heat was so great that one could not get very close. We pumped the well dry and hauled water, and finally, on the second day after, we got the fire out.

I saw Ward at his father's house. His mother was putting goose oil on his burns. She told me that since his outburst of tears as he fell on their floor after the fire, he had spoken but little of the disaster. In fact I found him very reticent and disinclined to talk. I sympathised with him and told him he had a miraculous escape. He thawed out a little and told me that he and his wife were awakened by the heat and jumped up and he got her as far as the door and had found the door difficult to open and when he finally opened it he turned for her, where she had stood beside him, but she was gone, and the flames were close upon him, their heat becoming intolerable. So he fled alone.

"'Poor Mary!' he sorrowed. 'I never can forget it.'

"His mother continued to dress his burns. I watched her and my eye lighted on a deep burn on the back of the neck at the base of the skull. The flesh was burned severely, but no hair was burned. That struck me as very strange. I examined the burn carefully Ward became uneasy. My suspicions were aroused instantly. I examined the other burns. They were deep, so deep and so similar as to strengthen my suspicions.

"I asked about Jennie Morrison, the fifteen-year-old domestic. She was at her father's home. I learned from her that on the morning of the night on which the fire occurred, Mary Ward was to have gone to visit her aunt in Toronto. Her husband had consented, but with reluctance. Before he started to drive her to the train he told her she had better send the Morrison girl home until she returned. Mary Ward said 'Nonsense,' but he insisted, saying the neighbours might talk, so Mary Ward, as she drove away, told Jennie Morrison she might go home for a few days and Jennie went.

"Ebenezer Ward drove his wife to the Caledon Station of the Canadian-Pacific Railroad. I learned there that after arriving at the station he changed his mind and told his wife she better not go that day but should wait a day or two and he would go with her. It seemed he could not bear the thought of having her out of his sight. She remonstrated reasonably, saying she was all ready to go, her aunt was expecting her, the train was about to arrive, and she should be glad to have him come that day or later. He insisted she should go back to the house and finally she obeyed and reluctantly gave up her trip that day and drove home again with him. They were alone in their house that night and at one o'clock in the morning the fire occurred and Ward ran naked from the house to his father's home.

"When the ruins had cooled so that I could go among them I had all the logs pulled out that were not burned. Then I began the supervision of a systematic sifting of the débris. I was hunting for traces of the remains of Mary Ward. I came across the stove. It was a fine Gurney range. I examined it and found it was burnt on the inside, burnt molten. I knew very well that cast iron could not be burned in this way except by artificial heat. I looked at the name on the range, Gurney. The letters were not molten nor had they been burned. Clearly it was not the heat of the burning house that had burned the stove inside, otherwise the outside and particularly the raised lettering of the name would have been burned. I took a piece of the stove and put it in an old bag. Then I had the men continue sifting the débris.

"I found a butcher's knife. The handle had been burnt off. The point of the knife was bent. I put it in the bag. I sifted for half an hour or more, and then found a piece of what resembled bone of a human body. I put this in the bag. I sifted on and found another piece of bone. I found some copper that had been melted. I also found a piece of feather-tick, matted, as if wet. As you probably know wet feathers are very hard to burn. All these finds I arranged carefully in the old bag, and that night I went to Toronto and called at the School of Practical Science. Dr. Ellis is there now, but Professor Croft was there in those days. I asked him if he could find traces of blood, if bleeding flesh had been burned in a stove and had stained it. He said he could, and that it was possible also to tell if it was the blood of a human being or the blood of an animal. I produced my piece of the stove and asked him to make an analysis. He did so and later reported that he discovered traces of the blood of a human being, and further that it was the blood of one who could nurse young, a female.

"The first piece of bone I had found was the sixth and seventh vertebræ of a human body. The second piece of bone I had found was a piece of ankle bone of a human body. These pieces of bone I had found some distance apart. The bent point of the butcher's knife seemed to say to me that it had been bent by disjointing Mary Ward's body after the blade had cut her into chunks. The matted piece of the bed-tick turned out to be matted with human blood. In the cellar I had found traces of the big barrels of tallow, and a speck or tallow spot on the range gave me the missing link. Mary Ward had been murdered in her bed, and her blood soaked the mattress and matted the feathers. Her body then was cut into pieces and the bones prized apart with the butcher's knife. The pieces were taken to the Gurney range and a copper bucket of tallow was placed upon them, and then more tallow, and then the whole was lighted and the terrific heat of the tallow consumed the body and melted the inside of the range. To conceal the crime the house was set on fire. Ward was a butcher. Such a mannered murder would be characteristic. For years he had butchered cattle, and when he decided to kill his wife the way naturally occurring to him was to butcher her as he would a steer. His jealousy, manifest in his unwillingness to have her out of his sight, his inability to have her go away, even for a day or two with her aunt, evidenced in the scene at the railroad station, threw light on the motive.

"I arrested Ebenezer Ward, charged with the murder of Mary Ward. It created a sensation. He was tried in Brampton in 1876. The late Kenneth Mackenzie, later a judge, prosecuted. Ward was defended by eminent counsel, one of the brilliant men of Canada, John Hilliard Cameron. It was the last case he had in court. Judge Morse, his first case on the bench, presided at the time. The Crown swore eighty witnesses. The case of circumstantial evidence was impregnable. The defence, after all else failed, fell back on a plea of insanity. Fourteen doctors were called by the defence to prove Ward insane. I had sixteen doctors and thus the Crown had the preponderance of medical testimony. Ward, despite the able fight made by his counsel, was convicted on May 12th, 1876, and was sentenced to be hanged. Subsequently the Minister of Justice commuted the sentence to imprisonment for life, owing to the difference of expert opinion.

"Ward was sent to Kingston Penitentiary. He acted strangely, and a great many believed he still simply was feigning insanity. He was removed to Rockwell Asylum in Kingston. There he became worse and died. His brain was examined by famous experts from the United States and Canada, including Dr. MacDonald, Dr. Workman, and Dr. Dickson. They found his brain was diseased.

"The burn on Ward's neck had been made purposely by him with a piece of iron, red hot. He had done it too well. A mere blister would have aroused no suspicion, but he had pressed the iron in so deep that if a flame had inflicted so severe a burn on the back of his neck, it would have scorched the hair off and blistered the back of the head. The piece of ankle bone and the vertebræ were buried decently later. They were all that remained of pretty Mary Ward, who used to laugh among the flowers opposite my window."

14

WHEN GLENGARRY WRECKED THE CIRCUS

THE men from Glengarry met Murray for the first time in the summer of 1877, and the acquaintance formed then ripened into friendship, and has strengthened throughout the years. The Glengarry lads were famous fighters in the bygone days, and it was through a fight, that lives to this day in the history of the county, that Murray went among them. There are firesides in Glengarry where old men sit in the winter evenings and spin, among their tales of prowess, the yarn of the great battle of 1877, when the men of Glengarry fought the travelling circus, and drove it, beasts and all, out of Cornwall. Many a scar is cherished as a souvenir of that fray. A thousand times beyond count have the children heard how Danny McLeod seized the lion by the tail and twisted it until the big beast roared.

John O'Brien, of Philadelphia, was the owner of the circus. It was travelling through Canada, and pitched its tents in Cornwall, the county seat of three counties—Glengarry, Stormont, and Dundas, fifty miles west of Montreal. The lumber-men and shanty-men had come out of the woods with their winter's wage in their pockets. They were stalwart lusty fellows, and they gathered from far and near to see the circus in Cornwall. They strode the streets in gorgeous red or rainbow shirts. They saw the grand parade in the morning, and joked about freak features that caught their eye. There was no talk of trouble, no premonition of a row. The men of the woods were out for a jolly day, expecting to bother nobody, and expecting nobody to bother them. They formed in a long line by the ticket waggon to buy the red pasteboards for admission to the tent. Some fell out of line to wrestle or spar good-naturedly, but all were waiting their turn.

A shout at the other side of the big tent steadied the line. It was the cry of a Glengarry man. Following it came the crack, crack, crack, of heavy blows, and around the side of the tent appeared one of their men, backing away, and whirling a long tent stake, as he came. Pursuing him were three circus-men, each with a club. Blood gushed from a big slash across the Glengarry's face. He was shaking it off as he swung the heavy stake. He dared not turn his head to look for help, but with eyes set and arms waving he whirled his weapon so that the three circus-men were held at bay. A flap in the big tent was raised as he passed; a fourth circus-man crept out behind the Glengarry, and as the stake swung around the new-comer dealt him a heavy blow with a club, and he went down like a log.

A roar burst from the line of lumber-men, a roar like that of the entire circus menagerie if the beasts had howled in unison. The line quivered, swayed, and broke. In a wild rush the lumber-men sprang forward, seizing clubs, tearing up tent stakes, jerking out poles and pins and stanchions. The four circus men yelled for help, and out of the big tent swarmed canvas-men, helpers, acrobats in tights, gymnasts in tinsel, clowns in paint and powder—every man the show could muster. They were needed, too. The lumber-men had formed in long open lines, like fire-fighters, and they moved into the thick of the tangle of men and ropes and canvas, beating right and left with their long clubs. The weapons rose and fell, whack, whack, whack, falling with terrific force, smiting whatever was within reach. When a man in the line fell another stepped forward into his place.

"Herd them! Herd them!" was the cry.

The lumber-men were striving to surround the circus-men and drive them into a huddled mass, and then—woe betide them! The force of the onslaught, the impact of the furious assault, drove the circus men back to the side of the big tent, so that when the lumber-men beat them in on three sides they had the tent behind them. There were mighty deeds of daring done that day. Shanty Donald, it is told, took five cracks on the skull and laid three circus-men out in a struggle where they had him three to one. Big McGregor seized an acrobat by the neck, and flung him skyward, and when he alighted he wildly begged for mercy. The strong man in the side show seized little Joe Sumac, and, when they fell apart, the strong man's left arm hung limp and useless, snapped below the elbow. One revolver flashed, and before it banged again, the circus-man who held it lay senseless, with his face trampled like a cleavered beefsteak.

The circus-men retreated under the flaps of the tent as the lumber-men crowded them. Knotty O'Brien, of Glengarry, one of the foremost in the lumber-men's line, dived under head first. His feet suddenly flew up, his limbs jerked, and he lay still. The lumber-men fought up to where he lay, and they smote the canvas side of the tent with mighty blows, ripping it to shreds, and as it tore away they saw little O'Brien gasp, half rise, choke and fall back dead. None spoke, none shouted as they beat before them. It was like a battle of mutes. Slowly they fought their way into the tent, when from the menagerie came the keepers with the elephants, and rushed the great beasts to the front, and ran them to and fro.

"'Tis like smiting a mountain!" quoth Big McGregor, as he drove his stake against the towering hulk. The next instant Big McGregor was flying skyward higher than he had tossed the tinselled acrobat. He came down with a thud, and plunged in again.

"The lions! the lions!" shouted the circus-men, and it is related that sure enough, a big beast came slouching forward with a keeper at his side.

In the tale as it is told, forward sprang Danny McLeod and faced the king of beasts. Even the men of Glengarry paused. The lion shook his massive head and tawny mane. Danny suddenly struck the keeper full in the pit of the stomach with his boot, and seized the lion by the tail and twisted it around and around. With a roar of rage and pain the king of beasts wheeled and fled, galloping pell-mell back to his cage, and clambering into it. But the elephants won the day. Both sides drew off, and the circus left Cornwall. Little O'Brien was buried, and the lumber-men sat them down to nurse their wounds and heal their scars.

" It was learned some time after the battle," says Murray, " that the man who struck O'Brien was Louis Kipp, a canvas-man, a fellow so short, and yet so stout, that he seemed as broad as he was long. He was about twenty-eight years old, and weighed about one hundred and seventy pounds. He had been one of the circus men who fought without flinching, blow for blow. The final evidence that it was he who struck O'Brien was obtained from a witness early in 1878, and in March 1878 I was instructed to locate him. I had nothing but his name and a poor description. I went first to Philadelphia and saw John O'Brien, the circus-man. He said he knew nothing of Kipp, that his head canvas-man hired men anywhere and paid them off anywhere. I found his head canvas-man at Newark, in New Jersey. He remembered the fight, and remembered Louis Kipp.

" ' He fought a good fight, too,' said the head canvas-man.

" He thought Louis was a Pennsylvania Dutchman from Bucks County or Lancaster in Pennsylvania. He had heard Louis speak of this section of the country, but knew nothing more about him, and said he had not seen Louis since the fight at Cornwall. He claimed the circus-men had fought in self-defence. I went to Easton, Pa., to an old friend of mine, Jake Johnson, chief of police. Jake knew that entire country. He had served in the Molly Maguire business, and was just voluntarily giving it up at that time. Jake agreed to go with me in a search of the two counties for Louis Kipp.

" Jake and I started out on Sunday, March 17th, 1878, St. Patrick's Day. It was raining hard. We had a cracking good team. We drove all day from place to place, and at nightfall came to a little tavern away up in the mountains, and decided to stay there all night. As we were putting up our team we got our first trace of the whereabouts of Louis. A lot of fellows were in the tavern celebrating St. Patrick's Day ; and one of them told us that a fellow named Louis Kipp worked for a farmer about ten miles farther on, over the mountain. We were forty miles or more from Easton. We pledged everybody's health in the tavern, and took the fellow with us to show the way. It poured like a deluge for the entire ten miles. Finally we came to a big farm with a great farmhouse and tremendous barns. We banged on the door, and my mind went back to Dixmont at the other end of the same State. A nightcapped head popped out of a window, and asked in German who was there and what was wanted. We answered that we wanted to see Louis Kipp, if he lived there.

"'He lives here, but he and his girl are out together for a walk,' was the reply.

"It was after midnight, and raining hard. The farmer, however, invited us in, and had us put up our team. Then he brought cider, and head cheese and gingerbread, and we sat in a huge room with a big fireplace, and sipped cider and munched head cheese and gingerbread while we waited for Louis. An hour passed, but no sign of Louis. Our host explained that Louis's girl also lived in the house, and that every Sunday evening they went spooning, rain or shine. Another hour passed. It was after two o'clock. Our host smoked on unconcernedly.

"'Sometimes they spoon till dawn,' he said in German. 'It is the way of unmarried love.'

"He told us of some fine currant wine he had in his cellar, and at length he insisted on getting some of it. He took a candle and disappeared into the cellar. Presently he reappeared without the wine, and in great excitement. He beckoned us to follow noiselessly. We did so, tiptoeing softly down the cellar stairs. It was a vast, cavernous place, with rows of huge hogsheads, like vats or cisterns. He led us among them to a remote corner, then held up his hand and pointed to a hogshead reclining on its side. We stepped silently up, and peeped in while he held the candle. I never will forget the sight. There sat Louis and his girl, their arms around one another, her head on his shoulder, both sound asleep, both with their mouths wide open, both snoring sonorously, inside this big hogshead.

"'Beautiful, is it not so?' said our host in German.

"He gazed enraptured on this picture of bliss. Then suddenly he sneezed a loud, resounding sneeze that blew out the candle. Louis, in the hogshead, awoke with a snort, as did his girl. We bumped amid the hogsheads until our host relighted the candle.

"'Pardon! pardon!' he exclaimed in German. 'Every time I see true love it makes me sneeze. I feel myself about to cry for joy, and when I would not cry, but almost, then I sneeze at the tickles of the nose from tears.'

"Louis and his girl, yawning and sheepish, followed us up to the big room. There Louis hugged his girl until I thought he would crush her short ribs, kissed her with a resounding smack, waited while she kissed him with equal explosion, and then said:

"'Goot night.'

"She went to bed. In the talk that followed I must confess I lied a little to Louis.

"'Louis,' I said, 'you were with John O'Brien's circus last year?'

"'Yah, yah,' grunted Louis, who spoke in broken English.

"'Do you remember a fight in Cornwall, Canada?' I asked.

"Louis's face lighted up.

"'Yah, yah,' he grunted. 'T'at vas te tamtest fight I efer see. Ve pull out t'e stakes und ve get t'e pest of it, but t'ey fight like t'e vild men ofer t'ere.'

"I said that one fellow had been badly hurt among the circus-men, and some fellows were arrested, and I wanted Louis to come over for the trial.

"I got no money,' said Louis. 'I gif it all to my girl.'

"I said I would pay all the expenses. Louis was delighted. The farmer said he could go. Louis called up the stairs to his girl, excitedly told her of the fine trip he was going to take, told her to take good care of his money while he was gone, and then hurried out, hitched up our team, and we started back to Easton at dawn. Louis was eager to go. I have often thought since, that he never realised, when the frenzy of the circus fight was over, that he had struck a fatal blow, and he honestly believed he was going back to Cornwall to testify for another. He stuck to me night and day, afraid lest he should lose me and miss the trip. We arrived in Cornwall on March 20th. There I told him that it was he who was to be tried.

"'Mein Gott!' said Louis. 'Von't I efer git back to my girl and my money?'

"That was all that worried him. He was very good, and gave me no trouble. He pleaded guilty to manslaughter, and I got him off with one year in gaol.

"'I remember now t'e little fellow vat I hit,' he told me, after hearing the details of the charge against him. 'It vas too bad he die. He vas a goot fighter. I vould radder it haf been one of t'e fellows who hang back and not fight.'

"When Louis got out of gaol he hied himself back to his girl and his money in Pennsylvania.

"Jake Johnson, of Easton, was glad to oblige me in the matter of finding Louis. For in January 1878, two months before I started after Louis, Jake had been over in Canada for a man by the name of Gillard, of Easton, who was a refugee from justice from Pennsylvania. Gillard had come to Canada, and found employment as a carriage maker with a man named Dixon, of Oakville, twenty miles from Toronto. The crime of which he was accused was serious, but did not come under extradition, although Jake Johnson was very anxious to get him.

"I had been laid up with typhoid fever, but in January 1878 I was able to get out, and Jake came to Toronto; and we went to Oakville and saw Mr. Dixon. He appeared to be quite willing to aid us after hearing of the serious charge against Gillard. Arrangements were made to land Gillard in some part of the United States. He would suspect if Suspension Bridge were chosen as the place, so Ogdensburg was selected. Mr. Dixon took Gillard with him, ostensibly on a business trip about waggons. I accompanied them. It was bitter cold weather. On January 23rd we crossed the St. Lawrence River at Prescott. Jake Johnson was on the American side. He had the papers for Gillard's arrest, with a requisition from the Governor of Pennsylvania on the Governor of New York. Instead of keeping these papers until train time, Johnson foolishly got a policeman in Ogdensburg, and had Gillard arrested and put in the lockup. I foresaw trouble. Gillard had no inkling of what was in store for him until he was arrested, and then he promptly sent for a lawyer, a prominent attorney named Kellogg. Gillard told Mr. Kellogg he had been kidnapped out of Canada. He told of my coming over, of Dixon's part in the matter, and of Jake Johnson. His lawyer caused warrants to be issued for the entire party. They arrested Dixon and Johnson, and were looking for your humble servant, but I was over the river.

"The first intimation I had of what was happening to Johnson was when this telegram from Jake was handed to me aboard the Grand Trunk train:

"'I am in the Ogdensburg gaol for kidnapping. What shall I do?'

"I answered, 'Employ counsel and fight.'

"At almost every station I received a frantic telegram from Jake, and I answered them all with the same advice. They had him locked up, all right. Dixon gave the affair away, saying he was induced to get Gillard over the line as a special favour to me. They released Dixon, but they held on to Johnson. Jake telegraphed me almost hourly. They committed him for the grand jury, and then released him on bail, and gave him no end of trouble. I looked into it in the meantime. When the matter finally came before the grand jury they ignored the bill against Jake. Gillard, in the interval, had been discharged, but he was arrested subsequently, and was held. After a great deal of trouble and litigation he was handed over to the Pennsylvania authorities. Jake Johnson had the satisfaction of seeing him tried and convicted.

"Gillard was very different from Louis Kipp. He was quite unwilling to go back to Pennsylvania, whereas Louis, during his year's sojourn in Canada, dreamed constantly of the big farmhouse and his rosy-cheeked, buxom Dutch girl, and his money, and the big hogshead in the cellar, where they spooned, and slept, and snored."

15

THE MILLION DOLLAR COUNTERFEITING

THE first five years of Murray's service with the Government in Canada were drawing to a close in 1880. They had been five eventful years. He had done his difficult work faithfully and well. He added to the name and fame, not only of the Department of Justice, but of himself. He had handled successfully scores of cases of varying degrees of importance, from atrocious murders to petty and persistent thievings The Government in no instance had called upon him in vain. But clever as he was, able and resourceful as he had proved himself to be, a still severer test of his qualities was about to come, and a task was to rise before him beside which all former cases seemed simple and insignificant. It was the Million Dollar Counterfeiting.

This crime is known as one of the boldest and greatest of its kind ever undertaken. It was a crime of genius. The man who solved its mystery and ran its perpetrators to earth, was a detective of genuine worth. His trophy of the chase rests on a stand in his library, one of the largest hauls of counterfeit plates ever made on the American continent, plates that are worth over $40,000, plates that set in circulation bogus money totalling over $1,000,000 so true to the genuine currency that to this day some of it is in circulation, and banks could not tell it was counterfeit.

"In the months of March, April, and May in 1880," says Murray, "Canada was flooded with the most dangerous counterfeit bills ever put in circulation. Banks took the bogus banknotes over their own counters, and could not tell they were not genuine. Officials whose signatures were forged could not tell the forged signature from the genuine. Good and bad bills were laid side by side, and experts had to resort to scientific methods to tell which were good and which were bad. The bills appeared all over Canada. It is known now that over $1,000,000 of them were sent out. In the far north-west $200,000 of this money was paid for furs that were shipped to England, Montreal, and New York from this remote country where there were no banks, and to the present time some of it is in circulation there, and is good money. The banks, as I have said, took them over their own counters to my positive knowledge.

"One of the counterfeits was a United States $5 bill of the Government issue of 1875. It was one of the first to be be discovered. It was detected in Washington by accident. An expert in connection with the Treasury Department happened to run across one of the new bills. He remarked that it was better work and a prettier bill than any he had ever seen. The one fault was the bill was too perfect. The expert took it to the Treasury Department to hunt up the series of numbers, and he found the bill was a counterfeit. Secret Service men were detailed at once. They set to work. Two or three were over here. This was before there was much talk of our counterfeits being in circulation. The Secret Service men got no trace of the counterfeiters.

"Then came the discovery of the Canadian counterfeits. Numbers on new bills on this side were compared, after the United States Secret Service men began to work and stir around, and the discovery was made that wholesale counterfeiting of Canada bills had occurred. The banks were in a stew. Everybody was stirred up. Business men were worried. The Government instructed me to get to the bottom of it, and above all to get the plates, and thereby stop further issue of the bills. I found the following Canada counterfeit bills in circulation:

"A $10 bill on the Bank of Commerce.

"A $5 bill on the Bank of Commerce, whose head office is Toronto, with branches all over Canada.

"A $5 bill on the Bank of British North America, of Toronto, with branches all over the country.

"A $10 bill on the Ontario Bank.

"A $4 bill on the Dominion Bank.

"A $1 bill Dominion of Canada, Government issue.

"There is any amount of this currency out still. Harrington, the signer of the Government issue, could not detect the forgery of his own signature. The counterfeiters were so bold and so daring that, as I have said, $200,000 was paid for furs and was accepted, and to this day part of it is in circulation in the north-west, and is as good as gold for all practical purposes out there. Even the banks whose bills were counterfeited accepted the counterfeits over their own counters. They denied that they ever paid any of them out again. The bills were afloat in all sections of the country and there was a great stir.

"It was my old line of work, although I was a little rusty, for I had lost track of some of the details of the whereabouts of the various people. I started out, and I knew at the outset that I was tackling one of the hardest cases of my life. The principals, not the small fry, alone held the plates. I went to New York, taking with me specimens of the Canada bills and of the United States bill, for the United States bill also was in suspiciously large circulation in Canada. In New York I went at once to the cooney places, and looked for cooney men. I found no one who had any information. From New York I went to Philadelphia, and there I made the usual rounds of the cooney places, and also called on the officers. I learned nothing. The Secret Service men had been over the ground before me without avail. From Philadelphia I went to Washington, and called at the Treasury Department. John Sherman, of Ohio, was Secretary of the Treasury. Jim Brooks, an old Englishman, was chief of the Secret Service then. I talked with the officers, and learned nothing. Back to New York I went empty-handed.

"In the old days in New York I had known some of the counterfeiters and ex-counterfeiters, and I got track of two or three of them in the cooney places or resorts they frequent, and finally I struck the trail of a man who was an expert in his day, and who was thoroughly up in counterfeiting and the work of counterfeiters. He had been a counterfeiter himself in the old days, and I had known him when I was working for the United States some years before. I showed him the bills. Counterfeiters often know each other's work. In using the word counterfeiters in this sense I mean the engravers, the men who make the plates. An expert engraver of counterfeit plates usually can tell within a group of men, if not the very man, who made the plate from which a bill was printed. They seem to recognise some bit of character, some intangible trait in the work that enables them to identify its maker, or the group from whence it came.

"My ex-counterfeiter in New York looked the bills over very carefully.

"'They are beauties,' he said. 'It looks very much like the work of old John Hill, but I think Hill has been locked up since he got the $10,000 for making those last plates of his. Yet it looks like Hill's work.'

"I knew Hill. He was an old, crooked engraver whose home was in New York, and who had done time twice. He charged a fee of $10,000 for making the plates for bogus bills, and would have nothing to do with shoving the queer—that is, circulating the money. I went to Albany, and thence to Troy to see another old cooney man who had reformed. He looked at the bills.

"'They look like Hill's,' said he, 'but I know Hill has not been situated in recent years so he had time to make them.'

"I thought the plates, wherever they might be, were the handiwork of Prussian Mark Ulrich, and that Pete McCarthy might have aided him, they were so perfect.

"'No,' said my cooney acquaintance whom I saw in Troy, 'they look like Hill, and next to Ed Johnson, Hill is the best man in the world to-day. They are not Prussian Mark's.'

"I ran down Hill's whereabouts, and satisfied myself that he had nothing to do with the Canada plates in this work. It required several years to make the plates, for a crooked engraver worked only at certain hours of the day, in a certain light, and the plates that made the bills I had were masterpieces from a master's hand.

"I decided to try Chicago, and see what I could learn there. I was on my way west from New York to Chicago, with Hill dropped from my consideration, when my mind turned to Ed Johnson. Where was he? I remembered the tales I had heard of him. He was an Englishman by birth, who was an educated man, and had married an educated Englishwoman. He learned the trade of an engraver, and the young couple moved to America, and he was supposed to be honest, and worked at his trade until, when the Civil War came on, some one made a fortune out of $100, $50, and $20 counterfeit banknotes, and Johnson had been mixed up in it, and later was reported to have returned to England. My Troy cooney man agreed, as a matter of course, that Johnson was the ablest man in the business, and the bills were beauties created by a master. They were the best ever seen, and unless a greater than Johnson had arisen, it was Johnson. I determined to account for Johnson as I had accounted for Hill. So I went on to Chicago, and there I learned that the last trace of Johnson in the business in that section of the country was in Indianapolis several years before. I learned this from an old time ex-counterfeiter whom I had known in 1867, and who had settled in Chicago. I conferred also with the United States authorities in Chicago. At every step in this case thus far, I had occasion to be thankful for my United States Government experience at the close of the Civil War, and for the acquaintance I built up at that time among officers and ex-counterfeiters and counterfeiters themselves.

"My next move was to Indianapolis, where I was well acquainted. I called on United States Senator McDonald, and others. I was on the hunt for trace of Ed Johnson. I learned that a family named Johnson had lived in Indianapolis about six years before in elegant style in a big house, with horses, carriages, coachman, footman, and quite a retinue of servants. They spent money lavishly, and lived luxuriously. Then came trouble in the form of an accusation that they were counterfeiters. The Johnsons promptly retained McDonald & Butler as their counsel, and I understood they paid the attorneys a $25,000 fee for defending them. They finally got clear, but the trouble had affected their position in Indianapolis, and they went away.

"In the family were Mr. and Mrs. Johnson, two beautiful

girls and five boys. The daughters were Jessie and Annie Johnson, both clever, accomplished girls. The boys were Tom, Charlie, Johnnie, Elijah, and David Henry. I knew three of them myself. I learned from friends of their counsel that when they left Indianapolis they moved to Cincinnati. I went on to Cincinnati, and found they had lived in Sixth Street there, and had occupied a big house over in Covington, Ky., for a while. They had left there several years before, and through one of their acquaintances I learned they had gone to Hartford, Ct. I went on to Hartford, and found the house there where they had lived in strict seclusion, seldom being seen on the street. They had moved from Hartford to a big, old house near Fall River, Mass. I located this house, but they were gone, bag and baggage, almost a year before, and there I lost the trail. I worked like a beaver trying to get some trace of them. But they had burned all bridges behind them.

"I finally went from Fall River back to New York, and saw the man I had seen there before.

"'Do you know old Johnson?' I asked him.

"'Yes, but I have not seen him in years,' was the reply. 'He is as clever as they make. He used to get on drunks, and his family had a desperate time watching him.'

"'Where is he likely to be now?' I asked.

"'They have money, Murray,' said he. 'Old Mrs. Johnson is rich. In the first two or three years of the war they rolled in it, and the old woman always is looking out for a rainy day. I heard they had left the country.'

"We talked the matter over fully. It was in a little restaurant. I remember well the little cubby-hole in which we sat. I told him to bring his glass next day, and study the bills. He did so. We had luncheon in my room, and he examined the bills minutely. For three hours or so he fussed over them, studying them under the glass. At last he looked up.

"'Well?' said I. 'Mark Ulrich?'

"'No,' said he. 'Hill may have done the States $5 bill, but Johnson did the Canada bills.'

"'Are you sure of Johnson's work?' I asked.

"'As sure as I would be of my own—in the old days,' said he.

"'And you have no idea where Johnson is?' I asked.

"'Not the slightest, Murray,' said he. 'I tried to get a hint of him last night, but the best I can learn is that he is out of the country—possibly in England, unless there is a job on the Continent.'

"I dug around in New York, and was baffled. I knew young Dave Johnson, and Tom, who was lame, and Johnnie. But the whole family had vanished when they left Fall River. I went to Buffalo and saw a retired man there, but nobody knew where Johnson was. From Buffalo I went to Detroit, and saw a man who used to be an expert bank-note engraver, and who had got square. He had no trace of the Johnsons, but agreed, as had my other acquaintances, to endeavour to find some track of them. By this time I was becoming satisfied that the Johnsons had gone abroad or had moved to Canada, and were in personal charge of the distribution of the counterfeit money. As a rule, the engravers or platemakers had little to do with shoving or passing the bogus money. I went up to my room in the hotel at Detroit. I intended to take a train an hour later, but became so absorbed in contemplation of the case that I missed the train. I thought it all over, and it became perfectly clear to my mind that the Johnsons, if they were to be found anywhere on this side of the Atlantic, were to be found in Canada, and probably right in or near Toronto, if they had not flown recently to other parts.

"Missing the train turned out to be a godsend. I took the next train for Toronto. When I alighted in Toronto I crossed to a saloon to get a welcome-home nip. I saw a figure at the other end of the bar. He turned. I stood face to face with Johnnie Johnson! If he had dropped from the clouds I could not have been more astonished, and if he had been the Recording Angel come to write my title clear, I could not have been more delighted. Johnnie was full. He stood alone at one end of the bar drinking.

"'I'll shadow you,' said I to myself.

"It was shortly after eleven o'clock at night. Johnnie

finished his drink, and went out. I went out by the other door. I was just in time to see Johnnie jump into a cab and drive away. He was out of sight and sound before I could get a cab. I spent that night, and the next, and the next looking for him. On the third night I spied him. He was just slipping out of Mitchell & Ryan's saloon on King Street, between Bay and York Streets. He walked quickly down Bay Street, jumped in a cab, and drove away. I had kept a cab within hail ever since I lost him the first night, so I jumped into my cab, and away we went after Johnnie. He drove north to Bloor Street, and at the corner of Bloor Street and Avenue Road, not far from where the Parliament building is now, he got out of the cab, paid the man and walked away. I go out of my cab and followed him on foot. He went around six blocks to Hazelton Avenue, turned into Hazelton Avenue, and, taking out a latchkey, unlocked the door of a comfortable brick house and went in.

"'There's where the Johnsons are,' quoth I to myself, as I heard the door softly close.

"It was a hard house to shadow, there being no sheltered place near by. I made arrangements with the occupants of an adjacent house, and kept the Johnson house under surveillance. For five days after Johnnie Johnson entered the house, no one passed in or out except the butcher and the baker and the milkman. I saw the baker down town, and asked who lived there.

"'An old lady and gentleman, two nice-looking girls, and a couple of sons,' he said.

"I saw the milkman. He had seen the girls, and had heard them play the piano and sing. The butcher saw the girls occasionally. I had no case on the Johnsons then, nothing beyond my certainty that they did the job. I kept watch of the house. One night lights burned in the parlour of the house all night, and the piano was played until an early morning hour. I sat watching and waiting. Days and nights had passed, and no one had appeared at the house. It was like a house where every one had gone away. But about seven o'clock in the morning, after the night of lights and music, the front door opened and old man Johnson himself, Edwin Johnson, the king of counterfeiters, appeared on the doorstep and walked jauntily down the street. I knew him the moment I saw him, for I had a dozen descriptions of him and a photograph, all of recent years. I had discarded the photograph, but my descriptions tallied to a dot. I trailed him. He stopped in almost every saloon on his way down town, but he paid for his drinks in genuine money. He got boozy, and finally he went to the railroad-station and bought a ticket for Markham. I sat six seats behind him on the train. We both got off at Markham. He went into a saloon, and bought a drink. When he came out, I went in. There was a young bar-tender—a saucy, smart aleck, but I had him call the proprietor, and through him I got the $1 bill that Johnson had given in pay for the drink. I paid silver for it, and had the proprietor initial it. I eyed it eagerly when I got it. It was a new Dominion $1 bill. I had my man at last.

"Johnson went into place after place, buying a drink or cigar, and paying in bad bills. I followed him from place to place, buying the bills as he passed them. He passed one of the $4 Dominion Bank bills in a store, where he bought a necktie. In fact, he kept busy until train time, when he went back to Toronto. I went on the same train. When he alighted in Toronto, I stepped up and tapped him on the shoulder.

"'How do you do, Mr. Johnson?' said I.

"Johnson was a gentleman. He was a very polite, polished old fellow, grey-haired, dapper, and of precise speech.

"'You have the advantage of me, sir,' said he. 'I do not know you.'

"'I've seen you often on the other side,' I said.

"'Oh,' said he, 'who might you be?'

"'I am Detective Murray,' I said. 'We might as well understand each other. You are my prisoner.'

"'All right, sir,' said old Johnson very politely, and not in the least flustered. 'What is the charge?'

"'Counterfeiting,' said I.

"We walked along as we talked. Edwin Johnson looked like a prosperous banker—as indeed he was, in bad money. He seemingly gave no heed to my answer.

"'Murray, Murray,' he mused. 'Oh yes, I've heard of you. This is rather unexpected. It takes me quite by surprise. I never had the pleasure before, sir.'

"'I have met several members of your family,' I said.

"'Indeed?' he said. 'A very fine family, sir. Do you not agree with me? A fine family.'

"We walked on to the corner.

"'Well, good day, sir,' said Edwin Johnson. 'Very glad to have met you.'

"'Just a moment,' said I. 'You are my prisoner, Mr. Johnson. You are a counterfeiter. I have in my pocket the bogus money you passed at Markham, and you have the equivalent of my good money in your pocket.'

"Instantly he ceased bluffing, and his manner became grave and earnest. He seemed to sober up.

"'Is there no way of arranging this?' he said. 'It appears to be a serious matter.'

"'We'll talk it over,' said I, and I called a cab and took him to the gaol.

"This was on Friday, June 11th, 1880. I held him without a commitment, for I wanted nothing known of it. In the gaol he said:

"'Murray, I'd like another word with you. Can we not arrange this matter? Give me your terms. I have money. I mean good money,' he added, with a smile.

"I searched him, and found more bad bills on him. Then I told the gaoler to treat him well, and left him cigars and the like, and told him to think the matter over until Monday, when he would be in better condition to discuss it.

"'The only thing you can do with me,' I told him, on leaving, 'is to deliver up to me the plates and whole paraphernalia of counterfeiting.'

"On Saturday, next day, he sent for me, and I went to the gaol. He renewed his proposition. He told me to name any amount. He did it in a very nice way, saying that his friends could raise a considerable amount.

"'Nothing for me except the plates,' said I.

"'A foolish fellow,' said Edwin Johnson.

"As I was leaving he said: 'Murray, if you ever get into

this line of business, don't drink. A man does things when he is drunk that he never would dream of doing when he is sober.'

"I knew he referred to passing the bills. Except when he was drunk Johnson never shoved or passed any bad bills. The shovers and the middlemen did not know him at all. Only the wholesale dealer knew him.

"'If I had not been drunk this would not have happened,' said Johnson, as I left him.

"On Monday I called again at the gaol. Johnson was as polite as if he were receiving me in the Indianapolis mansion of several years before.

"'Good morning,' said he. 'A very fine day, although a trifle hot outdoors, I should judge.'

"We talked a few minutes. I insisted that I must have the plates.

"'All I want is the plates,' I said.

"'I have thought it all over, Murray,' said Edwin Johnson. 'I sent for no lawyer. I sent no word home. I am going to turn everything over to you. We will have to go out and get it.'

"I had a cab. I sent for Detective John Hodgins, of Toronto Police Headquarters, and Johnson, Hodgins, and I drove away together. Johnson told the way. We drove out to Wells Hill into a piece of woods above Toronto. There we got out. The old man took observations. He spotted a large elm tree. As he sighted and moved around I thought of old Knapp and the buried plunder out of Erie.

"'There's where they are,' announced the old man.

"We took off our coats, got sticks, and began to dig. It was a blazing hot day. We dug and dug, and found nothing. I saw that the ground had not even been disturbed. I remembered Knapp, and told Johnson that he was mistaken. He went back and took another range, and tramped around, and finally pointed out another tree.

"'Here they are,' he said.

"'Sit down, Mr. Johnson, and cool off,' said I. 'Mr. Hodgins, you take the cab and go get a spade.'

"I was determined not to waste any labour on what might

be a fool's errand. During the absence of Hodgins I gently reminded Johnson that it was not a propitious time for a practical joke.

"'They are here, Murray,' he assured me. 'I vow they are here.'

"Hodgins returned with a spade, and he set to work. He dug while we waited. Finally he struck them. Johnson sprang forward and stayed his hand.

"'Careful, man! Careful!' said Johnson. 'They took years to make, and are worth over forty thousand dollars.'

"Johnson lifted them out as tenderly as a mother would raise her sick babe from a cradle. They were wrapped in oiled cloth, and were encased in solid coverings of beeswax.

"'Here they are, Murray,' said Johnson, handing them to me. They cost over forty thousand dollars to make. I don't own all these plates. A party on the other side has an interest in them.'

"They made a package the size of two big bricks, and were very heavy. I took Johnson back to the gaol, and then drove to the Attorney-General's Department with the plates. There I examined them, and saw they were the finest in the land. I marvelled at the firmness and precision of the strokes, the authority of the signatures, the beauty of the vignettes and medallions, the accuracy of following all the little whimsics of the engravers of the original, genuine plates. For each bill there were three copper plates—one for the front, one for the back, and one for the wedge. Each plate was about one quarter of an inch in thickness. I scored them criss-cross, and locked them up. Not only were the six Canada counterfeits in the lot, but the plates for the counterfeit States $5 bill were there. There were twenty-one separate copper pieces or plates, three each for the Bank of Commerce $10, the Bank of Commerce $5, the Bank of British North America $5, the Ontario Bank $10, the Dominion Bank $4, the Government issue $1, and the United States $5.

"I went to the gaol and saw Johnson.

"'Yes,' said Johnson, when I asked him, 'Hill made the States $5, and I made the others. It took me years to do them.'

"Johnson then told me the whole story. He made the plates in the States. His daughters forged the signatures. They had been trained in forging or duplicating signatures since childhood. They would spend hours a day duplicating a single signature, and would work at the one name for months, writing it countless thousands of times. Jessie was better on larger handwriting, and Annie was better on smaller handwriting. The boys were learning to be engravers, and one or two of them were so proficient that the old man spoke of them with pride.

"'I am the best,' he said proudly, 'and one of my boys may become better than I.'

"He said they had printed large quantities of the bills. They printed once a year. After each printing the plates were encased in beeswax and oilcloth and buried, and the other paraphernalia was destroyed. The bills were turned over to the wholesale dealer in the queer. The wholesale dealer, in turn, placed it with the retail dealer, who placed it with the shover.

"'The engraver, the man who makes the plates, is the only one who deserves credit or praise,' said Johnson. 'He has the skill, the creative genius. Yet, Murray, every time I get drunk the debased desire comes over me to descend to the low level of a shover, a passer of the queer. I cannot account for it. It is my lower nature. When I drink I indulge in it, and because I drank and indulged in it you got me.'

"I told him it was through Johnnie I came upon him, and he was much relieved to think that he had not been the first to give me the scent. Johnson said the half interest in the plates was owned in the States. He had lived in the Hazelton Avenue house a little over twelve months, and had been out comparatively seldom during the entire year.

"On August 19th, 1880, I went to Washington, and called on the Hon. John Sherman, Secretary of the Treasury, and told him the story and showed to him the $5 bill plates of the State issue. He congratulated me, and said it was one of the most valuable hauls of counterfeit plates ever made. Secretary Sherman sent for Jim Brooks, chief of the Secret

Service.

"'We want Mr. Murray used well in this matter,' said Secretary Sherman to Brooks.

"I gave to Brooks the names of the parties I had obtained from Johnson. They were arrested, and gave the names of Howard and Swanston and others. Their right names were not given, and I received none of the credit that otherwise might have occurred.

"Edwin Johnson was placed on trial at the Fall Assizes in 1880, in Toronto, before Chief Justice Hagerty. When he was arraigned, the Chief Justice looked down at him and asked:

"'Who is your attorney?'

"'Murray,' said Johnson.

"'What Murray?' asked the Chief Justice.

"'Your lordship, he means Detective Murray,' said Counsel Aemelius Irving.

"There was much laughter. Seven indictments were read, one after another. Johnson pleaded guilty to every one. The counsel for the Crown asked the Court to suspend sentence, and the Court did so. Johnson was released, and I took him and his daughters to the States, where the United States authorities desired to make use of them. The family jumped out of Canada. The son Tom, the lame one, had started a blind tobacco store in King Street, Toronto. He was arrested in Erie, Pa. He was searched, and nothing was found. He carried a cane. Its top was unscrewed, and the cane was found to be stuffed with bogus bills. Tom went to the penitentiary for shoving.

"Johnnie Johnson was arrested in Black Rock at Buffalo, and locked up for shoving. I called to see him when he was in gaol. He got counsel, and escaped conviction. Six years ago Tom and Charlie were arrested at Sarnia, in Canada, for having counterfeit money, and they were convicted and sent to the penitentiary. They had no business to set foot in Canada. Johnnie was arrested here in Toronto, after getting out in Buffalo. He was shoving the $10 Bank of Commerce bill, and he got ten years in Kingston. He too should have stayed out of Canada.

"After Charlie got out of the Canadian penitentiary for the

Sarnia business, he went to Detroit, and on August 12th, 1898, he and young Ed or Elijah were arrested. The old man was dead. The mother and sisters were living at No. 106, McGraw Avenue, Detroit. David Henry was living at No. 795, 26th Street, Detroit, and was married and had two children. Detectives Kane, Downey, and Reegan, with Webb, of the Secret Service, got them. They searched their houses, and found a hollow place in the base board which opened with a secret spring, and revealed a panel cabinet, in which was between $7,000 and $10,000 of counterfeit notes of the $2 Hancock issue and Windom issue of 1891 and 1893. On the bills the eyes had an upward stare, which was the only flaw. One of the family got away, and was caught at Blenheim, Ontario. The two girls were taken to Washington, as I had taken them in 1880. The mother was arraigned for disposing of counterfeit money. She always did the changing with the wholesale dealers.

"Old Hill in 1896 was still in prison in the United States, under the name of John Murphy. Part of the Johnson family is in prison, part is out and their whereabouts known, and part is dead.

"They were a wonderful family. Their biggest *coup* was the Canada counterfeiting. They placed over $1,000,000 of the Canada bills. Up in the Hudson Bay district the Johnson bills to this day pass as readily as gold. The capture of the plates put an end to the issue of more bills. The banks were delighted, of course. They had talked of a reward. I received it—in thanks. A meeting was held of the bankers in the Receiver-General's office in Toronto, and I was thanked formally for what I had done. At that meeting I laid some of the Johnson bills side by side with some of the genuine bills. Some of the experts failed to tell which were good and which were counterfeit.

"I treated old man Johnson fairly. The Canada counterfeiting was broken up, the plates were captured and incapacitated, and the Johnsons lived in the States, or if they set foot again in Canada, went to prison. Crime lost a genius when old man Johnson died."

16

HENEY, OF THE WELTED FOREHEAD

BENEATH the big trees in front of the farmhouse of John Morrison, chief constable of the county of Russell, who lived near the village of Bearbrook, a score of women were flitting to and fro on Friday, June 25th, 1880, bearing steaming dishes or plates or pitchers to a table that seemed spread for the feeding of a regiment. Some were singing, others were jesting or gossiping as they bustled about. From the woods near by came the sound of many voices, the shouts of men, the ring of axes, and the crash of falling trees. It was sunset time. A horn blew. An answering chorus of cheers came from the woods, where a great clearing had been opened since the morning. The ring of axe and crash of tree ceased. Out of the timber came a little host like the vanguard of a marching army. There were stalwart men bare-headed, bare-armed, bare-throated, with axes on their shoulders or in their belts. Teams of horses followed them, dozens of teams, with more men behind them. They swarmed into the road and came homeward enveloped in a cloud of dust. All halted at the barn and tended to the horses first, then left them and the axes and came empty-handed to the house.

The feast was waiting. They sat down amid laughter and shouts, and as they feasted they told the story of the day's work; of the race between champion choppers to fell mighty trees; of the rivalry between famed teams in the drawing of the logs; of the tricks of toppling trees in unexpected directions. Between stories they sang, men and women joining in the choruses. John Morrison sat at the head of the table—a fine host, a goodly man to look upon. He was in merry mood; for the axes had cut that day beyond his expectation, and the clearing was larger even than he had dared hope it would be. He pledged to his neighbours, that if ever they wanted five strong men and four stout teams, for a land-clearing bee, let them simply send a good word to John Morrison, who with his teams and men was at their command. The cheers that greeted this were dying away when a hoarse hail sounded from the roadway. Morrison stood up. His face grew stern. He left the table and walked down to his gate.

Two men were waiting at the gate. One was a bull-dog faced fellow with a deep furrow across his forehead, between his eyes and hair; and when he scowled, this furrow deepened to a purple welt. He was Bill Heney—Bad Bill, a tough fellow of the countryside, given to bullying and roystering. The man with him was his brother-in-law, Bud Harrison. Bill had not been seen for several months. In the past winter he had assaulted a neighbour, and a warrant for him had been placed in Morrison's hands with instructions to arrest Bill, if he did not keep out of the county.

"Morrison," said Heney, "you've got a warrant for me. Why don't you execute it? I'm tired staying away."

"You had better go away, Heney," said Morrison.

Heney's answer was a volley of oaths, which ended in the flash of a revolver shot. Morrison fell by his gateway. Heney turned and fled. The neighbours at the feast sprang up. Some carried Morrison into the house, others mounted and rode for doctors, others gave chase to Heney. They pursued him to the Harrison woods, a dense tract of timber, with an area of ten miles. In the centre of this tract, in a little clearing, lived the Heneys, father and mother of the refugee; and, since the winter-time, Mrs. Bill Heney had lived with them. Heney, with the neighbours close upon him, plunged into the thickets of the woods and vanished. The doctors worked in vain over Morrison. He died in agony. The neighbours set a watch on the Heney house, and meanwhile notified the Department of Justice.

"When I arrived at Morrison's," says Murray, "the neighbours reported that Heney's wife had been seen, day after day, sneaking from the house out into the thickets with a tin pail, and they were certain she was carrying meals to Heney. They were positive Heney was concealed in the woods. I decided to beat the woods. I called on the neighbours to rally the country-side. They came with a rush from every section of the district. I counted them off, and there were one hundred and forty-three men, with a host of boys and a legion of dogs. All the men had guns or revolvers. Some of them also had knives, axes, and clubs. A few had pitchforks, and I remember two had scythes. We divided them into squads and spread them out in a circle, surrounding the woods fairly well. We swore in the men as special constables. Every squad had a captain, and every captain had a separate section of the woods. At the word all advanced in the man-hunt, to beat the woods and capture Heney. I can hear them still as they moved forward, the dogs barking, the boys cheering. As they advanced they kept in touch. I left some watchers outside the woods on horseback; so if Heney slipped past the searchers and sought to escape, the watchers would see him and give chase.

"Hour by hour the circle drew in. Every yard of land in the Harrison woods was beaten. We travelled around the circle as it narrowed, and we saw the hunters searching even the bushes and the tree-tops. They were to capture Heney alive, if possible; but if he showed fight, they were to shoot him like a dog. Under no circumstances were they to shoot until they saw him and knew it was Heney. The circle closed in on the little clearing. Rabbits and wild fowl had been driven in, but no trace of Heney had been found. As the cordon of men, boys, and dogs stepped out into the little clearing and closed together around the house, Bad Bill's mother let out one of the most awful cries of human agony I ever have heard.

"'Oh, my poor boy! My poor boy! They'll hang you!' she wailed.

"She rolled over on the ground in her grief and howled forth her misery. We searched all the more diligently. The hunters stood in a solid circle around the house. Every man in the circle had a gun, and behind them stood the other men and boys, and on the far outside the dogs. We went into the house, the old woman begging us to spare her son's life. We searched in that shanty for an hour, and he was not there at all. I walked out, and when the old woman spied me she ceased wailing and began to grin. I called off the hunters and left the woods.

"I set men to watch the house for weeks. Heney never appeared. He was not in the woods at any time, since before the search. I began to watch the mails, and intercepted a letter from Heney to his mother-in-law. He told her he was writing in a schoolhouse in Fort Wingate, in New Mexico. He told her how he hid in the woods until nightfall on the day of the shooting; how he crept out in the darkness and boarded a freight train and got away to Boston; and how he went from Boston out to the south-west, where he was going to work for John Sullivan, a Boston contractor in the building of the Santa Fé Railroad. I knew a John Sullivan in Boston who was a railroad contractor, and I learned by telegraph that the John Sullivan I knew was the John Sullivan for whom Heney was going to work in New Mexico. In the meantime I had billed Heney all over the country; and I sent to John Sullivan, in New Mexico, a copy of the bill. It had a picture of Heney in the upper left-hand corner, and read as follows, in heavy, black type:—

$250 REWARD!

Is offered by authority of the Ontario Government for the arrest and detention of William Heney, for the murder of John Morrison, at Bearbrook, in the county of Russell, Canada, on the 25th of June, 1880.

William Heney is 34 years of age; about five feet ten inches high; weighs about 160 lb. His complexion is very dark, and he has raven black hair and small dark grey eyes. His forehead is a very peculiar shape, and has a furrow running across it midway between the eyes and hair; nose very low between the eyes, and then a rise, then a hollow, and the end rises again; one front tooth out; large dimple in the chin; shoulders a little stooped; walks with a shuffling gait.

Heney is a Canadian by birth, of Irish parents, and used to work as a farm labourer.

The above photograph was taken two or three years

ago--Heney was then stouter and fuller in the face than he is now.

When arrested, communicate immediately with

J. W. MURRAY,

Government Detective,

Toronto, Canada.

"I sent a second copy of this to my friend John Sullivan out in New Mexico, and early in December 1880 I received a reply from him that a man answering the description was in one of his gangs. On December 14th I started for Fort Wingate. As I was leaving the office on my way to the train, I received a telegram from Sam Farmer, city marshal of Fort Worth, Texas. It read:

"'Have arrested Heney here.'

"I went through to Fort Worth, and Sam met me when I arrived.

"'I've got your man, John, beyond doubt,' said Farmer.

"'Maybe so, Sam,' said I; 'but I'm afraid it is a mistake.'

"I looked the fellow over. He was almost Heney's double, but he was not Heney. Sam was crestfallen. That was on the evening of December 22nd. I was stopping at the El Paso Inn. A northerner came up, and it grew very cold. There was no adequate heating apparatus in my room at the hotel, and Sam sent word for me to meet him at Smith's saloon, a drinking place with a billiard-room beyond the bar-room, and with swing doors between. The bar-tender was alone in the bar when I entered. I told him Sam Farmer had sent word to me to meet him there. I sat down in a chair. All was very quiet. Some men were playing billiards in the adjoining room, and I could hear the click of the balls.

"'Come, sit behind the bar,' said the bar-tender to me, after a sudden silence in the billiard-room.

"'No, thank you; I'm very comfortable here,' said I, in my chair by the swing doors.

"'Come,' said the bar-tender abruptly. 'Sam Farmer wouldn't like it if a guest of his got hurt.'

"'Hurt?' said I. 'What's the trouble?'

"'Move over behind the bar,' said the bar-tender. 'Take

my word for it.'

"He seemed a decent sort of chap, so I moved. I sat on a beer keg behind the bar for about five minutes. The stove was red hot, and I began to perspire. I thought it was a joke. The bar-tender was squatting on a box back of the bar. Not a sound was to be heard except the quiet shuffle of the feet and the click of the balls in the billiard-room. I was dripping with perspiration. I stood it for another five minutes, and was about to step out and address a few remarks to the bar-tender when——

"'Bang! Bang!' went two revolver shots in quick succession in the next room, followed by a third, and then silence.

"'All right,' said the bar-tender cheerily, to me. 'She's all over. Pretty hot back in here, wasn't it? Too bad, but it was more dignified than squatting back of a box.'

"While he was speaking the swing doors of the billiard-room opened and a nice-looking fellow stepped into the bar-room with a revolver in his hand.

"'Has Sam Farmer got around yet?' he asked of the bar-tender.

"'No sir,' said the bar-tender, as if nothing had happened. 'He's due in a few minutes, as there is a friend waiting for him.'

"The man with the revolver in his hand turned to me. I dodged behind the stove and reached for my own gun. He smiled and held up his hand.

"'No, no,' he said gently. 'Come, join me in a cigar.'

"The bar-tender nodded to me.

"'It's all right,' he said. 'The shooting's all over.'

"Just then Sam Farmer entered. The fellow bade him good evening, and then, without an explanatory word, handed Sam his revolver, a 44 Colt.

"'Ah,' said Sam quickly. 'You've done it, have you?'

"'In the billiard-room, sir,' said the bar-tender briskly.

"'I'll have to lock you up,' said Sam, and turning to me, invited me to accompany him.

"We walked to the lockup, where Sam threw open the door and said: 'Wait for me, Charlie.' My new acquaintance went in and sat down while Sam and I returned to the saloon. They were just carrying the corpse out. The judge had arrived and went to the court house, and a dozen men offered to go bail. The bonds were filled out, and Sam sent word to the lockup for the fellow to come out.

"'It was an old score,' said Sam. 'They happened to meet and they settled it.'

"Business went on as usual. The next morning a paragraph in the paper simply stated the shooting had occurred. The shooter was acquitted. The dead man had gone back to his pistol pocket first.

"'There is little hanging for murder here, unless it is murderous robbery,' said Sam Farmer. 'But they hang for stealing mules.'

"Two days later I was on my way to Albuquerque, and I arrived in Fort Wingate, New Mexico, on December 29th. I learned that my man Heney had worked for a week there, and then had gone on to the front of the new railroad. I called at the United States Army headquarters there, and the officer in command was a gentleman, through and through. He said he would give me every assistance in his power. Lieutenant Watson, a bright, intelligent officer, was sent for. He got a sergeant and three horses, and we started to ride out to the front, where the railroad was being built across towards the coast. We rode about forty miles, and on beyond where the rails had been laid, out to the farthest outpost gang, for Heney had kept in the van. They were a tough crowd, these road-builders, culled from all parts of the country, some of them, like Heney, fled from justice and buried in the wilds of the south-west. Sullivan, of Boston, was at the front. He said Heney had started out alone with another fellow, the pair saying they were going to hoof it to Lower California.

"The Army men and I rode on out, and stopped and looked ahead to where the earth and sky seemed to meet. In the intervening reaches of space no living man or beast or bird was to be seen. The heat hovered over the waste places as if a vast furnace lay beyond. Sullivan had said that one of the two men who started out had been shot by an Indian, and that from what he heard of the raven-black scalp it was

Heney, as the fellow who had started with him had red hair. We turned and rode back to the rude outpost of civilisation, the shelter of the van-gang of road builders. On every side stretched the seemingly endless expanse of earth. I looked to the western skyline, where the strange roads went down.

"'Poor Heney!' I thought, and I turned homeward.

"He never came back."

17

THE TOOKES'S REVEL IN RICHES

CHARLIE TOOKES was a school teacher. He had a younger brother, George Tookes, who decided that he would be a millionaire. All that was necessary was to get $1 and add $999,999 to it; the sooner he began, the sooner he would finish. So in the tender years of his youth, George Tookes set forth to accumulate seven figures of worldly wealth. He pottered around at odd jobs for a couple of years, and then struck a balance. He had $16 of the $1,000,000. At the rate of $8 a year he would be over a hundred thousand years old before he could sit back in his private car and gaze out upon the world through the window—a millionaire.

George Tookes's father was a minister—a good man, of ancient family and respected name—who lived east of Brockville, and who gave little thought to laying up treasure where moth and rust would corrupt, and where thieves would break through and steal. He gave both of his boys a good education, and had taught them faithfully that the love of money was the root of all evil. George Tookes grieved the good man by painting a motto for the wall, declaring that the lack of money was the root of all evil. When the lack fell heavy on George, he would fall back on his brother Charlie. On these visits the dead-broke George would confide in the school-teaching Charlie his plans to wake up some sunny morning and have the bank telephone him he was a millionaire.

Charlie was a bookish sort; he would listen to George's dreams and would blink. Money, to Charlie, was something to read about, with an occasional glimpse of a sample of it on its way to the landlady or the clothing store. But such a thing as having $15 in his inside pocket was something beyond the range of Charlie's imagination. When George, therefore, descended upon Charlie after two years' travelling on the highway to becoming a millionaire and produced $16 Charlie was dazzled. George was affluent beyond Charlie's wildest dreams of riches.

"It's very easy," said George. "Once you get money started your way it comes of its own accord. All money wants is a leader; it follows the leader."

Charlie blinked many times and looked again at the fortune of $16 in the hands of George.

"For instance," said George, "it is very simple for you to make money. In your own particular line of business—this educating line—what do the most people want most at the present time?"

It was June 1881. The examinations in the high schools and colleges were about to be held throughout all Canada. Charlie gravely pondered George's question.

"Advance papers," he answered.

"What's that?" asked the embryonic emperor of finance.

"Advance copies of the examination papers, so they will know what questions they will have to answer," said Charlie.

George thought the matter over.

"A good idea," he said. "A capital idea."

"What is it?" said the confiding Charlie.

"Why, we'll furnish them the papers," said George.

"But where will we get them?" asked his brother.

"Leave that to me," said the future millionaire.

George went away. He visited various high schools and educational institutions and, by one pretext or another, obtained lists of those about to be graduated, and more particularly of those who expected to apply for admission. He represented himself as a book agent and stationery seller, and in other ways managed to get copies of the lists. Then he returned to Charlie, and his $16 had dwindled to $3.

"It takes money to make money," he explained to Charlie, when the latter asked for a glimpse once more of the fabulous sum of $16.

George set Charlie to work preparing a set of questions and answers.

"Make them precisely as if you were preparing a set of

examination papers, marking the standard for the high schools of Canada," said George.

Charlie worked day and night on the task. George, meanwhile, was making scores of copies of a letter he had drafted. It was marked confidential, and stated that the writer was glad to inform the reader that a complete set of the questions and answers in the examination of such and such a school might be had for the simple pledge of confidence and the small amount of——. George left the price blank, as it would vary according to the school or college. For some the price was $10, for others it ranged as high as $50. Charlie had suggested a fee of 50 cents for high schools and $1 for colleges; but Charlie was ambitious to become worth $16, while George aimed $999,984 higher. George's scale of prices prevailed. The letters were written, the papers prepared by Charlie were copied. George took a big bundle of envelopes to the post office and dropped them through the slot.

"In a few days you will be a rich man," said George to Charlie.

"I have my doubts," said Charlie to George.

The few days passed. Letters began to pile in; every mail brought a batch, and every batch brought a bundle of money. Every enclosure of money was answered with a copy of the papers prepared by Charlie.

"What did I tell you?" said George, as the banknotes overflowed Charlie's sack, in which they had decided to keep them. "Money flows in. You are worth $500 already."

"I feel that I have enough," said Charlie.

George smiled pityingly on him.

A few days later they moved on to another post office address, Charlie leaving his school. From their new headquarters they sent out a second batch of letters and the answers poured in, and in a few days they moved on again.

"I heard of them in the form of a dozen complaints from honest, straightforward, righteous folk who had sent them money to buy examination papers and had found the papers worthless," says Murray. "I heard of them in Kingston, Belleville, Coburg, Port Hope, and all along. I suppose those who bought the bogus examination papers did so, not to use for themselves, but to destroy them without looking at them, and thereby keep them out of the hands of others. However, their course did not affect the attitude of the law toward the Tookes brothers. I set out to learn their next probable headquarters. I intercepted some letters in Brantford, identified by the return mark and I sent a decoy letter to them at Paris, Ontario, in which I wrote as a tender young lady of high hopes and advancing years, who did not dread the examinations, but nevertheless preferred to make sure. On the day I mailed the letter I went to Paris and secreted myself in the post office to await the call of one of the Tookes brothers.

"It was a rainy day, the streets were muddy, and the skies were pouring down a modern miniature deluge. In due time a fine-looking young fellow entered the post office and asked for letters for Charles or George Tookes. The clerk asked him again for his name, and he said 'Charles Tookes.' Thereupon the clerk handed him my letter from Brantford and one or two others. Their lists were thinning out, and their mail was not as big as it had been. I moved out from where I was concealed in the post office. Whether Tookes knew me or whether he suspected something was wrong I do not know, but he made a leap for the door and bolted down the street in the rain. I sprang after him ; he could run like a greyhound.

"Away we went through the streets of Paris, mud flying at every leap, water splashing, Tookes running as if his hope of glory depended on his smashing all the world's records. Some dogs saw us and they dashed forth in pursuit ; that summoned the small boys, and soon there was a howling horde of dogs and youths trailing after us. I have chased many men, but Tookes was one of the fastest runners I ever saw. I realised I could not catch him by greater speed, for he was swifter than I, so I settled down to wear him out. Block after block we ran. My feet seemed to weigh two tons apiece ; the sticky mud clung to them. If I was impersonating justice I certainly was leaden heeled. But Tookes was no better off than I. I could see him flounder at times and strive to shake his feet free. He was turning a corner when his feet clogged, he slipped and fell flat in a puddle of mud and water. I came up panting and waited for him to rise. He was a sight: mud-coated from head to foot with a face like a Comanche Indian's. He spluttered and gasped to get the muddy water out of his mouth. I handcuffed him, found the papers, including my letter, on him, and started back through the town at a proper gait.

"Twice he tried to break away. The second time I stopped, and, placing my mouth close to his ear, I informed him what would happen if he tried it a third time. He looked at my feet, big as gunboats with their armour of mud, and he surrendered.

"As we walked up the street I saw a fellow on the other side of the highway that looked so much like him that instinctively I felt it was the brother.

"'There's your brother over there,' said I.

"'No,' said he. 'I never saw him.'

"'Oh yes it is,' said I; and I called to the man across the street, 'George! Come over here; Charlie wants you.'

"George crossed the street, and I promptly handcuffed him to Charlie.

"I took them to Brantford. Old Mr. Jimmy Waymes was magistrate. He was a sympathetic old gentleman, with a tender heart, which constantly pleaded for mercy to be mingled with justice. They gave the name of Tookes, and Magistrate Waymes had heard of their father and mother and sisters, and he was moved to have compassion on them. Yet justice was justice, and he finally sent them to the Central prison for six months apiece.

"Charlie Tookes, when liberated, resumed a sedate life in the rural districts. George Tookes resumed his planning to become a millionaire. The last I heard he was still in the vicinity of the $16 mark. But his hopes were high."

18

JOHN DOBBIN, FROM BEYOND THE QUICKSANDS

WILD DOBBIN was a name given by some to John Dobbin of Bracebridge, when he skipped out of the district of Muskoka and settled across the Red River in the western country, away out in Manitoba, seventy miles beyond Winnipeg. He won the nickname by flying into fits of rage and chasing those near him helter-skelter, while he pursued with club or gun or whatsoever he laid his hands upon. Dobbin was about fifty years old, five feet nine inches tall, with a sandy beard. He was a wiry fellow with an ungovernable temper.

"The reason for his skipping out of the district of Muskoka," says Murray, "was his treatment of John Breckenridge, a Scotchman, who came from the old country. Breckenridge had some money, but knew nothing of farming. He went to the District of Muskoka and settled near Bracebridge. He wanted to buy a farm. John Dobbin heard of it and went to see him and sold him a farm. Breckenridge paid Dobbin part cash and gave him a note for the balance, pending the arrival of a remittance from the old country. When the note came due, Dobbin told Breckenridge he had lost it, and made an affidavit to that effect. Thereupon Breckenridge paid him the amount of the note. Dobbin went away and was seen no more. After he disappeared it transpired that, instead of losing the note, he had sold it to a man who gave it to another man to collect, and this man sued Breckenridge for the value of the note and got judgment. The Scotchman saw he had been swindled by Dobbin, and applied for assistance to the Government. He was directed to me.

"I went to Dobbin's old home at Bracebridge. I could find no trace of him. I nosed around until I learned that his sister had gone away some time before and had bought a ticket to Winnipeg. Through a friend of the sister in Winnipeg I learned that she had gone to Morris, at that time the end of that branch of the Canadian Pacific Railroad, and at Morris she had disappeared. I got my warrant and went to Winnipeg. There I got an officer, Mackenzie, now a private detective, and went to Morris, where the railroad ended. I arrived in Morris on a stifling hot day in July, 1883. I inquired right and left for trace of John Dobbin, but no one seemed to know of him. I decided to try the open country beyond the Red River. I walked for three miles down the river, asking at every house if they knew John Dobbin. No one knew him. After trudging another mile and finding no way to cross the river I sat down in the shade to cool. The river was not so wide but you could be heard on the other side, so while I sat in the shade I bellowed at the top of my voice, at frequent intervals. I became interested in the echoes and shouted lustily. Then I whistled and listened for the echoes and finally I screeched and roared. I was lying flat on my back.

"Suddenly I heard an answering screech. I sat up and looked across the river. On the opposite bank stood a woman screaming to know what was the matter.

"'I want to cross the river,' I shouted.

"'How much will you give if I take you over?' she screamed.

"'I'll give you $1,' roared I.

"'All right! I'll call my man from the field!' she shouted.

"I waited. She moved back into a field and presently I saw a man at the water's edge and he pushed off in a boat and paddled over. He stood off shore about fifteen feet and I looked him over. He was a funny little Frenchman, burned almost black by the sun.

"'Give dollair," he said, keeping his boat away from the shore.

"I stood up, took out a paper dollar and was about to walk down the sandy shore to the water's edge, when he let out a terrific whoop and waved me back with frantic flourishes of the paddle.

"'Queeksand! Queeksand!' he yelled.

"I stopped short on the very edge of a treacherous pit of quicksand. I tested it cautiously with one foot and while it looked like dry sand it yielded readily and sucked in the foot greedily. The little Frenchman all the while shrieked for me to keep back. He would not come nearer shore but motioned for me to give him the $1 first. I cut a long stick from a tree and fastened the $1 to an end of the stick, then climbed out on a limb of a tree overhanging the water and tried to hand the money to him in this way. The limb bent and suddenly broke clean off and down I went in a quicksand by the water's edge. I began to sink. My ankles had disappeared in the sand and my knees were vanishing. I had struggled to an upright position as I fell. The little Frenchman backed his boat over near me, but just beyond my reach.

"'Back in here quick and let me get hold!' I shouted.

"He smiled at me with a sweetness born of the angels.

"'How much you give?' he asked.

"'Back in here! Name your price later but give me a grip of the boat!' I said, for I could feel myself settling and I knew that to struggle would involve me all the deeper.

"My little Frenchman paddled a foot nearer but still kept beyond reach, even if I had flung myself forward with outstretched arms.

"'How much you give?' he asked again, with a voice that seemed to tremble with divine pity. Then, as a thought struck him, he added: 'You give to me, not to her,' and he nodded to the woman who calmly waited on the opposite shore.

"'Yes, yes!' I roared. 'Back the boat in, you fool!'

"'But how much you give?' he insisted, holding himself just out of reach.

"Figures flashed through my head. A goodly sum trembled on the tip of my tongue. I felt myself slowly settling.

"'Name your own price,' I said.

"The little Frenchman eyed me with sparkling eyes.

"'It must be one dollair! No less!' he cried.

"You could have knocked me down with a feather. I had been thinking of hundreds.

"'All right! Back in!' I said.

"'But please give it me,' he said sweetly. 'Give me please the dollair!'

"I was sinking well up the hips and beginning to settle fast, too, but I had to go down in my pocket and dig up another $1, and toss it out to the little Frenchman, who had rescued the first $1 when the limb broke and the stick fell in the water. The Frenchman whirled his boat around and shot the light end in to where I could reach it. I clutched it and kicked and heaved while the little boatman paddled valiantly. I came up like a cork out of a bottle and the boat shot out into the stream with me dragging along in the water behind it. I clambered in and the little Frenchman, with the perspiration pouring down his shining face, paused in his paddling to take the two $1 bills out of his mouth. He folded one in a tiny wad and tucked it into his left ear. The other he rolled in a ball and as he was about to hide it in his mouth, under his tongue, he smiled to me and said:

"'Please, you do not tell her,' and as if to make doubly sure of my good will he added: 'if you had not been in such hurry I would have done it for feefty cents—maybe.'

"I smiled, and he paddled us to shore. The woman was waiting and the little Frenchman took the $1 out of his ear and gave it to her. She shouted at him to give her what he had in his mouth, but he darted beyond reach and defied her. I told her I was buying farms.

"'I understand a man named Dobbin lives near here and has a farm to sell," I said.

"'Buy ours,' she said.

"'I'll buy a lot of farms,' said I. 'But I must see Dobbin's first. Where does he live?'

"'The only Dobbin I know is four miles back cutting hay,' she said.

"'Can your man show me?' I asked.

"The commercial instinct popped out again instantly.

"'For $1·50,' she said.

"I paid her the money then and there. She shouted to

the little Frenchman and he nodded, and away we started to find the man Dobbin, who might or might not be my Dobbin. The little Frenchman walked ahead and I followed. We trudged along in the blazing sun for an hour through brush and across prairie. At last we came upon a man in a field cutting beaver hay.

"'There's Dobbin,' said the little Frenchman, keeping aloof, for it seemed all thereabouts feared Dobbin.

"Dobbin stopped mowing as we drew near. He was dripping wet and his face was crimson from his labour.

"'Are you John Dobbin who lived near Bracebridge?' I asked, while the little Frenchman listened intently.

"'Yes, why?' said Dobbin.

"'Dobbin,' said I, 'I have a warrant for your arrest.'

"'Arrest me!' exclaimed Dobbin, and then slowly he turned on the little Frenchman. 'And you brought him here to arrest me? You French —— ——!'

"With a roar of rage Dobbin went after the little Frenchman with the scythe. With a shriek of terror the little Frenchman sped away, Dobbin in hot pursuit and I after Dobbin. As the little Frenchman ran he squealed with fright, and as Dobbin ran he bellowed in fury. I began to laugh. The ludicrous side of it struck me. There scooted my little Frenchman like a rabbit, bounding over ditch and bush, while Dobbin thundered after him like a savage hound or an avenging demon. They ran until Dobbin dropped the scythe and settled down into steady chase. I trailed along for I saw that the little Frenchman was heading for the river. The terrific pace was telling on both of them, and their gait fell bit by bit until it was a lagging trot, then a walk, then a stagger. And so they tottered on, not twenty feet apart, both gasping and well-nigh exhausted, the Frenchman unable to go forward and Dobbin unable to overtake him. They ran themselves to a standstill. I came up and caught Dobbin and started him back toward his house, which was beyond the field where he had been mowing. I heard the little Frenchman crying after me piteously. I turned back to see if he were hurt.

"'The dollair!' he lamented. 'I did swallow it!' and his

grief burst forth afresh.

"As I started away he cried after me: 'Think, oh think! The queeksand! I save you! I do eat the dollair! Give to me a dollair!'

"Dobbin, furious as he was, laughed scornfully back at the little Frenchman.

"Dobbin's wife was out when we arrived at his house, but she came in presently with her sister. She was a terror. The moment she spied the handcuffs on her husband she made a break for the woodpile and the axe. The sister ran down in the cellar. Dobbin and I were in the kitchen, he on a chair in one corner and I on a chair in another corner. In a moment in marched Mrs. Dobbin, axe in hand, and up from the cellar came the sister with a cleaver.

"'What does this mean?' said Mrs. Dobbin to me. 'Explain yourself, or I'll chop you into mincemeat.'

"She was the kind of woman who could have made first-class mincemeat out of a man. I carefully changed my revolver to my left hand, and began to reason with her. But it seemed there was to be no such thing as reason. She advanced towards me with the axe. I drew a second gun.

"'Dobbin,' I said, 'call off your wife. I dislike to shoot a woman. I can arrest her and take her to Winnipeg and lock her up and send her to prison. She's a fool.'

"The woman stopped in the middle of the kitchen floor. There she stood, axe in hand, while her sister guarded the door with the cleaver. It was twilight, and darkness came. I could discern the three figures as they stood. A clock struck nine.

"'Time's up,' I said, rising. 'Strike a light!'

"There was silence. I turned to Dobbin.

"'I've had enough of this,' I said. 'Axe or no axe, woman or no woman, this stops now. Call her off.'

"Mrs. Dobbin burst into furious ragings.

"'I'll die before Dobbin crosses the Red River to-night,' she shouted.

"I'll take him, you, and your sister,' I replied; and I advanced, preparing to dodge the axe and seize it.

"She raised the axe and planted herself to strike. I stepped forward, and with my left hand holding a revolver and my right hand free, I feinted to draw her blow. Dobbin, who had watched it all, saw the beginning of the end, and stood up and called his wife aside and tried to pacify her. The sister sought to slip outdoors, but I called her in, mindful of men who had been shot in the darkness through an open window.

"'Be quick,' I said to Dobbin. 'I've dallied too long. I'll get a boat three miles up the river.'

"'I own a boat on the river,' said Dobbin sullenly.

"'It's mine, not yours,' said Mrs. Dobbin.

"I thought of the commercial instinct.

"'You can make some money out of your boat,' I said to her. 'Dobbin must go over the river with me. Some one will make the money.'

"'What will you pay?' she asked.

"'I'll give you a dollar,' I said.

"I dropped four silver quarters on the kitchen floor, one by one. She leaped for a candle, lighted it, and gazed at the money.

"'Who will bring the boat back?' she asked.

"'You can send for it,' said I.

"She thought it over.

"'For $1.50 I'll do it,' she said.

"I dropped two more quarters on the floor. She clutched them eagerly, and the woman who was going to die before Dobbin should cross the river—and meant it, too—capitulated for six quarters shining in the candle-light on her kitchen floor. Truly, the power of money is magical at times.

"I took Dobbin away in the night, and we crossed the river and hired a team and driver at Morris and drove the seventy miles to Winnipeg, getting a midnight meal on the way. Dobbin kicked in Winnipeg. He employed a lawyer, the famous Fighting Mackenzie. This lawyer took Dobbin before Chief Justice Walbridge on a writ of *habeas corpus*. I employed the present Judge McMahon to fight the writ. The Chief Justice dismissed the writ, and ordered the prisoner into my custody. I started back with Dobbin.

I had to take him by way of the Sault Ste. Marie Canal, and the boat went through the American side. Fighting Mackenzie told Dobbin to keep quiet until the boat was in the Soo; then to yell and demand protection, and he would telegraph the American sheriff to be there and compel me to liberate Dobbin, as I had no papers authorising me to hold him in American territory.

"Dobbin and I embarked on the steamer *Campana* at Port William, which at that time was Port Arthur. Captain Anderson, now of the steamer *Manitoba*, was her commander. I got a hint of the job put up to save Dobbin in the Soo. I knew everybody aboardship. The crew and officers all were my friends. I said to Captain Anderson: 'Before we get to Sault Ste. Marie, land me with Dobbin in a small boat above the rapids, and I'll pull for the Canadian shore.' I told him of the job.

"'I know the sheriff myself,' said Captain Anderson, 'and instead of risking it in a small boat above the rapids, I'll put Dobbin in the hold and shut the hatches before we get to the American side.'

"John Burns of Toronto was steward of the boat. Captain Anderson and Burns and I talked it over, and the captain selected a room on the port side farthest from the American shore, and told me to get Dobbin in there and Burns would lock the door.

"'He can yell like a Comanche in there and no one will hear him,' said Captain Anderson.

"Dobbin was all primed for the job. As we drew near the locks he even cleared his throat for the yells that he was to pour forth. The steward came to me.

"'Mr. Murray,' he said, 'would you like a little good whisky?'

"'Yes, indeed,' said I. 'Dobbin, want a drink?'

"Dobbin smacked his lips. He had time, before the boat entered the locks.

"'Why, yes,' he said.

"'We went down to the room. It was a little cubbyhole of a place with no window or outlet but a little porthole. A decanter of whisky and glasses were on the table. We went in. The steward stepped out and slammed the door.

"'What did he shut the door for?' asked Dobbin, with sudden suspicion.

"I eyed him.

"'Why don't you holler, Dobbin?' said I.

"He glared at me. I could see the crimson dye his face, the veins swell, the eyes grow small, as his temper rose. He grabbed the decanter. I flipped out my revolver. We stood face to face with the little table between us. I eyed him, look for look.

"'Take a good drink, Dobbin,' I said.

"The boat was in the locks. Dobbin drank.

"'Why don't you holler?' I said.

"He looked at me, at the locked door, at the porthole; then he sank into a chair.

"'Murray, I've lost my voice,' said Dobbin.

"He sat with eyes closed for an hour or more. When we were through the locks and out into Canada waters and away from shore, the steward unlocked the door and said:

"'Dinner, gentlemen!'

"Dobbin awoke, as if from a dream.

"'I'm hungry as hell,' he said, and went in to dinner.

"We landed in Collingwood, and went to Barrie, where, on August 13th, 1883, I turned Dobbin over to the authorities. As I bade him good-bye, he said: "Just wait till I get back to Red River and meet that Frenchman!' At times, when weird noises sound in the night, I think of Dobbin, and wonder if he has caught the little Frenchman at last."

BALDY DRINKWATER

DRINKWATER'S first name was Archibald. His friends called him Baldy Drinkwater. He was a travelling nursery-man, and he drove from county to county doing business with farmers. He had a wide acquaintance. His speciality was selling trees and fancy shrubbery. He was persistent, and clung to the guileless farmer until he had him for a customer. Cash or notes, it was all the same to Baldy Drinkwater. In fact, he seemed to prefer notes from many of his customers.

"He finally began to discount notes in the banks, and eventually he disappeared," says Murray. "When the signatures were investigated it was found that Baldy Drinkwater was a forger, and had faked the signatures to bogus orders and to notes. The farmers were angry, and it was just as well for Baldy that he was out of the country. The case came to me, and I set out to find him. He had a brother-in-law in Illinois, and it was quite probable Baldy had skipped to him. Refugees frequently flee to relatives in other countries, instead of braving exile alone or apart from any one who knew them before. I billed Baldy all over the country, too. While I was waiting for trace of him, I prepared the necessary extradition papers, and when no clue to his whereabouts developed I started for Chicago. There I called on the United States Commissioner and the marshal, and he assigned a German deputy to assist me. The deputy and I went by train to the village of St. Ann's, about one hundred and fifty miles from Chicago. Baldy's brother-in-law lived near St. Ann's.

"The German deputy was a funny fellow. He spoke quaint English, and was full of proverbs. Also he had a love affair, which demanded much of his thought, and of which he spoke frequently and fervidly. I remember we were riding serenely along, and the train passed a farmhouse painted sea-green. My German friend grasped my arm and shook me out of a pleasant doze, and pointed excitedly out the window.

"'See it! See it!' he cried.

"'That house? What about it?' I asked, wondering if Baldy Drinkwater's face had appeared at the window.

"'Her eyes are yust t'at colour,' he exclaimed, and sank back with a happy sigh.

"'The colour of that house?' I said, craning my neck for another glimpse of the sea-green farmhouse.

"'Yah,' he said sweetly. 'Heafenly blue!'

"A lot of things along the road reminded him of her. He was not backward to tell me of them.

"'Say, Peter,' said I finally, 'does she ever cry?'

"'Vunce,' said Peter sadly.

"'What did you do?' I asked.

"'I yust let her cry till she dried herself up,' said he.

"'Don't you know that the books tell of how the fond lover kisses the tears away?' I asked.

"I remember Peter's expression to this day. His face puckered up.

"'Ah, yah!' he said. 'I yust tried it, und it was salty like t'e mackerel—o-o-oof!' and Peter spat mightily at the mere memory of it. 'She iss very salty, iss Katrina.'

"But he turned out to be a brave man, did Peter. We arrived at St. Ann's about six o'clock in the evening, and I had no trouble in learning that Baldy's brother-in-law, who was a county constable named Goodfellow, lived about twenty miles out in the country, and was quite well known there. I hired a team, and Peter and I started to drive from the little village. It was a fine road, and we made good time, and about ten o'clock at night we drove up to the cross-roads saloon of a little country-corners town. We hitched the team and walked into the saloon. There were six men in the place apart from the bar-tender. The seven were drinking together, and all were half-drunk. The moment Peter spied them he whispered to me:

"'T'at is Big Polley, und t'e little fellow und he yust got

out of t'e penitentiary.'

"'I never had seen Drinkwater, but I had a fairly good description. The first man I spied answered the description to a dot—big, burly, rough, with facial marks to make sure. As they all turned, when we asked the bar-tender for a drink, I saw to my amazement that the second man was almost a duplicate of the first. Never have I seen such a remarkable likeness between two men. I was positive one of the two was Baldy, but which one? I could not tell. They were playing pool, and resumed their game as the bar-tender went behind the bar to serve us. There was a mirror behind the bar, and I could see them clearly as I stood with my back to them. Peter ordered a whisky. As he did so an idea struck me.

"'What's yours?' asked the bar-tender.

"'I'll drink water,' I said, rapidly and distinctly; and added, "with whisky on the side.'

"As I spoke I watched the six men through the mirror, and saw one of the pair glance up quickly, shift uneasily, eye us a moment, and turn again to the game. I believed I had learned which was Drinkwater. Peter and I finished our drink. How to get the man, without a fight and perchance a shooting, was puzzling me. Peter read my thoughts. We stepped outside and untied the horses, and drove the team close up to the saloon and beyond the door.

"'Peter,' I said, 'you saw the two men who looked alike, and you know the big one with the grey hat?'

"'Ah, yah,' said Peter.

"'Step in and tell him a woman wants to speak to him at the door,' said I. 'Be sure you come out ahead of him, and when you get out jump for the waggon and the reins.'

"Peter went in. I stood close by the door, holding the reins loosely and ready for the door to open. Peter popped out, leaped in the waggon, and caught the reins. Right behind him came the big fellow.

"'Where is she?' he said, as he stepped through the door.

"'Without a word I grabbed him and heaved. He was caught unawares, and landed sprawling in the light waggon. Peter sat on him in a jiffy, and I snapped the handcuffs on him and jerked his revolver out of his pocket. The moment he felt himself seized in the dark he yelled for help. Out rushed his friends. They sprang to the horses' heads in the interval of our struggle in the waggon. Two of the crowd drew revolvers. So did Peter and I. The bar-tender ran out with a light.

"'T'ank you, kint frent,' said Peter. 'I kin see to shoot.'

"'Stand back from the horses,' I said.

"They answered with a chorus of oaths. I told them I was a United States Marshal from Chicago. One of them began to yell for a magistrate. My big fellow lay in the waggon swearing like a trooper and beseeching his friends to kill us. A man came out of the back room of the saloon. He seemed to be a magistrate. He told me to show my papers. I told him I was a United States Marshal, and would not show my papers to him or any one else.

"'If anything happens here, you will be held responsible,' I said to him.

"He called three of the gang into consultation. That left three men.

"'Loose the horses' heads,' I commanded.

"They laughed. I aimed as close as I could for an ear of one of the horses and fired. With a snort the two horses reared, tore loose from the men, and flew down the road at full gallop. I caught the reins while Peter sat on the big fellow, who raged and swore and kicked. The horses were headed for St. Ann's, and I gave them full rein, and they sped through the night like swallows. Peter's human cushion yelled and howled all the way, struggling to free himself, and calling on his friends to follow and kill us. As we neared St. Ann's I tied a kerchief round his mouth, so he would not rouse the whole village. He bit and snapped at it as if he were a mad dog.

"We drew up at the hotel in St. Ann's in the dead of night. The horses were fagged out, and stood panting, wet, drooping. We had to carry our prisoner, kicking and swearing, into the hotel and into a back room to wait for the Chicago train. I expected pursuit, and told the landlord I was a United States Marshal and for him to lock the doors. Hardly had he shot the bolts when we heard the hoof-beats of galloping horses, and then we heard men's voices, and finally they halted outside the hotel and began to bang on the door and fire revolvers.

"Landlord!' they shouted. 'Open this door in the name of the law. We are officers!'

"The landlord wavered, and finally said he would have to admit them. I had sent Peter into the back room with the prisoner. I had two revolvers, one in each hand. I stood by the door, and when the third of the gang outside had entered I shut and locked the door and faced them.

"'Hands in front of you, please,' I said, and they obeyed. 'Now, who are you, and what do you want?'

"'We are officers, and want to see your authority for holding the prisoner you have,' said their spokesman.

"'I am a United States Marshal from Chicago, and I have a warrant from the United States Court for this prisoner, and I am not obliged to show my authority to county constables, bailiffs, or anybody else,' I answered.

"While this was occurring, the prisoner kept yelling for them to shoot me, to rescue him, to kill me like a dog.

"'Peter,' I called to the deputy marshal, 'if you hear a scuffle or a shot out here, shoot the prisoner first through the head, and then come out.'

"'Ah, yah,' answered Peter from the back room.

"The three men turned to form a group, ostensibly to confer.

"'Face me, please, and keep your hands in front,' said I.

"'May we speak to the prisoner,' said their spokesman.

"'One at a time, from the doorway,' I said.

"One of them went to the doorway, and spoke to the prisoner, who answered with a volley of oaths and a demand that I be killed and he rescued.

"'I guess that's all,' I said, when the prisoner had finished his tirade, and the three filed out at the door.

"As the last one went out he flung himself against the door. I was expecting it, and there was a moment's scuffle, then the door banged amid curses and shouts. Suddenly a shot rang out in the back room, followed by a moan, and then all was still except for a faint ' Ah, yah,' from Peter. I hung on to the door, struggling to keep it shut and lock it. When the shot sounded, the noises outside ceased. I bolted the door, and sprang for the back room. There lay the prisoner, gagged and unhurt, while Peter smilingly eyed a hole in the wall which he had made with the bullet he fired to cause the gang outside to think the prisoner had been killed.

"The Chicago train was due in thirty minutes. I slipped upstairs, and through a window I could see the gang drawn back down the road, and they were drinking. I looked out the back way and saw a rear road leading to the station. I softly opened a back door. I went back to Peter, and we took the prisoner, and lugged him out, and away we went to the station. We laid back by a fence corner near the station until the train came in, and then we picked up the prisoner and made a rush for it. We got aboard all right, and the train moved out, while we could see the crowd riding to and fro by the hotel, occasionally shooting into the darkness.

"The prisoner was sullen. He kicked at Peter until finally the good-natured German got a pin, and every time the prisoner kicked him Peter drove the pin into him. About the third pin-drive the kicking ceased.

"'Herr Trinkvater, v'at a foony name you haf,' said Peter.

"The prisoner turned to me.

"'I'm Drinkwater,' he said. 'Now take that Dutchman away.'

"Peter instantly began to tell him of his beloved Katrina, and all the way to Chicago little Peter told big Baldy of the beauty and the goodness of his sweetheart.

"'Ven I sat on you in t'e vaggon, I t'ought of Katrina, you vas so big and soft,' said Peter.

"Drinkwater swore. When we arrived in Chicago, Baldy fought extradition determinedly, but it was no use. Back he came to Owen Sound in Canada, and he was sent to Kingston penitentiary for seven years. He and Herres, as I have said, were the meanest prisoners I ever had. I have thought since of the absence of any sense of sorrow when I heard Dutch Peter's shot ring out in the back room of the hotel at St. Ann's. A hole in a wall looks different from a hole in a man's head. But the temptation had been strong on Peter, and he shot as close as he dared. The hole in the wall was about an inch from Baldy Drinkwater's head. Peter was a good shot, too. He could miss a man closer than most marksmen. He reminded me, in some of his quaint ways, of John Klippert, who died recently, full of years, and with his life's work well done."

20

THE SHANTY CITY OF SLABTOWN

SLABTOWN is a sprawling settlement of shanties along the feeder to the Welland Canal on the outskirts of Dunnville in the county of Haldimand. It is a Government reserve, and the residents are squatters. They are a motley population, who pay no rent, and fish or loll through life with an occasional industrious man among them. They are as distinct, in their way, as a nation apart from Canada, for they seem to have a code of morals all their own, and their customs in business are unique. One of the flourishing features of trade in Slabtown is in wives. They trade wives like knives in Slabtown, a fair swap and so much to boot. The women do not object, and the families increase and multiply upon the bank of the canal, one mother and several fathers.

This results in quite a tax on the memory of Slabtown society. Mrs. Sallie Poney, for instance, using fictitious names, had seven children. One was Johnnie Poney Scollie. another was Mickey Poney Ready, another was Luella Poney Stott, another was Mabelle Poney Watkins, another was Thomas Poney Colter, another was Samson Poney Pettingil, and another was Tillie Poney Scollie, for in the end Mrs. Sallie had been traded back to the father of Johnnie Poney Scollie. Tobias Stott could point, as could other men of Slabtown, to a fine family of sons and daughters scattered through the shanties. Not all the élite of Slabtown were of the Stott or Scollie kind, of course, or the population would have become hopelessly mixed. As it was, a man was living with his great aunt, while an uncle traded for his niece's daughter by his aunt's son. In fact, one Slabtown dame once said that she had become her own mother.

"Shure, Patty Scollie is his own grandfather for he traded

for his father's great aunt's mother's son's daughter," said she.

A stranger appeared in Dunnville on October 31st, 1888.

"He was an old gentleman," says Murray, "about fifty-five, well dressed, apparently respectable. He had money. About eleven o'clock at night John Upper, living near the canal bridge on the edge of Slabtown, heard a loud scream and a splash in the water, then a clatter on the bridge, as if a man ran across it to Slabtown. Upper spoke to several persons about it, and in the morning they looked for signs of a struggle but nothing was to be seen. Nine days later a body was found floating in the canal west of the bridge. It proved to be that of the old gentleman who was in Dunnville on October 31st. He had been murdered before the body was thrown into the canal. There was no water in the lungs, and the base of the skull was fractured. The pockets were turned inside out, his money was gone, no papers were found on him, and there was no clue to his identity. He was last seen about five o'clock in the afternoon on his way to Slabtown, slightly under the influence of liquor. I sent out his picture and long afterward I learned that he was a harness maker named Lowrie, from Toronto.

"The autopsy I ordered, when I had the body exhumed on my arrival, showed that the man not only was dead when put in the water but the body was still warm. This was shown, said the doctors, by the fact that what a layman calls gooseflesh, was visible. This appears and remains when a warm dead body is put in the water. Thus it was evident that the old gentleman had been attacked, had screamed, had been struck on the head with a blunt instrument and killed, then had been robbed and the body thrown in the water.

"I became a frequenter of Slabtown. I collected a marvellous mass of information. You can get all kinds of information in Slabtown. Anything you want to know, they will tell you. I learned from a Slabtowner, named Henry Overhold, that three hours before John Upper heard the scream and splash in the night, Joe Clemo, of Slabtown, had stopped at Overhold's, and told him that before morning he would be a rich man. Joe Clemo then went out and returned to Overhold's house at seven o'clock in the morning, and drew a big roll of bills from his pocket and slapped them down on the floor.

"'Hanky,' said Joe Clemo, 'I made that since I saw you last.'

"Overhold told this to me solemnly. I looked up Joe Clemo's record and found he was a bad egg, and for so young a man he had spent much time in the penitentiary. I learned from an hotel man in Dunnville that, two days before the murder, Joe Clemo had borrowed five cents. He always was broke.

"I called on the aristocracy of Slabtown. They received me with open arms and soapsudsy hands or fishy fingers. Huldy Smith led me out to the bank of the canal, and there told me that Joe Clemo had called on her when John William Smith was out.

"'Joey showed me the squidge of bills, and he shook them to me so's I smelt 'em, and he says to me: "Huldy, fly with me to the United States." Joey says it to me.'

"'Was that all he said?' I asked.

"'Oh no,' said Huldy. 'He says he love me and I smelt the bills again. Bills has a funny smell.'

"'Didn't Joey tell you where he got the bills?' I asked.

"'No; I didn't ask,' said Huldy.

"'But if Joey really had loved you he would have told you where he got them,' said I.

"Huldy bridled up.

"'Huh!' said she. 'So he did tell me. While I was smelling the bills Joey Clemo whispers to me: "Huldy I love you; fly with me; and I killed an old man because I had to hit him to rob him, and I hit him harder than I meant, so when he wouldn't come to I pitched him in the canal. Fly with me." I told Joey that was no way to get money, and for him to go on about his own business and fly himself, but he wouldn't fly me with him. I stood by for John William, who ain't hitting people too hard on the head and pitching bodies into the canal.'

"I found Joe Clemo had skipped out a few days after the murder. I hunted him for months, and finally heard of a fellow answering his description near Essex Centre, in the county of Essex. I went there late in March, and on April 4th I arrested the man, who was Joe Clemo. He had stopped at a farmhouse and was on his way to the United States. I handcuffed him, but said nothing about the charge against him.

"'What are you arrested for?' asked the farmer's wife.

"'Oh, I am arrested for murder, that's all,' said Joe Clemo.

"He had excellent power of divination. He evidently expected to be arrested for a murder. Men who have done no murder seldom expect to be arrested for killing a man. I took Joe Clemo to Cayuga before Squire Wintermute, and I summoned a number of Slabtown witnesses, and the magistrate was satisfied of Joe Clemo's guilt, and on April 16th, 1889, Joe Clemo was held for trial. Sam Smith, who, it was said, had been seen in Joe Clemo's company, also was remanded. I arrested Sam in Dunnville, but later no bill was found against him.

"In making ready for the trial of Joe Clemo, I found the Slabtowners eager to be called in the case. Every time they told their story they made it stronger, as if they feared they would be overlooked unless their testimony was sensational and positive. They seemed to enter into a competition to see who could tell the most damaging story against Joe Clemo. This rivalry became so keen that Joe Clemo, according to the tales of the witnesses, had waved the banknotes before several women and while they smelt them, Joe said: 'Fly with me.' When Huldy Smith said Joe had asked her first, another promptly declared Joe Clemo had asked her three times and had showed her how he had killed the old gentleman and had dived with the body to the bottom of the canal, and had stuck it head first in the bottom so it would not come up, and had robbed it under water so no one would see him do it. One of the women finally said that Joey embraced her and said: 'You need not fly with me, if you don't want to. I love you so that you can take the money and not fly.' She added that she refused the money. This aroused other witnesses to still greater efforts.

"I conferred, finally, with Crown Prosecutor Colin Macdougal, and I explained the situation to him and said frankly that it was one of the strangest cases I ever had encountered. Meanwhile, the grand jury, after calling only a few of the witnesses, had found a true bill against Joe Clemo, and his trial came on before Chief Justice Armour. We were in an awkward position. While I thought Joe Clemo did the deed, I did not think the witnesses were telling the truth, as they kept changing their stories constantly, and finally, as I have said, got into a competition as to who could tell the strongest story. Joe Clemo was defended by an able counsel, the present Judge Snyder, of Hamilton. I had a conversation with him, and he had very little hope of getting Joe Clemo out of his trouble. I had another conversation with the Crown Prosecutor and advised him to speak to Chief Justice Armour about the matter. I knew there would be no restraining many of the witnesses, once they got on the stand. They simply would vie with one another to tell the biggest story and make the grandest appearance on the witness stand. She who carried off the honours would be queen of Slabtown, and her various children would bask in her glory. However, we hit on a plan of our own.

"First we proved the death of the old gentleman. Then we selected some of our choicest Slabtown witnesses. Sarah Scollie was one. Sarah Scollie and Sally Poney were not the same woman. Sarah told her story. It was just grand to see her swell before the Slabtowners on the benches. Then came her cross-examination.

"'Are you married, Sarah?' asked Mr. Snyder politely.

"'None of your —— business,' replied Sarah haughtily, with her nose elevated and her head held high, as a sign of utter disdain.

"Sarah meant to squelch her cross-examiner. So she gave him the Slabtown snub. Her answer gave the judge and jury an idea of Sarah's character. She was instructed to answer the question.

"'Not by a —— sight,' said Sarah.

"She was asked with whom she was living at that time.

"'Sam Smith,' said Sarah, sniffing.

"'How long have you lived with Sam?'

"'Two years,' said the haughty Sarah.

"'With whom did you live before that?'

"'Ben Hughes,' said Sarah, glaring.

"'How long?'

"'About a year and a half,' said Sarah.

"'Was there not a dicker between Sam Smith and Ben Hughes about your transfer?'

"Sarah tossed her head and looked unutterable scorn.

"'What transfer?' she snapped.

"'Of you to Smith.'

"Sarah glared. The court instructed her to answer.

"'Yes,' exclaimed Sarah. 'A cow and a couple of dollars.'

"Sarah stepped down. Next came Mrs. McCann. She was of the same stripe, only she was better natured than Sarah. She had lived with one man after another and there had been bargains and barter. After a few more of these witnesses the judge asked Mr. Macdougal if that was the kind of witnesses the Crown proposed to produce throughout the prosecution.

"'We take the witnesses just as they come," said Mr. Macdougal.

"'Well, I would not hang a dog on the testimony of such witnesses,' said the court.

"We had some respectable witnesses, but they were not our main ones. Joe Clemo went free. He was the hardest-looking man in the dock I ever saw. He was cross-eyed, so that he seemed to hold his head sidewise to see you. He was so well known as a bad character that the jury would have been apt to convict him. I was under the impression he was guilty, but I did not think it right to convict a man on the testimony of people whom the Crown officers did not believe; and, under the circumstances, I was glad he was acquitted.

"Numerous unsuccessful efforts have been made to break up Slabtown. The ministers and county councils and others have tried it, but there it is and there it seems to stay. There are honest, industrious folk in Slabtown. It is not a nest of thieves or a mere place of dissolute people. They simply are traders, even in wives."

21

WHY TAMBLY SLEEPS IN GEORGIAN BAY

HIGH on a hill overlooking the waters of Georgian Bay stands a white farmhouse. It may be seen from afar, shining like silver in the sunlight. Mariners know it as the White House on the Hill. They point it out, across the waters, a mere white speck ; or, when nearer, they nod toward it, as if to the marble tomb of some mighty chieftain. A lad once lived at this White House on the Hill—a fair-haired, blue-eyed, merry lad, whose grandfather carved small boats for him and taught him to sail them, first in the watering trough, then in the duck pond, and finally in the creek. The old man and the boy were wont to sit for hours in the shade, looking out over the bay, where the waters shimmered and sparkled, where the ships came gliding up out of the nowhere, beyond the line where the sky dipped down to the earth. Stories of terrible tempests, tales of phantom ships, yarns of gallant seamen and how they went to their death were spun by the old man, while the boy listened, wide-eyed and open-mouthed.

"The waters rock them to sleep," the old man would say. "The ships that go down are the cradles in which the seamen sleep."

A great love for the water came to possess the boy. The land seemed a hard and desert place. He yearned for the life of a sailor. He used to tell his mother of his dreams, when golden ships came sailing over shining seas with a ship for him on which his name glittered. He plodded on about the farm, toiling in the soil and dreaming of the sea.

"When he was twenty-two years old," says Murray, "he packed his duds in a bundle and went to Owen Sound, determined to be a sailor. The *Baltic*, a steamer plying on Georgian Bay, between Owen Sound and Sault Ste. Marie, was in port at that time. He went aboard. It was in September 1889.

"'I want to ship as a sailor,' said he.

"'What's your name?' they asked him.

"'George Tambly, of the county of Grey,' said he.

"'Ever been afloat?'

"'No, I've lived on a farm near Wyerton.'

"'They laughed; but they hired him. He shipped as a deck-hand, and it was the proudest moment of his life when he went ashore and sent word home that he had shipped and was going to be a sailor. The *Baltic* carried a crew of about ten deck-hands, four firemen, two wheelsmen, two engineers, and a chief cook. Captain Robinson was her master. Many of the crew were rough-and-ready fellows, hardened to the life they led, reckless and devil-may-care. They were a different crowd from the gay adventurers who manned the shining ships in the farmboy's golden dreams. They were no gentlemen with velvet coats and jewelled daggers and bags of gold. Instead, there were slovenly, grimy, hard-spoken toilers, to whom life was a stern and merciless task-master, to be greeted with a sneer or a guffaw.

"The crew quickly learned of young Tambly's high ideals, and they gibed him constantly. The green country boy shrank from them, and sought to be alone. There was liquor in the cargo on this trip. It was alleged that some of the crew pilfered and that a group of them broached the cargo. Certain it is that they hunted out Tambly and dragged him from his hiding-place, and sat him down in the centre of their circle and bade him drain a cup of liquor. He refused. They seized him, to force it down his throat. He set his jaws, and they could not open them. So they drank around the circle, each draining the cup that Tambly had refused. They spat on the country boy, and kicked him until he broke away and hid again.

"'He knows of the broached cargo,' said one.

"'Aye, and he refused to join us,' said another.

"They debated it in their drunken way. Their contempt for the country boy grew to dislike and deepened to a deadly hatred.

"'Let's coat him, and make him dance," said one.

"With a shout they leaped up to carry out the suggestion. Two went for tar, one stole a pillow, and slit it open and made ready the feathers; the others began a search for Tambly. They found him hid near his bunk. He fought and kicked, but they choked him and dragged him out in the moonlight. They stripped off his clothes and beat him, and then the hot tar was brought forth and they tarred him, slapping it on with paddles and smearing it over his naked skin. In agony he broke from his tormentors and ran around the ship. He shouted to the ship's officers for mercy, he pleaded with his pursuers to have pity. He fell on the deck and writhed as they chased after him, slapping tar on him and thumping him with the paddles. He knelt in anguish, and begged them to desist. Their answer was taunts oaths, and more tar. The captain was aware of the persecution, but made light of it. Then they chased him again. Around and around the deck he fled, a hunted, tortured being, the tar stiffening and smarting. In despair he sprang upon the rail, and struggled to climb beyond reach. They gathered below him like a pack of hungry, snarling wolves.

"Tambly looked down at them and then out across the water. High on the hillside he saw a light shine out, bright as the evening star. It was the light of home. He knew the old man was there, and probably had the glad note spread out before him, reading of how George had shipped as a sailor. A door in the farmhouse opened, and a stream of light poured forth like a beacon to beckon him home. The boy, for he was only a boy, hesitated. The waters looked cold and dark in the night. The drunken crowd beneath him clamoured for him to come down. One started to climb up after him. The door in the farmhouse on the hill closed. The light went out. His cry rang out in the night, and he leaped. There was a splash, and the ship went on.

"The bodies that go down in these waters never come up. The water is too cold, and the depths are far, far down. Tambly sank, and never rose again. Quiet fell aboard the *Baltic*.

"A passenger who was aboard the steamer on this trip heard of the outrage. He notified the proper authorities, and on the next trip I boarded the *Baltic* at Wyerton. I made the trip, and I drank with some of the crew and got the story and the names, and I arrested six of them, including Russell, the second engineer; Tripp, the chief cook; a deck-hand named Jennings, and others. I took them to Owen Sound and locked them up, and they were committed for trial for manslaughter. Later four of them were sent to prison. The captain's licence was revoked for a year.

"I went to Tambly's house. I asked what they last heard from the boy. They told me that they had received his note about shipping as a sailor; and the old man had taken it out again, for the hundredth time, to read it, and as he read he thought he heard a cry in the night.

"'I thought George was calling,' said the old man, and he opened the door and stepped outside and listened.

"Far out on the water he could see a steamer's lights. He heard nothing, and went indoors.

"'I thought George called,' he said, 'but I was mistaken. George is where, even if he called, I could not hear.'

"The old man was right. George, far down in the icy waters, was where, even if he called, the old man could not hear."

22

REGINALD BIRCHALL: OCCUPATION, MURDERER

THICK grow the briars in Blenheim Swamp. Fallen logs and tangled thickets mingle in a maze, impassable save where paths penetrate the dense underbrush.. Desolation and loneliness pervade the place. The spirit of solitude broods over the marsh. Wild creatures are its only habitants. They flit to and fro, their weird cries echoing in the stillness. On an edge of it is a deep and silent pool, Pine Pond. Its inner fastnesses for many years were an undiscovered country, from whose bourne at least one traveller did not return. The bones of dead men had been found in the swamp; but not until February 1890 did it reveal a body lately dead—a body that lay like a bundle, half concealed. Two woodsmen passing came upon it and rolled it over. Two long arms flapped lifelessly, two glassy eyes stared vacantly, and a cold, white face turned skyward, with a purple blotch to tell where a bullet bored its fatal way.

Only the wild creatures of the swamp had beheld the tragedy. From the treetops and the moss lands they saw a young man, a gentleman, come walking up an old narrow trail. Gaily he came. He was smoking, and gazed eagerly ahead as if the bush-grown road were a golden highway to a promised land. They saw him point forward and press on. They saw death walking at his elbow—a second figure, handsome and alert, swift of movement, stealthy, noiseless. They saw the glitter of steel, the flash of flame, the puff of smoke, and heard the explosion ring out through the forest. They saw the blithesome young gentleman lurch forward, sway and fall, as a second shot went echoing over the marsh. They saw the murderer coolly feel the pulse, quietly search the pockets, then deliberately produce a pair of scissors and clip from the dead man's clothes all tell-tale traces of his identity or of the place whence he came. Nothing was done hurriedly. The noise of the shots was the rudest part of it. All else was done softly, placidly. The murderer raised the body by the arms and started toward Pine Pond, but the way was choked with tangles, and the blood left a crimson trail. So he laid the body down in a lonely spot, hid it as best he could without too great exertion, washed his hands in a pool, and walked briskly out of the swamp, whistling softly a merry tune.

The murderer neither hurried nor lagged. He cast no furtive glances around him. Perfect self-possession marked his mien. He seemed to have no fear. He skirted Pine Pond, whose unfathomed depths would have told no tale if the body had been buried there. All was silent, for picnic parties had not visited the pond since a fire and storm felled trees and blocked the way. He vanished down the picnic road, where the year before jolly parties journeyed on merry outings, and where Lord and Lady Somerset, spending some months at Woodstock, eight miles away, were fond of coming to explore the Blenheim Swamp before they returned to England.

"The body was found," says Murray, "by the Elridge brothers, Joseph and George. They lived in that vicinity, and were out chopping on Friday, February 21st, and one of them, in the tangle of the bog, amid a snarl of logs, and vines, and briars, and brush, stepped on the body, slipped, and almost fell upon it. They bore it out of the swamp, and, in response to a telegram to the Department of Justice, I went immediately to the township of Blenheim, in the county of Oxford, and saw the body. It was the body of a young man, smooth shaven, of refined appearance, and clearly a gentleman. The clothing was English in style and cut, with a check caped mackintosh. The underclothing was of English make, for I had ordered some of the same kind and make in England some months before. There was no clue to his identity. The name of his tailor and the label on his clothes had been cut out carefully. The label of his brown Derby hat had been removed. Even a possible tell-tale button had been severed. I sat down with the body, placing it in a sitting posture opposite me. I looked at it as if it were a man asleep. He was little more than a big boy, a gentle lad, a youth just out of his teens, a refined son of refined parents. In the back of his head was the purplish black hole of the bullet, and near the nape of the neck was another. He had been shot from behind; perhaps he never knew who shot him. Death crashed upon him from the rear, and he fell without a glimpse of his murderer.

"What could have brought this young Englishman of gentle birth to this desolate spot, and what could have been the motive for his murder? Possibly he had been murdered elsewhere, and the body taken secretly to the swamp and hid, to shrivel and wither and crumble away until only a string of dead men's bones remained to tell of the tragedy.

"'Who are you?' I asked the dead body as it sat facing me; but, in answer, it lurched forward and fell on its face.

"I had it photographed. I gave copies of the photograph to the newspapers of Canada, and requested them to print the picture and to ask other papers throughout the United States and England to reproduce it. I hoped that some one somewhere in the world, seeing the face of the unknown dead, would recognise it, and thus solve the mystery of his identity. Even in death he was so typically English, so characteristically British, that I said at once he was not from Canada or the States, but was from England. But where had he been murdered?

"I went to the snarl in the bog in Blenheim Swamp where the body had been found. I saw where it had lain, half hid, where only an accidental stumbling on it would have revealed its presence. I pondered on the mystery of Providence in guiding the Elridges to the precise spot where the body lay. A regiment of hunters might have tramped through the swamp and not come upon it, yet one of these two brothers, by favour of good fortune, had slipped and stepped on it, and so discovered it. I saw the crimson stain where the head had been. I crawled on hands and knees over the surrounding ground, and I found a crimson trail. I followed it back a few paces, and it stopped in a blotch of blood. Beyond the blotch there was no further trace of blood. Here the murder had been done, here the shot had been fired, here the victim had fallen. His murderer had borne him to the denser place and hid him there. I crawled about the scene of the crime. I went over the ground inch by inch. On three separate visits I did this, hoping that some clue, some bit of a label, some little button, some shred out of his past life, might be lying in the swamp-land. On my last search I came upon a cigar-holder with an amber mouthpiece marked 'F. W. B.' It was half buried, as if it had been stepped on. It was the first clue.

"Five days had passed since the finding of the body. No identification came. The picture was in all the leading papers in Canada, and in a few days more it would be published in England. The body was buried at Princeton, a town a few miles from Blenheim Swamp. On the sixth day a man and woman arrived at Princeton, and asked to see the body of the young man who had been found in a swamp, and whose picture had been printed in the papers. They said they had crossed from England recently, and on the same ship was a young man who resembled strongly the picture of the dead man. The body was dug up on March 1st. The lady and gentleman looked at it, and both identified it as the body of their fellow-passenger, and both were shocked deeply.

"'His name, we think, was Benwell,' they said. 'He was merely a casual acquaintance aboard ship, and we knew nothing of him.'

"The lady and gentleman returned to Paris, about ten miles from Princeton. I had been to the swamp and out among the people living in that section, seeing them one by one, and I returned in time to join the lady and gentleman at Paris. We met in the hotel. I introduced myself, and the three of us were alone in the parlour upstairs.

"'I am J. W. Murray, of the Department of Criminal Investigation,' I said. 'You are the gentleman who has been out looking at the body of the young man found in the swamp?'

"The gentleman was dressed in perfect taste. He was handsome and easy in manner, with a certain grace of bearing that was quite attractive. He came toward me, and I saw he was about five feet nine inches tall, supple, clean cut, well built. His hair was dark and fashionably worn ; his forehead was broad and low. He wore a light moustache. Two dark-brown eyes flashed at me in greeting. Clearly he was a man of the world, a gentleman, accustomed to the good things of life, a likeable chap, who had lived well and seen much and enjoyed it in his less than thirty years on earth. The lady stood by the window looking out. She was a slender, pleasant-faced blonde, a bit weary about the eyes, but evidently a woman of refinement. She half turned and watched us as the man advanced to meet me.

"'Yes,' said he, in quiet, well-modulated voice ; 'my wife and I were out at the grave and saw the body.'

"The lady shuddered. The man continued that he was very glad to meet me.

"'You knew the young man?' I asked.

"'Yes, very slightly,' said he.

"'Ah, I am very glad to hear it,' said I. 'At last we may know who he is. Where did you meet him?'

"'In London,' said he.

"'London, Ontario, or London, England?' said I.

"'He came from London, England,' said he. 'A mere casual acquaintance. I met him, don't you know, on the ship—aboard ship, in fact.'

"'His name?' I asked.

"'I think it was Bentwell, or Benswell, or Benwell,' said he. 'I knew him very slightly.'

"'What ship?' said I.

"'The *Britannic* of the White Star Line,' said he. 'We arrived in New York on Friday, February 14th.'

"'When did you last see the young man alive?' I asked.

"'He was on his way to London, Ontario, and as we were travelling to the Falls our way was the same. I last saw him at the Falls. He had a great deal of luggage down there. He left some of it, in fact.'

"'I'm very glad to know this,' said I gratefully. 'You will be able to point out his luggage?'

"'Yes,' said he. 'I'll be very glad to aid you. I am

returning to the Falls to-day. We came, you know, because we saw the picture in the paper.'

"'Will you take charge of the luggage for me?' I asked.

"'Gladly,' said he.

"'Your name, so that I may find you at the Falls?' I asked.

"'Birchall,' said he. 'Reginald Birchall, of London—London, England.'

"'Very glad to know you, Mr. Birchall; very glad indeed,' said I.

"During our conversation he became quite familiar and talkative. His wife was very nervous, as if the sight of a dead body had upset her. She began to pace up and down the room.

"'How was the young man dressed when you last saw him?' I asked.

"I had a navy-blue overcoat on at the time. Mr. Birchall put his hand on the coat sleeve. There was no tremor in it. I noted it was rather a dainty hand.

"'Like that,' he said.

"'A whole suit of that colour?' I asked.

"'Yes,' said he.

"'Would he take a glass, do you know?'

"'Oh, yes, he used to get very jolly,' said he.

"'That London, Ontario, is a bad place,' said I. 'They'd kill a man for a five-dollar note there. And this poor young man went to London, eh?'

"I could see the wife's face clear with an expression of relief. The man reiterated his pity for the young man, and his desire to be of any service possible to me. We chatted quite cordially.

"'Were you ever on the continent before?' I asked.

"'Yes, New York and Niagara Falls, but never in Canada,' said he.

"After further conversation I produced my note-book.

"'I am greatly indebted to you, my dear sir, for your kindness,' said I. 'This information is most valuable. It tells us just what we wish to know. May I trouble you to repeat it, so that I may note it accurately?'

"The lady began to pace the floor again. The man told once more the story he had told to me. He made occasional pauses to ask the lady a question, as if his own memory had failed to note certain desired details of a casual acquaintance. She answered in a weary, anxious voice.

"'And I bade him good-bye at the Falls,' he concluded, 'and he went on to London, Ontario.'

"'Did you hear from him?' I asked.

"'Just a line,' he said.

"'Have you got it?' I asked.

"'Have I got Fred's note, my dear?' he asked his wife.

"'No,' said the lady, 'but I remember seeing it.'

"'It was just a note to get his luggage through,' said he.

"'His first name was Fred?' I asked.

"'I think so,' he said quietly, as we eyed each other. 'It was so signed in the note.'

"His manner changed to even effusive cordiality.

"'Mr. Murray, come down and spend Sunday with us at the Falls,' he said heartily.

"'Delighted, but I must go to Toronto,' said I.

"'Toronto!' said he. 'I'd like to see Toronto. My dear, will you go to Toronto on Sunday as Mr. Murray's guest?'

"'Unfortunately I will not be home on Sunday,' said I. 'Will you meet me at nine o'clock on Monday morning at the Falls, and get all the luggage at the Customs House?'

"'Delighted to aid you,' said he.

"We shook hands and bowed. The tired lady bowed, and I withdrew. I walked straight to the telegraph office. On the way I thought it over. The man was lying; I was sure of it. Yet, if he knew aught of the crime, why should he come to Canada at least a week after the deed was done and identify the body? The autopsy had shown the young man had been dead a few days, but not over a week; so it was within eight or ten days after the murder that this suave, handsome Englishman and his gentle wife had come from the Falls to Paris and thence to Princeton to view the body. Why had they come? This story of seeing the picture in the paper was quite plausible. If he were telling the truth I could understand it, but I was satisfied he was lying. Yet the London, Ontario, part of it might be true. I wanted a few hours to investigate it and make sure. So I entered the telegraph office and sent a telegram to the Falls, describing Birchall and telling of his return to the Falls later that day.

"'Shadow this man,' I telegraphed. 'Do not arrest him unless he tries to cross the river to the States. I will be there Sunday night.'

"I jumped to London, Ontario, and called on acquaintances there for trace of this young Fred Benwell. Among those I saw was Edward Meredith, a lawyer, to whom I spoke of Benwell and the steamer *Britannic*, and he told me that Barrister Hellmuth, of London, Ontario, had returned from England on the *Britannic*. I made sure that Benwell, or whoever the young man was, had not been to see Attorney Hellmuth; in fact, I scoured London, and satisfied myself he had not been there at all. Birchall and his wife, meanwhile, had returned to Niagara Falls, Ontario; and on March 2nd Birchall was arrested, his wife being taken into custody two days later. They were remanded until March 12th.

"I found that Birchall and Mrs. Birchall and a young man named Douglas Raymond Pelly were stopping at Baldwin's at Niagara Falls, and had arrived there the day after the murder. I saw Mr. Pelly. He was a handsome young fellow, about five feet nine inches tall, slight build, small light moustache, and a decided English accent. He told me he was the son of the Rev. R. P. Pelly, of Walton Place, Vicar of Saffron Walden, Essex, England. He was twenty-five years old, a graduate of Oxford, and a cousin of the beautiful Lady Pelly, who was one of the suite of Lord Lansdowne, formerly Governor-General of Canada. He told me he knew both the dead man, whose picture was in the papers, and Birchall.

"'Benwell, Birchall, Mrs. Birchall, and I all came out from England in one party,' said Pelly. 'Birchall and Benwell left us for a day, and Benwell never came back. I saw the picture of the dead man in the paper a few days later, and I told Birchall it was Benwell, and that he ought to go and identify the body and make sure.'

"I sat down with Pelly, and for several hours he talked,

telling me what he knew of Benwell and Birchall. Among Birchall's papers, found in searching his effects, were letters corroborative of what Pelly said. Pelly, with his Oxford course finished and the world before him, was looking for an opening in life when, in December 1889, he read an advertisement in London, England, newspapers as follows:

> 'CANADA.—University man—having farm—wishes to meet gentleman's son to live with him and learn the business, with view to partnership; must invest five hundred pounds to extend stock; board, lodging, and 5 per cent. interest till partnership arranged.—Address, J. R. BURCHETT, Primrose Club, 4, Park Place, St. James', London.'

"Pelly saw this advertisement, and wrote to J. R. Burchett about it, asking for particulars. He received in reply, on December 9th, a telegram from J. R. Burchell, stating that he would go down to Walden Place, Saffron Walden, on the following Thursday. Pelly answered with a note, which was found with other letters in Birchall's effects, hoping he would stay all night as it was a long way to come for such a short interview, and also as he desired to have his father meet J. R. Burchell. On the appointed day J. R. Burchell arrived at Walden Place, and later met Pelly in London, and won over both Pelly and his father. He pictured to them a large farm one and a half miles from Niagara Falls, Ontario; a farm with large brick houses and barns, the former heated by steam and lighted by gas and the latter by electric light, with lights placed around the farm. He told of the big and profitable business, and mentioned the fine fishing, shooting, and other sports to be enjoyed on the farm. He explained that the business carried on was buying horses in the rough and grooming them to sell for profit; that the farm was used to raise horse feed; that during J. R. Burchell's absence, his overseer, a Scotchman named McDonald, and several hired men looked after the farm and business; that he had a branch business at Woodstock, and had rooms there, where he and Mrs. Burchell lived at times. He said a number of Englishmen lived around

Niagara Falls, and that a club had been created in which the members lived in English style and had English servants. J. R. Burchell said he organised the club. The country was an earthly paradise, with wealth to be had for simply sojourning in the land. This glowing description captivated Pelly, and on January 11th, 1890, he wrote from Hollington, St. Leonard's-on-Sea, to J. R. Burchell, saying: 'Please consider all settled. If you will have the agreement drawn up, I will sign it and forward you a cheque for one hundred and seventy pounds at the same time. I shall look to meeting you on February 1st. When you get my steamer tickets would you be so kind as to forward me some steamer labels at the same time?'

"References had been exchanged. Pelly had referred J. R. Burchell to Edward Cutler, Esq., Q.C., 12, Old Square, Lincoln's Inn; Godfrey Lawford, Esq., 28, Austin Friars, E.C., and the Rev. Alfred Rose, Emmanuel College, Cambridge. J. R. Burchell referred to David Stevenson, Bainbridge, Maberley Road, Upper Norwood, master of transportation of the London and North-Western Railroad. J. R. Burchell drew up the following agreement:

> 'Memorandum of agreement, made this day of , 1890, between J. R. Burchell, of Niagara, Ontario, Canada, and Bainbridge, Maberley Road, Upper Norwood, England, on the one part, and D. R. Pelly, of Walden Place, Saffron Walden, in the county of Essex, on the other part, to the effect that the said J. R. Burchell agrees to provide the said D. R. Pelly with board, lodging, washing, and household extras for one year, also with travelling expenses in Canada and United States, use of horses, carriages, sleighs, and such things as he may require pertaining to his business; also for the space of one year: the said D. R. Pelly in consideration of the same, one hundred and seventy pounds, agrees to pay the sum of one hundred and seventy pounds sterling, the money to be invested in stock (horses); this sum to be repaid together with interest at five per cent. per annum in case the said D. R. Pelly does not stay beyond

the year before mentioned. If the said D. R. Pelly should stay for a longer period, then the aforesaid sum to be repaid or applied as the said D. R. Pelly shall determine.

'The year mentioned to date from the signing of this agreement.'

"A copy of this agreement I found in Birchall's handwriting, and beneath it were scribbled various names, including A. Sloden Jones, 18, Talbot Road, Bayswater; J. R. Birtwistle, Fred Beteor, H. H. Foxby, J. B. Simons, Dear Miss Lovett, the Rev. J. Readon, and Alfred A. Atkinson.

"Pelly continuing his story, told me that he met Mr. and Mrs. Birchall on February 5th, and boarded the *Britannic* at Liverpool. To his surprise he found a fourth member of the party, a young man whom Birchall introduced to him as Fred C. Benwell, son of Colonel Benwell, of Cheltenham, England. Birchall intimated to Pelly that Benwell was not much of a fellow, but that he was simply crossing with them to a farm, and that it would be just as well for Pelly to have nothing to do with him. So Pelly treated Benwell rather distantly, and devoted himself to Mrs. Birchall and Birchall on the voyage. Benwell seemed to reciprocate by treating Pelly coolly, so Birchall deftly kept the two young men from becoming familiar and confidential. Finally Benwell and Pelly chatted together and Benwell told Pelly he, too, was to join Birchall in the horse business. Pelly went to Birchall and threatened to withdraw. Birchall pacified him, saying: 'Never mind, I shall find some way to get rid of him.' Birchall enlivened the voyage with glowing pictures of the profits awaiting them.

"The *Britannic* arrived in New York on February 14th. The Birchalls, Pelly, and Benwell went to the Metropolitan Hotel. While there they met a fellow from Woodstock, Neville H. Pickthall, who greeted Birchall and his wife.

"'Why, Lord Somerset and Lady Somerset,' exclaimed Pickthall, the moment he saw them. 'Delighted! Are you on your way back to Woodstock?'

"Birchall got free from Pickthall with little ceremony. Later some people supposed Pickthall had gone to New York to meet Birchall, but it turned out that green goods men had persuaded Pickthall to borrow $1,000, on his farm and go to New York to buy a lot of bogus money. Pickthall went, and happened to be there when the Birchall party appeared at the hotel. The same day the green goods men got Pickthall's $1,000, and sent him out to Denver, Colorado, on a wild-goose chase, and he turned up in Denver broke, and wrote to friends in Woodstock, and I had him back to testify at the trial.

"Pelly said their party stayed overnight at the Metropolitan Hotel, and the next day, February 15th, they went to Buffalo, arriving there on the morning of February 16th, and registering at the Stafford House. Each young man was eager to see the mythical farm. It was only a couple of hours from Buffalo, said Birchall. Mrs. Birchall preferred to wait in Buffalo until sure everything was all right at the farm for her reception there. Pelly gallantly agreed to tarry with Mrs. Birchall while Birchall and Benwell went on to the farm to surprise the employees. If all was well at the farm, Benwell would remain there, and Birchall would return and take Mrs. Birchall and Pelly to the farm. Benwell and Birchall were to start at six o'clock the next morning. They did so, leaving the Stafford House bright and early on the morning of February 17th, to take a Grand Trunk train to the farm.

"Birchall returned to the Stafford House in Buffalo alone at half-past eight that evening. He was in good humour, pleasant and laughing. Pelly asked where he had left Benwell. Birchall said he took Benwell to the farm and introduced him to McDonald, the overseer, and later in the day Benwell had told him he did not like the place, and did not care to associate with such people, and that Benwell had eaten nothing all day, but had stayed at the farm when Birchall left for Buffalo. Birchall said he gave Benwell some addresses before leaving, so he could visit folk in the country roundabout, including Attorney Hellmuth, of London, who had been a passenger on the ship. Pelly began to ask too many questions, and Birchall said he was tired and went to bed. The next day they went to Niagara Falls, taking their luggage with them. They crossed to the Canada side and stopped at Mrs. Baldwin's, Birchall arranging for rooms and board there.

"'Soon after our arrival,' said Pelly to me, 'Birchall invited me to go for a walk. I went. We walked along the river road which goes from the village up to the Falls. I had told him about ten minutes before that he was failing to fulfil the representations he had made to me. He had replied with a shuffling explanation, and I mentally decided to give him another week, and if matters did not change I would leave him. On our walk we came to a place where Birchall said a religious body in past years had held camp meetings, and it was thought it would be nice to bathe in the river, so a stairway was built down over the cliffs with the idea that they could go down it to bathe, but it had been found impossible to bathe there because the current was too strong. Birchall said to me: "Oh, you have never been down here; you ought to go. It is the best way to see the Falls." I told him I should like to go down, and he stepped aside for me. I went down first and soon noticed it was a rotten, unsafe stairway. It led down close by the Falls. "Birchall," said I, "this is a horrid place." He was following and said: "Go on; it will pay you." I wondered afterwards that I did not slip or miss my footing. We landed at the bottom finally. To my great surprise, there stood a man gazing into the swirling water. This man turned and looked at me. I sprang past Birchall and started back up the stairs. The man turned and resumed his gazing into the water. Birchall seemed nonplussed when we came upon this stranger in this lonely, secluded spot, with the roaring waters ready to sweep a dead body away. Birchall followed me up the stairway, and all that day he was moody and silent.

"'He invited me for another walk the next day,' continued Pelly. He led the way down to the cliffs close to the cantilever bridge. Underneath this bridge you cannot be seen. You get in between the brickwork of the span and the edge. Birchall took me in there so as to get a better view of the rapids. He tried to persuade me to stand close by him at the edge, but his manner seemed so coldly quiet, so repellent, that instinctively I drew back and made my excuses for not going near the edge and went away. This was the second time. A little push and all would have been over. We returned to our rooms. I saw in the papers about a murder near Woodstock. On the next morning Birchall proposed I should go to Woodstock and look at the body and see if it was Benwell. That alarmed me, and I got a revolver and put it in my pocket. Birchall and I went to the station, but the train had gone. I wanted to telegraph to New York, thinking Benwell might be there. Birchall refused to do this, and persuaded me to go over to the American side to see about some supposed matter of baggage. It began to rain while we were there, and he wanted to stay on the American side, but I said that was absurd, because his wife was at the Baldwin's boarding house and would expect us back. We started to walk back to Canada across the lower suspension bridge. It was storming and blowing. When out near the centre of the bridge, Birchall walked over by the edge and looked down at the roaring rapids. "Come, see the view; it is superb," said Birchall, beckoning me close to the edge. I drew back. He grew white and walked on. I lagged behind, out of his reach. "Come, walk with me," he said, halting. "Your great coat will help keep off the rain." I shook my head. He repeated his invitation. I declined. He stopped, turned squarely and looked back. Then he advanced a step toward me. I stepped back and was about to run over the bridge when two men came walking across and Birchall turned and walked on to Canada. I see these things in a clearer light now that I know Benwell's fate.

"'The next day,' continued Pelly, 'Birchall went to Buffalo to see about some message he said was from Benwell. When he returned he said Benwell had sent a message to forward all his heavy luggage to the Fifth Avenue Hotel in New York. The next day I saw the awful picture of the dead man in the paper. I took it to Birchall. "That looks like Benwell," I said. Birchall said it was impossible, as Benwell was to be in New York. I told him he should go and see the body, and I would go to New York to see if Benwell was at the Fifth Avenue Hotel. I saw him leave for Paris with Mrs. Birchall to see the body. Then I went to New York on the next train. I could find no trace of Benwell, so I returned. Birchall and his wife had been to view the body and it was Benwell, and the arrest followed.'

" Pelly was telling the truth from first to last," says Murray. " In going through Birchall's effects I found this note, written in a big, boyish hand :—

'20, PORCHESTER GARDENS,
'BAYSWATER,
'LONDON, W.
'*December 3rd*, 1899.

'DEAR SIR—

'My father thinks I had better see you as soon as possible. I will be at my club, " The National Conservative," Pall Mall, at the corner of Waterloo Place and opposite the " Athenæum " at three o'clock on Thursday afternoon, and will wait there till five o'clock ; or if you prefer it I will go down to Norwood or any place in London you like to name, soon, if you will drop me a line.

'I am, dear sir,
'Yours faithfully,
'F. C. BENWELL.

'J. R. BURCHELL, ESQ.'

" I found other letters from Benwell to Birchall, and in Benwell's luggage I found letters from Birchall to Benwell. Here is one :

'PRIMROSE CLUB, 4, PARK PLACE, ST. JAMES';
'BAINBRIDGE, MABERLEY ROAD,
'UPPER NORWOOD, S.E.,
'*February 2nd*, 1890.

'MY DEAR BENWELL—

'We sail Wednesday next, February 5th, in the White Star S.S. *Britannic.* I have got you a ten-guinea berth for the eight pounds and ten shillings you sent me. So that is pretty good, I think. The ship sails in the afternoon early. I am going up first thing in the morning to ascertain the exact time of sailing. If the ship doesn't sail till after three, we shan't go down overnight, as there will be lots of time in the morning, if we leave here by an early train. Your heavy baggage must be taken on board by the tender on Wednesday, or shipped in the dock on Tuesday. However, I fancy it will be best to have it consigned to c/o the White Star Company, per S.S. *Britannic.* I will wire you in the morning, how to act. Of course, if we haven't time we must leave on Tuesday night. This you shall hear further of. Your labels shall be posted to-morrow morning.

'I fancy the storms are gone over now and we shall have a good voyage. You will be able to meet us on the voyage. Of this I will inform you to-morrow.

'Kind regards to Col. Benwell and yourself.

'Yours very sincerely,

'J. R. BURCHELL.'

"The letters showed conclusively that Benwell, like Pelly, had been caught by Birchall's advertisement, and that he had arranged with each without notifying the other. Benwell and Birchall had met and talked over the farm business. Young Benwell talked to his father, who had travelled considerably and he advised his boy to go and see the farm and then draw on him for what he required. Birchall had taken Benwell with him to this side, Benwell paying the passage money to Birchall and having an ample amount of money with him for expenses and the authority to draw on his father.

"I cabled and wrote at once to Scotland Yard for information about Birchall and his reference, David Stevenson, as well as Pelly and Benwell. I also advertised all over this continent for the stranger who stood at the foot of the old stairway by the Falls when Pelly and Birchall descended to the water's edge. The stranger never answered the advertisement. He may not have seen it or he may have seen it and desired to avoid notoriety. I doubt if he were an accomplice or acquaintance of Birchall. He probably was a sightseer enjoying the view.

"The replies from my friends in England informed me that J. R. Birchall was none other than the younger son of the Rev. Joseph Birchall, late well-known Vicar of Church

Kirk and Rural Dean of Whalley. The Birchalls had a sort of hereditary connection with Brasenose College, Oxford, where the father held a foundation scholarship or fellowship. Wherever the young Birchall had lived he achieved notoriety. In his younger days he was at Rossall School for some time when the Rev. H. James, late Dean of St. Asaph and then head of Cheltenham College, was head master. He left there suddenly and entered the Reading School, boarding with the Rev. Mr. Walker, head master. He earned a reputation in these schools that preceded him to Oxford where he went in the autumn of 1885. His name vanished from Oxford's calendar in the spring of 1888. His college was Lincoln, and the dons remembered him with sad headshakes. He was a rake and a wild one. He was an organiser of carousals, in and out of college, day and night. He had plenty of money, and kept a number of horses at college. No one was cleverer than he at evading punishment for his pranks. Often merciless in his pursuits of mischief, he would do his fellows a turn with good grace. He was hail-fellow-well-met with a number of men, who knew little of him except that he was full of humour and fun and had singular conversational gifts. His notoriety was due in no small part to his loud style of dress. He wore gaudy waistcoats, and his costume rarely lacked some adornment of flaming hue. He established at Oxford a club called The Black and Tan. It attained such a reputation for noisiness and boisterousness that it became extinct. At Oxford, Birchall showed, in his class work, great powers of mind, with an exceptional memory. He was being educated for the Church. His father's church at that time was in Lancashire, and his brother had a church near Lechlade. His father died while he was at Oxford, and the property was divided between the two sons and a daughter. Reginald's share was over $20,000, but by the provisions of the will he was not to come into possession of it until May 1891. In June 1889 he had been notified by Clement, Cheese, and Green, solicitors, of London, that his creditors proposed to throw him into bankruptcy. He replied that he had sold his interest in his father's estate for $15,000 to pay other creditors.

"After leaving Oxford he went to London. There he eloped with Florence Stevenson, daughter of David Stevenson, for fifty years master of transportation of the London and North Western Railroad. This explained the reference to Mr. Stevenson when Birchall exchanged references with Pelly. Birchall's father-in-law knew nothing of the use of his name. He was a respectable, honest man, seventy-six years old. In his daughter's effects were found some pathetic letters from the old man to his son-in-law. On November 25th, 1888, when he heard of the marriage, he wrote saying: 'Let me at once recognise your perfect right to get married in the form you preferred; but we were a little grieved that we did not see our daughter take the most important step of her life.' Other letters were marked with tender solicitude. Birchall had dabbled in theatricals before his marriage and was well known to many stage-folk in London. His favourite club at this time was the Badminton Club, 100, Piccadilly, W. When he made ready to leave England after his marriage, he cashed cheques for £25, or $125, at the Badminton Club, and C. Stewart Sproat, secretary of the club, wrote him on January 7th, 1890, when he was back in England, to send the cash without further delay. He and his bride sailed for America in the fall of 1888, after their marriage. They wrote to David Stevenson from America, and early in 1889 Birchall wrote from Woodstock, Ontario, to creditors at Oxford, saying he was in the employ of Somerset & Co., Brock Street, Woodstock, and had a lucrative position and would pay his debts promptly. While he was in Woodstock, solicitors in England were advertising in the newspapers for his whereabouts. His father-in-law called on the solicitors and asked what such scandalous advertisements meant. When he was informed of his son-in-law's conduct the old man wept bitterly. In the summer of 1889 Birchall and his wife returned to England and lived with Mr. Stevenson. Then it was that Birchall began advertising, under the name of J. R. Burchett or Burchell, address the Primrose Club, for young men with money to go to Canada and learn farming.

"My information from England proved Pelly and Benwell

to be just what Pelly had said, two victims of Birchall. Pelly's father was vicar of Saffron Walden, Essex, and Benwell's father was Col. Benwell, of Cheltenham. The parents of both confirmed the stories told by the letters I found in the luggage.

"At Woodstock I learned that Birchall and his wife had arrived there from England in the autumn of 1888 to look over farm lands and enjoy the country life of Canada. His name was not Birchall then. He was Lord Somerset, Frederick A. Somerset, some day to be one of the lofty lords of England. His wife was Lady Somerset. They boarded at Mrs. John McKay's in Woodstock, lived gaily, dressed loudly, and became familiar figures in the country round about. They seemed to have money like the lord and lady they were supposed to be. They were fond of driving and picnics, and one of the spots Lord Somerset visited on various occasions was Pine Pond, with the Blenheim Swamp around it. This was eight miles from Woodstock and Lord Somerset came to know it well. When they left Woodstock to return to England, Lord and Lady Somerset were called away suddenly and left numerous unpaid bills behind them. Lord Somerset, from across the sea, wrote to a Woodstock acquaintance as follows:

'MIDLAND GRAND HOTEL,
'LONDON, ENGLAND.

'MY DEAR MAC,

'You must have been surprised to find me gone. I went down to New York for the wife's health and while there got a cable the governor was suddenly taken ill. I rushed off, caught the first steamer over, and got here just too late, the poor chap died. So I have been anyhow for some time. I am coming out to Woodstock shortly, I hope, as soon as I settle up all my governor's affairs. I owe you something I know. Please let me know, and tell Scott, the grocer, to make out his bill, and any one else if I owe anybody anything. I was in too much of a hurry to see after them. I have several men to send out to you in August. Tell me all news and how you are. Many thanks for all your kindnesses. 'FREDK. A. SOMERSET.'

"Lord Somerset did not return to Woodstock promptly. The next time he sailed for America was under his right name with Lady Somerset under her proper name, Mr. and Mrs. Reginald Birchall, and they had with them the two young men, Pelly and Benwell, and the four arrived in New York on the *Britannic*, on February 14th, and the first person they saw in New York, by the merest accident, was the farmer Pickthall of Woodstock on his way to meet the green goods men. He recognised Lord and Lady Somerset and went his way to be fleeced by others. I verified at the Metropolitan Hotel the date of their arrival and departure. I verified at the Stafford House in Buffalo the fact of the arrival of the party of four on February 16th. I verified also at the Stafford House the fact that, the next day Pelly and Mrs. Birchall stayed at the hotel, while Birchall and Benwell were called before six o'clock and went away. Birchall returned in the evening. Benwell never returned.

"I took up the trail of Birchall and Benwell when they walked out of the Stafford House about six o'clock on the morning of February 17th. I saw Conductor William H Poole, who had the run on the Grand Trunk Railroad between Niagara Falls and Windsor. He had two passengers who got off at Eastwood, a station four miles from Blenheim Swamp. Their description answered that of Birchall and Benwell. The train stopped at Eastwood at 11.14 that morning. Matthew Virtue, a bailiff of Woodstock, was on the train. As the train left Eastwood he saw two young Englishmen walking away from the station, one of them wearing a cape coat. Miss Lockhart, of Blandford, was on the train. A couple of seats ahead of her in the car sat two young Englishmen. As the train approached Eastwood her attention was drawn to them by the manner in which they were talking abut the land. They were admiring fields which were in no way to be admired. One wore a big astrakhan cap. It was easy to identify him by it. She noticed the man in the cap was very quiet and twitched in his seat, yet always was attentive to his fellow-traveller, the younger man. She saw them alight at Eastwood and start off briskly to the north, the man with the fur cap in the lead. I found others who saw the pair on the train. Alfred Hayward and his wife saw them leave Eastwood station. John Crosby, a young farmer, living in Blenheim township, was driving in Governor's Road about noon when he saw the two young men walking toward Blenheim Swamp. Miss Allie Fallon, who lived with her mother a short distance from Blenheim Swamp, saw two young men pass the house on the road leading past the swamp. There was a ball at Princeton that night and she remarked: 'There go two dudes to the Princeton ball.' One, in a cape mackintosh, walked ahead. The other was walking behind. She had come to know Lord Somerset by sight the year before and she thought the man walking behind was Somerset. They were walking in the direction of the swamp. James Rapson, owner of a swamp adjoining Blenheim Swamp, was out with his men cutting timber about one o'clock in the afternoon, when he heard two pistol shots in quick succession in Blenheim Swamp. He was a little less than a mile away but heard the shots distinctly.

"Thus I traced them, step by step, to the swamp and to the very hour of the murder. Then comes an interval when the murderer is alone in the swamp with his victim. The shots are fired about one o'clock, within about half-an-hour after Miss Fallon saw the two men going to the swamp. Birchall evidently had been pointing out land from the car window, as part of his farm, and had told Benwell they would take a short cut through the thick woods and surprise the men at the farmhouse. Benwell was a credulous young fellow and innocently entered the swamp and started up the abandoned winding trail, Birchall readily finding a pretext for dropping behind a moment and Benwell eagerly pressing on for a sight of the farm—the farm he never was to see.

"An hour passes. At half-past two Charles Buck, a young farmer living on the road between Eastwood and Blenheim Swamp, about half a mile from the swamp, was driving home from Woodstock, when, at the cross-roads leading to Eastwood, a man turned the corner from the Blenheim Swamp road and started for Eastwood. The man wore a fur cap, and he stopped and asked Mr. Buck the way to Gobles Corners, as he wished to get to Woodstock. Buck told him he was within much less than two miles of Eastwood and he could get to Woodstock from there as easy as from Gobles Corners. The man thanked him and walked on toward Eastwood at a rapid pace. At three o'clock Miss Alice Smith arrived at the Eastwood station to post a letter. As she was going into the station gate she came face to face with Lord Somerset, who had been in Woodstock the year before and who had called at her grandfather's, John Hayward's, home at Eastwood. Somerset wore an astrakhan cap. He came up to Miss Smith and shook hands pleasantly, saying: 'How do you do? Don't you remember me?' and asked after her family and the 'old governor,' meaning her grandfather. He told Miss Smith he was coming back later and then bought a ticket for Hamilton. Miss Mary Swazie, another young lady of Eastwood, also was at the station for the three o'clock train. She saw the stranger. His trousers were turned up and his shoes were muddy. Miss Ida Cromwell, of Eastwood, also saw him at the station. James Hayward, an Eastwood storekeeper, saw him at the station and recognised him as the so-called Lord Somerset.

"At 3.38 the train for Niagara Falls arrived at Eastwood. The stranger in the fur cap boarded the train. George Hay, a train brakesman, saw him and remembered him distinctly, and identified Birchall positively as the man. Other witnesses also identified Birchall, and I established a perfect chain of evidence showing his whereabouts from the time he left London and from the time he left the Stafford House on the morning of the murder until his return there at 8.30 that night. Witnesses identified the dead body of Benwell as that of the young man with Birchall on the train to Eastwood and on the road to the swamp. I traced them together to the swamp, where Benwell was found dead the next day, and I traced Birchall away from the swamp and back to Buffalo, after the pistol shots had been fired. He had four hours and twenty-four minutes in which to walk the four miles from Eastwood to the swamp, do the murder, and walk back to Eastwood. He arrived at 11.14 in the morning and departed at 4.38 in the afternoon. If he took three hours to walk the eight miles, he still had one hour and twenty-four minutes for the crime.

"To clinch Birchall's guilt, I heard from London at this time that Colonel Benwell had just received from Birchall an undated letter, headed with the address of Niagara Falls. The postmark revealed its date was February 20th, three days after Birchall left Benwell dead in the swamp. In this letter Birchall asked that the agreement be set aside, and that $500 be sent him at once. 'I have been talking to your son to-day about arrangements, and he is so well satisfied with the prospects here that he is ready to go immediately into partnership, and he is writing to you to-day on the subject,' wrote Birchall. This was three days after he left Benwell dead in Blenheim Swamp. The $500 was to be the first payment on $2,500 which Colonel Benwell was to send to his son for Birchall if the farm and prospects pleased young Benwell. Pelly identified the body found on February 18th as Benwell's body, and thus Birchall could not have been talking to him on February 20th. Instead of writing to his father on February 20th, Benwell lay dead on a slab with none to know his name.

"I brought creditors of Lord Somerset from Woodstock to see Birchall. They identified Birchall as the bogus Lord Somerset. One of them, William MacDonald, denounced Birchall as a dead-beat, a swindler, and a faker. Birchall haughtily declared that such language offended and insulted him. Later a lunatic in the gaol approached him and said: 'Tell me why you killed Benwell.' Birchall laughed merrily, and was neither offended nor insulted. I brought witnesses who said Birchall was the same man who, as Lord Somerset, had made frequent visits to Blenheim Swamp the year before, and had learned the path to Pine Pond, the lake in the swamp that is supposed to be bottomless. I studied all the data I had in hand, and worked out the theory on which I was certain we could convict this clever murderer.

"Birchall had embarked in business as a murderer. He had adopted life-taking for revenue as a profession promising rich returns. He had become deliberately a professional murderer. For a year he had planned the crimes, and fitted himself for the practice of his profession. While masquerading as Lord Somerset he had selected the bottomless lake, known as Pine Pond, for the grave that would tell no tales. The Blenheim Swamp he selected as the place of slaughter, his chamber of death. He was familiar with the emigration business, through his father-in-law's knowledge of it. He conceived the idea of taking rich young men instead of poor emigrants. He created an imaginative farm, and he went back to England to select a victim. He made the mistake of taking two instead of one. Even then his plans were well laid. He would kill Benwell in the swamp and shove Pelly into the rapids at the Falls to be pounded to pieces. Neither body would be found, for he would bury Benwell in the bottomless lake and Pelly would vanish in the whirlpool. If one of the Elridges had not slipped in the Blenheim Swamp all would have been well. He stepped on Benwell's body, and the crime was known. Birchall had not intended to leave the body where any one could step on it or see it. He was heading for Pine Pond when he killed Benwell, and meant to drag the body thither; but since his last visit to the swamp, a fire and storm had swept it and choked the way to the bottomless lake. He was relying on water to hide both his victims. Neither body was to be found. The two young men were to vanish from the face of the earth. The professional murderer would have collected, by bogus letters to fond parents, the sum still due from the victims, and would have gone back to England for more victims.

" He had no grudge against either Benwell or Pelly. They never had wronged him. No flame of fury leaped up within him inciting him to crush out their lives. It was purely and simply a matter of business. The life of each young man represented so much ready money, and Birchall was a murderer for the money there was in it. He went about it in a practical, quiet, methodical way. Eventually he might become rich. No bodies could be found, and lost dead men are as good as live men whom no one can find, he reasoned. As he increased his capital, he might buy a farm with a bottomless lake and a dismal swamp, and kill his victims without trespassing on other people's property. He could vary his name and address and keep the families of his victims far apart, and thus minimise the risk of detection while the bottomless lake swallowed the victims one by one and kept their bones icy cold through endless years.

"Fate was against the murderer for revenue only. Fire and storm had blocked his way in the marsh. Providence guided a woodman's step to the very spot where the body otherwise would have lain undiscovered, and crumbled away. Fate placed the stranger at the foot of the rotten stairway at the Falls where Pelly was to die. Fate put the two strange men on the lower suspension bridge the night Pelly was to be hurled into the rapids. Pelly lived, and he compelled Birchall to go to Princeton and view the body. It may be that Birchall believed he would brave it through, and still kill Pelly at the Falls, and then throw the crime of Benwell's death on the missing Pelly. But it all failed. The hand of Fate reached out of the world of chance, and destroyed the whole fabric this professional murderer had constructed so carefully. He planned well, but Providence swept his plans aside.

"The case had all the elements to make it a famous crime. It involved immigration, in which both England and Canada were interested vitally. The high connections of young Pelly, the refined associations of young Benwell, the notoriety of Birchall and his previously picturesque career, combined to give it prominence. Some folks declared the murder of Benwell was but a part of a plot of wholesale killing of rich young men of England by an organised band of red-handed villains, who enticed their victims to Canada. This I never have believed. Birchall had no male confederates, and he acted single-handed. I looked up his life thoroughly, year by year. John Emery, a London actor, wrote to me of Birchall's theatrical career. He was treasurer of one company, and appropriated some of its funds to his own use. Later he was assistant manager of a company playing *A Child of the West* in the provinces in England. Emery was in the company, and when a difference arose over failure to pay salaries, Birchall and the manager called Emery into a room and drew a pistol, and advised him to cease being dissatisfied. Other episodes showed Birchall a desperate man if occasion demanded. His crime at Blenheim Swamp aroused Canada. Great crowds attended the inquest at Princeton on March 8th. Pelly testified against Birchall. Mrs. Birchall was discharged. Public sympathy had been awakened for her. Birchall was committed for trial. Mrs. Birchall's father, David Stevenson, cabled $500 to me for his daughter the day after she was arrested. I gave it to Mrs. Birchall and her counsel, Hellmuth and Ivey, of London, Ontario.

"The trial of Birchall stands out as one of the great criminal trials of Canada. It attracted world-wide attention. On September 20th the grand jury returned a true bill against Birchall. His trial began on Monday, September 22nd. It was held at Woodstock. Justice McMahon presided. B. B. Osler, a truly brilliant lawyer, prosecuted for the Crown, assisted by J. R. Cartwright, Deputy Attorney-General. George T. Blackstock ably defended Birchall, making a desperate effort to save his life. Cable connections led direct from the Court House to London, England. The English newspapers, as well as those of France, Germany, and Italy, printed columns upon columns of the trial, some of the English papers printing the full testimony, the lawyers' pleas, and judge's charge. The gist of the defence was that in the four hours and twenty-four minutes between his arrival at Eastwood and his departure on the day of the murder, Birchall could not have walked four miles to the Blenheim Swamp, shot a man, and walked four miles to the station. The verdict was inevitable—guilty. The evidence simply was overwhelming. Birchall was sentenced to be hanged on November 14th.

"During his imprisonment in Woodstock gaol, Birchall was the recipient of much attention from some people. There were people in Woodstock who bared their flower gardens to send him nosegays every day. Silly girls wrote silly letters to him. He sent me word on various occasions that he wished to see me. Indeed he became quite offended if I went to Woodstock and did not call and take him for a walk in the gaol yard.

"'I found you always a gentleman,' were his last words to me; 'and you did your duty, and I have no hard feelings against you.'

"During his last months of life he wrote an autobiography, in which he omitted many salient facts of his career, and in which he did not confess the crime. However, I may say that, while Birchall went to his death without a public confession, the last possibility for doubt of his guilt was swept away before he was executed.

"He was hanged on November 14th—a cold, grey morning. He went to his death ghastly white, but without a tremor. He walked out in the prison yard in his own funeral procession, unsupported, and mounted the scaffold with a steady step. 'Good-bye, Flo dear; be brave,' was his farewell to his wife. The *Domine cum veneris judicare noli nos condemnare*—'O Lord, when Thou shalt come to judge, do not Thou condemn me'—was uttered by the Rev. W. H. Wade, of Old St. Paul's. The Lord's Prayer was said. And then—a crash, a creak, and a lifeless body dangled where a man had stood. It swayed gently to and fro in the chill November wind. So ended the Birchall case as it had begun—with a death.

"Pelly returned to England after the trial. He had desired to go home after the preliminary hearing, but the Government decided he should remain, and he stayed with me until after the trial. He arrived at Saffron Walden at seven o'clock in the evening of October 27th. An English newspaper, telling of his home-coming said:

"'The knowledge of the arrival had become known, and the result was that a crowd of some thousands had assembled in the vicinity of the railway station in order to give a welcome to the returned voyager. The arrival of the train was signalled by a *feu de joie*. Mrs. Pelly, with Miss Geraldine and Miss Daisy Pelly, were on the platform when the vicar stepped out with his son, and the greetings between mother and son, sisters and brother, were very warm. These over, a move was made for the carriage in waiting, and as soon as Mr. Douglas Pelly appeared on the outside of the station he was received with prolonged and deafening cheers. The horses were unharnessed, and the car was drawn to Walden Place by willing hands, preceded by the Excelsior Band, playing

" Rolling Home to Dear Old England," and men carrying lighted torches. In addition to the large following, crowds had assembled all along the line of route, and as the carriages passed along, the occupants were repeatedly cheered. Flags were hung from various private houses, and the residence of Mrs. Bellingham was illuminated with coloured lights. At the entrance to Walden Place a triumphal arch had been erected, having on the front the words " Welcome Home." '

" Pelly was drawn home by a rope in many willing hands; Birchall was drawn home by a rope in hands he did not know and never saw."

23

THE FOUR BARN BURNINGS OF CHATHAM

FOUR thrifty farmers lived on four adjoining farms with four big barns all on the same side of the Chatham Road, in the township of Chatham, in the county of Kent. Beyond them lived a settlement of negroes who lolled and laughed through life, with occasional days of labour as hired hands on the farms roundabout. On the night of October 15th, 1894, the four barns were burned to the ground.

"The County Attorney, Douglas, immediately called my attention to it, and I went to investigate," says Murray. "Many of the country folk were satisfied the four fires were accidental. I drove from farm to farm and learned that the four fires had occurred about the same hour, two o'clock in the morning. This coincidence settled in my mind the belief that the fires were of incendiary origin. I inspected the premises closely, and found fastened to the gatepost of each barnyard fence a notice, roughly scrawled in lead pencil, on slips of paper about the size of pages from a small memorandum book. They were identical in writing and read: 'We will burn you out from the Arthur Road to the Chatham Road for insults you white trash gave our coloured folks.'

"I carefully preserved these notices. It seemed strange to me that if negroes had fired the barns they would have left such deliberately made traces of their identity. Such action simply would have provoked further insults. The notices looked like a blind to me, a false clue to cast suspicion on the negroes. There had been one or two little incidents of friction between whites and blacks, but there was no bad blood and no feeling to incite arson so far as I could learn.

"Beginning at the first of the four scenes of the fire, I went over the ground methodically, foot by foot, within a radius of five hundred feet of the fire. Leading into what had been the door of the first barn I found footprints in the earth of the barnyard. I measured them carefully, and covered them up and marked them so that none would molest them. Then I drove to the second barn and went over the ground carefully, and there also I found footprints leading to the barn. I measured them, and they tallied to a dot with the footprints at the first barn. I drove to the third barn, and after a long search I found, near a corner of the barn where the fire had started, footprints identical with those at the other two barns. Then I drove to the fourth barn, and to my surprise I found many such footprints around the barn. I marked the tracks carefully and arranged to have plaster casts made of them. I was confident they were the footprints of the incendiary and that one man alone fired the four barns. This strengthened me in my belief that the notices indicating negroes had fired the barns were a blind.

"Nevertheless, I visited the darkey settlement and, armed with the accurate measurements of the tracks, I investigated the size of the feet and shoes of the darkies. Not a single foot or boot or shoe or slipper did I find to match the footprints.

"I went again from farm to farm, beginning at the one where the first fire broke out. Each farmer talked freely, answering all questions, telling of waking up to find night turned into day with four monster fires blazing and throwing showers of sparks skyward, while the country for miles around was illuminated. The fourth farmer, Edward Kehoe, dwelt on the splendour of the scene. When I began to question him as to his idea of the origin of the fires he began to curse the darkies. I stood listening and thinking of the notices found on the gateposts.

"'Was your barn insured?' I asked casually.

"'You're not the insurance agent, too, are you?' he answered.

"The tone of his voice caused me to glance quickly at him. In so doing my eyes fell upon a pair of old ragged boots he was wearing. The footprints had been made with comparatively new boots or newly soled boots.

"'Where are the boots you wore this morning?' I asked.

" Kehoe started as if I had stuck a pin in him.

" 'These are the boots,' he said shakily.

" 'Where are the boots you wore yesterday?' I asked.

" 'They were burned in the barn,' said he.

" I told him the first farmer wished to see him about a clue. He started off. When he was out of sight I entered his house and began a search for the boots. I could not find them. As I rummaged in out-of-the-way nooks and corners, I came upon a small memorandum book, a milkman's book. I opened it, and instantly the pages reminded me of the notices found on the gateposts. There was writing on some of the pages. I took out the notices and compared them. The hand that wrote in the book also wrote the notices. Page by page I turned the book from cover to cover. Pages were missing. I inserted the four notices. They fitted, even to the irregularities in the edges. They had been torn out of the book.

" I hunted anew for the boots. I could find no trace of them. An idea came to me. I went out and looked at a field where wheat had been sown. A farmer near by told me Kehoe had sown it. I went down to the field. There were the tracks of the sower marked in the soil. I measured them. They matched the footprints leading into Marshall's barn, one of the four that had been fired. They were the footprints of Kehoe. My case was complete.

" I started down the road, driving. I met Kehoe coming back afoot. He was passing me by without speaking.

" 'Hold on!' I called.

" 'What do you want?' he growled.

" 'Whose field is that?' I asked.

" 'Mine?' said he.

" 'Who sowed it?'

" 'I did, every foot of it,' said he.

" 'Thank you,' said I. 'Now if you will get in I will drive you to Chatham gaol and lock you up.'

He quailed, but laughed and told me not to crack any more jokes like that.

" 'I mean every word of it,' said I sternly. 'Come here and get in.'

" He obeyed, and I took him to Chatham and locked him up. I spent days hunting for those boots. I never found them. Kehoe must have buried them. He was tried for arson, and was convicted and sent to Kingston Penitentiary for seven years. He had insured his barn heavily and I guess he needed the money. He claimed falsely that thirty-five acres of his farm had been planted with peas. I rooted for the boots, but they seemed to have walked off the earth. If Kehoe burned them he must have thrown them into his own burning barn and then walked barefooted on the air to leave no tracks. But if he buried them may their soles rest in peace."

ALMEDA CHATTELLE, THE HAIRY MAN

CHUNKS of a human body were found in a clump of woods near Listowel, in the county of Perth, on Friday, October 19th, 1894. They were fitted together and proved to be about two-thirds of the remains of a beautiful young girl. They had been found by searchers hunting for trace of Jessie Keith, the fourteen-year-old daughter of respectable country folk living three miles out of Listowel. Jessie had started in the morning for Listowel to get some groceries.

"Hours passed and she did not return," says Murray. "Her parents investigated and learned she had not arrived at the grocery. Searching parties were organised and they divided the country into sections. The party hunting beyond the Keith home came upon the pieces of a body lying in the woods. Newly turned earth showed them where parts had been buried. Other portions were spread out while others had been tossed into the brush. Tightly wrapped around the neck was a white petticoat, soaked crimson. The head was uncovered and the pretty face of Jessie Keith was revealed. The girl had been disembowelled and carved into pieces. The Department was notified instantly and I hastened to Listowel. I found the folk greatly excited.

"Bands of men were scouring the country calling upon every man they met to give an account of himself and prove he was not near Elm Bush, the dense woods where the body had been found. One of the searching parties met a man beyond Listowel, and as he was a stranger to them they led him back and sternly bade him tell whence he came and by what road. The fellow answered frankly that he had been working near Ailsa Craig and was on his way to another job. They had been ready to deal severely with him but when he told his straightforward story they felt that they had wronged him and they took up a collection for him, and released him to go his way. I heard of this and started immediately to get the fellow and have a talk with him, but he was gone. I telegraphed all over the country to keep a lookout for him and striking his trail on the road he had taken, I drove night and day for two days to overtake him. He went through Wallace township, then north to Palmerston, stole a ride on a freight train, was seen the next morning at six o'clock in Peel township, county of Wellington, twenty-six miles from Listowel. He was travelling afoot on the gravel road from Guelph to Port Elgin, where Charles Quinn gave him breakfast. From Guelph he went to Erin, known also as Cataract Station, forty-four miles from Listowel. My telegram had preceded him. He was heading for the United States when he was arrested and taken to Stratford gaol.

"When I looked at him he reminded me of a gorilla. He was as hairy as Esau. As I studied him he seemed to look less like a gorilla and more like a donkey. He had huge ears and his face actually resembled the features of a jackass. He was very dark. He was not tall, but was broad and powerful, being under medium height, yet weighing one hundred and ninety pounds. He wore a woman's knitted jacket that had been stretched to bursting to cover his bulging muscles. On the back of his head was tilted a Glengarry cap. He walked with the peculiar swaying motion of a baboon when it rises on its hind legs and toddles across its cage. In fact, if the wild man of Borneo had been clipped close as to his hair, he would have been mistaken for this fellow's twin brother. He had a knife. I looked at it. There were stains on it—blood stains. He tallied exactly to the description given by Robert Morris, a neighbour of the Keiths, of a man he saw on the morning of the butchery walking toward the scene of the crime and within a mile of the bush. The man seen by Morris had carried a little valise. A small satchel had been found hid in the bush, near the pieces of the body.

"'What is your name?' I asked this hairy man.

"'Almeda Chattelle,' said he.

"His voice was soft and low and sweet, a gentle voice. I was astonished. He spoke as a gentleman.

"'Be seated,' said I.

"We sat down.

"'Where is your home?' I asked.

"'In Lower Canada,' said he. 'That is, I was born there. The world is my home. But I spent my boyhood near St. Hyacinthe, in the Province of Quebec. I have travelled some. I sailed out of Boston, and I know the West Indies well.'

"He spoke almost sorrowfully. He hesitated, looked up half timidly and smiled.

"'I was in a lunatic asylum in Massachusetts for a time, he said. 'They sent me there from Boston. I thought there was no need to do it. After they had me there for some time they said I was all right and they let me go. I agreed with them, and I think I am all right now.'

"I then went over his movements step by step before and after the crime.

"'Chattelle,' I repeated, 'you were walking near Listowel on Friday and you met a little girl.'

"The hairy man looked at me wistfully.

"'Yes, mister, I did,' he answered as simply as a little child.

"'What did you do?'

"'I grabbed her around the waist and carried her to the woods,' he answered, all the while looking at me as a dog would look at a man it liked. 'She screamed and dug her heels into the ground, so I tied a white skirt around her neck. She still struggled, so I took out my knife and I cut her across this way and then down this way, and I threw away the parts of her I did not wish, and the parts I liked I treated considerately, and later I buried them under a tree. I was not unkind to the parts I liked.'

"The hairy man told this horrible tale of butchery in a gentle, tender voice, illustrating on his own body how he had carved and hacked the body of the young girl.

"'You see,' he continued, 'I had stopped at a house farther

back on the road and a red-haired girl gave me a handout. I was all right until I met the red-haired girl. I looked at her red hair and then I went away, and when I met the pretty little girl it all came over me like a flash and I just grabbed her and carried her across the fields to the woods and cut her up. I do not think I was right just then, although I was all right before it, and I am all right now, and I remember all that I did.'

"The hairy man paused and his eyes sought mine.

"'I am very sorry,' he said softly. 'I know it is too late to be sorry, but I am very sorry. I got sorry at once, and I was trying to get to the other side. I was starting for Niagara Falls when they caught me and took me back ; but they accused me of it, so I lied to them and they believed me and gave me money and let me go.'

"I looked at Almeda Chattelle, the hairy man. I looked at the big, gentle eyes, at the huge hands that had torn the child to pieces. He waited patiently for me to speak. I stepped to the door and sent for the County Attorney, who came in, and to him Chattelle repeated his confession. His memory was perfect as to every detail.

"I set out to prove the crime against him precisely as if he never had confessed. I took the woman's knitted jacket that he wore and the white skirt found wrapped around the young girl's neck and the valise found hid in the bush, and I undertook to find their owner or owners. I knew the house of Donald McLeod at Ailsa Craig had been robbed on Tuesday, October 2nd. A valise and other property had been taken. I telegraphed for Mrs. McLeod and she came to the gaol. She looked at Almeda Chattelle and said at once that she had seen him before, that he had dug a cellar for a new house near Ailsa Craig. I showed to her the valise, the jacket, and the skirt. She identified them all as property stolen from her home. She pointed out also the Glengarry cap that the hairy man wore and said it, too, had been stolen from her house.

"'Yes, I stole the valise and what was in it,' said the hairy man to me.

"Robert Morris and others proved Almeda Chattelle was

going to the bush and later was coming from the bush where the crime was committed.

"I took Almeda Chattelle to Listowel on October 25th, and he was held for trial. Stones were pelted through the windows of the place where I had him. One of the stones struck the hairy man.

"'If they are going to hang me, why do they not hang me now?' he said. 'I'd rather be hanged to death than stoned to death!'

"I knew that some of the enraged people were aroused and that a crowd might try to lynch Almeda Chattelle. Sure enough, a crowd began to gather in the evening. They had a rope. A train left for Stratford at 10.25 that night. I had a carriage drive to the door just before train time and I jumped into it with the hairy man, and we were off at a gallop for the station. I had him out of the carriage and into the rear car before the crowd could get at him. Some of them sprang up to uncouple the car. I told the hairy man to get down between the seats if there was trouble, and then I stepped out on the car platform and faced the crowd. It was a delicate situation, but the train pulled out a moment later and the hairy man was saved from a premature hanging.

"Almeda Chattelle was hanged in Stratford in the spring of 1895. He raised no question as to his sanity, and his plea at his preliminary examination had been 'Guilty.' All he said was: 'I am sorry.' From the moment I was satisfied that he was aware of what he was doing, at the time he did it and thereafter, no doubt of his full responsibility for his crime presented itself to me. He, indeed, was horrible, hairy, human, with hands like the paws of a bear. Yet his voice was as gentle as his crime was brutal."

25

THE MIDDLEMARCH MYSTERY

A CLUMP of timber near Middlemarch, three miles from St. Thomas, in the county of Elgin, became known throughout all Canada in 1895. For years it had stood on the county maps as Wardell's woods. It was good for squirrels and firewood and that was about all. But in the closing days of 1894 came a tragedy that caused people to travel for miles simply to tramp through this fragment of a forest and gape at the scene of blood. The crime has passed into the records as the Middlemarch mystery, although its mystery long since was solved.

"William Henry Hendershott, a name which its owner always wrote or pronounced in full, as if he were proud of its extent and its euphony, was a young man, unmarried, well known among his neighbours, and a skilled hand about a farm," says Murray. "He boarded with his uncle, John Hendershott, a farmer. A fellow-boarder was young William David Welter, who was engaged to Mary Hendershott, the pretty daughter of John Hendershott. On the morning of Friday, December 14th, 1894, John Hendershott and his daughter Mary drove away to Eden, forty miles from home, leaving his nephew and Welter on the farm. About three o'clock that afternoon Welter went to the house of his cousin, Charles Welter, who lived near the Hendershotts, and told his cousin that a tree had fallen on William Henry Hendershott, while they were chopping in Wardell's woods and had killed him. The uncle was notified by telegraph at Eden, and the next day he drove home, and after a post-mortem, the body of William Henry Hendershott was buried on Monday, December 17th. Welter told at the inquest how the tree had fallen and crushed his companion to death. I was telegraphed for the next day and I arrived on Tuesday.

"I got Drs. Gustin, Lawrence, Fulton, McCarty, and Wilson, and drove to Fingal cemetery and exhumed the body of William Henry Hendershott and looked at the wounds. The only marks were on the head. There was not a scratch on the remainder of the body. Clearly, if a tree fell on him it must have fallen on the head alone. Moreover there were various wounds on the head. Instead of a complete crushing it showed numerous contusions, so that the tree would have to bounce up and down on the head to make them. They looked to me as if they had been made by many heavy blows instead of by the single smash of a falling tree. I had the head taken off and requested the doctors to preserve it.

"We then drove to the scene of the tragedy in Wardell's woods. I had a constable bring Welter to the place. Welter came striding through the woods, a massive fellow, over six feet tall, deep-chested, broad-shouldered, powerful. We were waiting for him by the fallen tree.

"'Welter,' said I, 'show me the exact spot where William Henry Hendershott stood, and where you stood, and show me precisely where you were when the tree fell.'

"Welter walked over by the stump of the tree.

"'I stood here,' he said. 'Hendershott had left his vest with his watch in it over there on the ground, and when he saw the tree falling that way he ran to get the vest out of the way, and the tree killed him.'

"'Show me where the vest lay,' said I.

"Welter walked out along the fallen tree to a spot about forty feet from the stump.

"'Here it was, and here he was killed,' said Welter.

"At this point on the tree trunk was a large knot, the shape of a cocoanut and bigger than a half-bushel basket. When the tree fell this knot had been buried in the springy soil. The buoyancy of the limbs had raised it up, leaving a hole in the ground beneath the knot.

"'I found Hendershott lying dead in the ground beneath this knot,' said Welter.

"'Get down on the ground and place yourself exactly as he was lying when you found him,' said I,

"Welter demurred, but finally sprawled flat, face down, his head in the hole beneath the knot.

"'Stay there now,' I said.

"I called the doctors to take careful notice. I had Welter, lying on the ground, explain it all again. Then I bade Welter step back.

"'Would there not be a smashed head and a great deal of blood,' I asked the doctors.

"'There certainly would,' they said.

"The doctors examined the soil, a rich loam. There was no blood. One by one the doctors made sure of this. I then took samples of the earth. Blood was on the knot. But it had been smeared on and had not splattered at all. The doctors examined it and said it had been rubbed on the knot. On the top of the tree as it lay, I found a large quantity of blood.

"'How do you account for that?' I asked Welter.

"'I don't know,' he said.

"I began to circle the tree in ever widening circles, and one hundred and ninety feet from the stump I came upon a little pool of water. Around it were spots of blood, and a zigzag trail of blood drips led to a place fifty feet from the stump, and there I found a lot of blood. Hendershott had been killed there, then put under the top of the tree, and then removed to where the knot was. The murderer had washed his hands, and perchance his weapon, in the little pool. Thus I accounted for the various crimson stains. I believed the weapon used was the axe that chopped the tree. I searched the woods thrice and could not find it, but at last it was revealed. It had been shoved in between the bark and the log of an old tree trunk. It never would have been discovered if one of the searchers had not stumbled on the log and smashed the bark off so that the axe fell out. It had been partially washed, but there were tell-tale traces on it. John Hendershott had given me previously an old axe, saying it was the one used to chop the tree. It was not.

"When I again came to the woods I found a lot more blood splattered about in confusing quantities. I investigated and found an old dead horse in a field near by. During the night some of Welter's friends had drawn blood from this carcass and sprinkled it around in Wardell's woods. They were too late. I already had taken my samples of the stained soil.

"I learned that Welter and John Hendershott had negotiated $11,000 insurance on the life of the dead man. Several months before, they had taken out two policies, one for $6,000 in a Galesburg (Illinois) Company, and one for $5,000 in the Mutual Reserve of New York. Both policies were in the name of John Hendershott as the beneficiary. I knew many of the people in that part of Canada, as it was my old headquarters when I was at St. Thomas with the railroad. Among my acquaintances was a worthless fellow named Patrick Fitzpatrick, who was known as Paddy the Diver. He was the St. Thomas town drunkard. Paddy the Diver told me Welter and John Hendershott had spoken to him about insuring his life. I investigated among the insurance companies and found the two men had tried to insure Paddy the Diver, but the applications had been refused. Then they had taken Paddy the Diver to Aylmer before another doctor, and had changed his name slightly, and he passed the examination and the application was approved, but when it reached the insurance company's head office the trick was discovered, owing to the failure to make a greater change in the name, and the policy was cancelled. So they then effected the $11,000 insurance on Hendershott's nephew. This was done several months before the murder.

"These circumstances left no doubt in my mind that John Hendershott, the uncle, was a party to the crime. I went to Eden, where John Hendershott had driven, with his pretty daughter, on the morning of the murder, and where he had stayed all night. I saw those who were with him when he heard of his nephew's death.

"'It's just like that fool to leave his watch some place, and in going to get it he might get hurt,' said John Hendershott when the telegram came stating his nephew was dead.

"This settled it. Welter had told us of the watch and had stated on the day of the murder the same version of how young Hendershott met his death. But how did John Hendershott, forty miles away, happen to give the same version as Welter, although John Hendershott knew nothing of how it had occurred? They had fixed up the story beforehand. John Hendershott, in Eden, also showed the insurance policies to friends. He had taken the policies with him when he drove away to Eden. Why? When he heard his nephew was dead he produced the policies from his coat pocket.

"'Will got killed, but I am not so badly off,' he told his friends.

"I re-opened the inquest. I arrested Welter and John Hendershott on December 21st, 1894. They were tried before Chief Justice Meredith. B. B. Osler prosecuted, ably assisted by D. J. Donahue; and Norman Macdonald and John A. Robinson defended. Mr. Macdonald made a good fight in behalf of his clients. It was a long-drawn-out trial. We swore eighty-five or more witnesses for the Crown. On Friday, March 15th, 1895, both Welter and John Hendershott were convicted. They were hanged on June 18th at St. Thomas. Welter was a heavy man on the gallows."

26

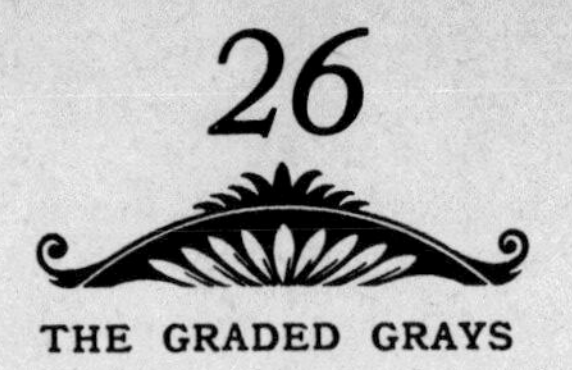

THE GRADED GRAYS

DAVID SCOLLIE was an old man with a long white beard, and Tommie Gray was a tow-headed boy. David Scollie was six times as old as Tommie Gray, and Tommie was eleven years old. David Scollie lived alone on a little farm in the township of Otonabee, in the county of Peterboro. Tommie Gray lived across the road with his parents. Thomas Gray, the father of Tommie Gray, was a farm labourer, with a wife and six children, the oldest being a girl of twelve. Thomas Gray worked for various farmers, chiefly for John Graham Weir. Tommie Gray spent most of his time with his friend David Scollie—in fact, Tommie and David spent most of their days together.

" Scollie was so old that he got Mrs. Gray to do baking and occasionally set his house in order for him," says Murray. " He was very fond of young Tommie Gray. Finally Tommie's father struck up a bargain with old Scollie. They agreed that if he gave them his farm they would keep him and care for him as long as he lived. To Scollie it meant an end of worry over housekeeping, and above all, life with Tommie would be unbroken. The old man went to Peterboro and had the papers drawn up transferring his farm to the Grays. The deed was executed and the Grays moved to Scollie's house. Early on the morning of February 23rd, 1894, the house was destroyed by fire. Gray had gone to Maydock, forty miles away, on the previous day to see his brother, and was absent when the fire occurred. Mrs. Gray, Tommie Gray, and the other children escaped and were cared for by neighbours. Old David Scollie was found in the ruins dead. He was buried and soon thereafter the Grays sold his farm to Michael Fitzgerald for $1,000, squandered the money, and disappeared with all the children.

"Months passed. Over a year later, in May 1895, W. J. McGregor, a brother-in-law of Thomas Gray, told of a talk between Mrs. Gray and Mrs. McGregor shortly before the fire.

"'If something isn't done with that old divvle of a Scollie he is as likely to live as long as I will,' Mrs. Gray said to Mrs. McGregor.

"'I suppose he will live as long as God will let him,' replied her sister.

"'No. I'll be —— if he will; I won't let him,' said Mrs. Gray.

"'Be very careful or the law will get you,' said her sister, Mrs. McGregor.

"Then had come the fire, with old Scollie's body found in the ruins.

"Almost sixteen months later the matter was reported and the Government sent me to Otonabee to investigate. I looked over the case. I took doctors and went to Peterboro, and had the body exhumed. I found the head completely severed or burned from the body. I was surprised to find so few traces of burns on the remainder of the body. A head cannot well be burned from a body without the trunk showing evidences of the intense heat. However, the body had been buried so long that it was very hard to make a satisfactory post-mortem. I learned also that the body had been found in the cellar after the fire in an opposite corner from that beneath Scollie's own room. He could not very well have fallen from overhead to the spot where he was found, with his head severed. How had he come there?

"It was decided to locate the Grays and bring them back. A letter had been received from them by one of their old-time neighbours, saying they were living near Ocala, Florida. I prepared extradition papers and went to Florida. I found them living in great poverty and squalor. Their house was a shanty, some of the children were running around practically naked. I looked at the six little ones, dirty, clothesless, and hungry. I could not take the parents and leave the six children alone in this shanty. They would have starved to death or perished of neglect. So I took the entire family to Ocala and registered them at the gaol. The sheriff and his wife and townsfolk washed the children and made up a purse and bought them clothes. Tommie Gray invested five cents, given to him by a lady, in candy known to Tommie as Red Dave's jawbone. Tommie would begin to suck on a jawbone after breakfast, and along toward sundown it would melt away.

"I can see my party now as it looked when we started north. I was the tallest, then came Thomas Gray, then Mrs. Gray, and then six little Grays. We made a human stairway, with my head the top landing and a Gray baby no taller than my knee the bottom step. Tommie Gray, his pockets bulging with all-day suckers, *alias* Red Dave's jawbones, was the fourth step from the top and the fourth step from the bottom. Despite all my efforts to form them in column of two, the Grays persisted in walking Indian file, the tallest first, the smallest last. I led this parade of graduated progeny through the streets of Ocala with a horde of shouting pickaninnies trailing in the wake of the procession. Tommie Gray sang at the top of his voice all the way to the station.

"On the train I found the Grays still bound to arrange themselves according to age and size. The moment the train started Mrs. Gray began to boohoo, and the six little Grays burst forth into a chorus of caterwauling, and Thomas Gray blubbered, while Tommie Gray opened wide his cave of the winds and poured forth frantic howls. Of course this was not pleasant for the other passengers, and several men promptly left the car after glaring at me. A gentle old lady arose and crossed to the seat of the wailing Tommie.

"'Poor little mannie,' she said tenderly.

"'G'way, darn you!' howled Tommie. 'Don't you dare to try kiss me!'

"'What ails the mannie? What's the matter?' said the old lady soothingly.

"'Can't you see I'm crying, you old fool?' howled Tommie.

"For answer, the sweet old lady suddenly reached down and seized the weeping Tommie, and, despite his kicks and struggles, lifted him up and laid him across her knees and spanked him soundly. To my utter astonishment and the amazement of the Grays, Tommie suddenly ceased his howling and looked up and smiled.

"'That's better,' said the old lady, and Tommie Gray grinned as he rubbed his tingling seat of chastisement.

"At sight of Tommie grinning, all the other Grays promptly stopped howling. The old lady returned to her seat, while the eight Grays eyed her. Suddenly a long loud wail broke forth. It was Tommie Gray.

"'She bruk me jawbones!' he howled. 'She bruk me jawbones!'

"The other Grays took up the wailing. They shrieked and bellowed. Over all could be heard Tommie Gray, howling:

"'She bruk me jawbones! She bruk me jawbones!'

"The old lady paled, then flushed. At length she arose and came over to me.

"'Sir,' she said, 'I trust you do not think I injured him. I did not strike him on his face, so his jawbone is unhurt. I struck him not on the face, but on his—on the—on the appropriate place provided therefor, sir, and it was—I—it was with my open hand.'

"'Oh, it's all right,' I answered. 'I can have his jaw set when I get him home.'

"Tommie meanwhile had produced one of the broken jawbones and was sucking it contentedly. One by one the tribe of Grays fell asleep. The old lady dozed in her seat. I looked at my eight slumbering charges. I had travelled many miles with many prisoners, but never did I have such a cargo and such a trip. It was a long series of snorings and shriekings. When they were awake they howled, and when they were asleep they snored, and Tommie Gray kicked in his sleep and had dreams that called for wild acrobatic feats. It was stifling hot weather, too, and the presence of the Grays could be detected, even by a blind man, if his olfactory organ did even half its duty.

"I landed them in Peterboro on Friday, July 5th, 1895. Mrs. Gray was tried at the Fall Assizes. A seventh Gray child was expected soon after the trial. Tommie Gray went on the stand, and his testimony saved the day for his mother.

Tommie testified her right out of it. Mrs. McGregor's statement of Mrs. Gray's talk with her duly appeared. All things being considered, including the expected seventh Gray, the verdict of acquittal perturbed no one. Thomas Gray left his wife after the case was over and went his way alone. Mrs. McGregor's cow was poisoned by an unconvicted hand. What became of Tommie Gray, the guardian angel of freckle-faced, tow-headed jawbone-suckers only knows."

27

GEORGE ALGER'S GRAVEYARD POLICY

GRAVEYARD insurance is as old as the insurance of life itself. On a small scale it is practised year after year with varying degrees of success. Occasionally a big raid is planned on the insurance companies ; but the larger the amount involved, the less apt the plan is to work out. In Canada, however, in the year 1895, a scheme to mulct the insurance companies out of many thousands of dollars was engineered and was beginning to materialise, when it was detected and broken up. A number of persons doomed to die were insured by fraud and misrepresentation, through a conspiracy involving agents of some companies.

" The case that brought the whole conspiracy to collapse was located in the township of Pickering, in the county of Ontario, ten miles from Whitby, the county seat," says Murray. " A farmer, named George Alger, and his wife lived there on a fine, big farm. Mrs. Alger was a delicate woman. In the same neighbourhood lived Dr. Charles Henry Francey, who was medical examiner for a number of insurance companies, one of them being the Equitable. In 1894 Alger and Dr. Francey effected an insurance on the life of Mrs. Alger in the Equitable for $7,000, and on July 11th of the next year application was made for $5,000 in the Home Life. The application was approved, as it was regular and favourable, owing to the conspiracy. Before the policy could arrive Mrs. Alger was dead. She died on August 13th, 1895, and, while she lay in her coffin in the parlour, the $5,000 policy on her life came to her husband.

" Alger set out to collect the insurance. An action was begun, and finally came to trial in Toronto. In the meantime the Home Life policy, so closely connected with her death, led to an investigation. I had the body of Mrs. Alger exhumed in Brougham cemetery, and had it examined by Dr. Ferguson and Dr. Bingham. They found death had been due to consumption. She had been ill for several years I learned from others. Alger went on the stand in the trial in Toronto, and gave evidence clearly contrary to the facts. I was satisfied there was a conspiracy afoot. I arrested him and took him to Whitby, where he was committed for trial for conspiracy. Dr. Francey, who had acted in the dual capacity of medical examiner for the insurance companies and Alger's physician, had left the country. He went to Buffalo. After staying there some time I located him and saw him, and he was persuaded to return and give evidence under the protection of the Crown. When this had been accomplished, it simplified the whole matter. We needed Francey to prove other cases.

"We showed at the trial of Alger that Dr. Eastwood, in 1888, had examined Mrs. Alger, and had told Alger that his wife had consumption and would die in a few years, if she did not have a change of climate. The years passed. Mrs. Alger grew worse. Her husband sat by as she coughed her life away, and as the end drew near took out insurance by fraud and then waited for her to die. It must have been a pleasant household where this weak woman sat suffocating day after day, each day being harder than the day before, while the man with the big farm and perfect health sat quietly by, waiting for her to smother to death so that he could grow richer by her dying! His so-called friend came and went, but the woman was left to die. Instead of sending her to the mountains or to California to live, as he could have done, he speculated on her death, cheating her in her life and endeavouring to cheat the companies by her death. But, by the irony of fate, after lingering so many suffering years, she died too soon. She was very patient and brave during her agony and endeavoured to make her husband as little trouble as possible. She never knew of his villainy.

"Alger was tried in March 1896, and was convicted and sent to Kingston for seven years. Dr. Francey not only testified against Alger and revealed the entire dastardly plot, but admitted his own part in it and acknowledged he was a rascal. He confessed also that he had acted with equal dishonesty in a number of other instances. There was considerable excitement over the revelations.

" The result was a wholesale overhauling of a number of policies. The Equitable cancelled two policies on the life of A. E. Thornton of Whitevale; a policy on the life of Donald Beaton, a policy on the life of J. H. Besse, and a policy on the life of James Sadler, of Greenwood. Other companies cancelled other policies and the conspiracy collapsed.

" Nicholas L. Brown, an Ontario agent of the Home Life, came to me and told me how he got into it. He got off. Joseph Hortop, agent for the Ontario Mutual Association, also got off. In the trial of the case, Crown Attorney Farewell prosecuted, while Alger was represented by G. Smith Macdonald, T. Herbert Lennox, C. Russell Fitch, and S. Alfred Jones. The case marked the end in any concerted efforts in the Province to mulct the insurance companies on an extensive scale. Alger's seven years stands as a powerful deterrent to others. Dr. Francey left the Province. He went up into the North-West, and later I heard he was practising medicine in the western part of the United States.

" Mrs. Alger developed consumption in 1888 and died in 1895. That was seven years of suffering. Alger went to the penitentiary for the same length of time—seven years."

28

THE VOICE OF THE HAUNTED HOUSE

IT is a far cry from Paris, in France, to Hagersville, in Canada, but soon after Murray's return from abroad a telegram called him to the little town in the county of Brant. The people were talking of a tragedy. There had been a funeral, and they believed the closed coffin hid the evidence of a murder. They had gathered at the house on the day of the burial, but few, if any, saw the face of the dead. The women spoke in whispers, and some vowed there was no body in the coffin. Others thought the body might be there, but in pieces. A few were in favour of lifting the lid boldly, but others shuddered and shook their heads. Among them were those who said the coffin held the dead intact, and not in pieces. But as to the manner of death they were mute. It was a gruesome mystery.

"The dead was a woman," says Murray. "I went to Hagersville on receipt of the telegram to the Department. I had the body exhumed and a post-mortem made. She was a young woman, but was so emaciated that she seemed to have been simply a yellow parchment drawn tight over a skeleton to masquerade as a human being. The body had not begun to disintegrate, and there were traces of a bygone beauty. I marvelled at the emaciation. It reminded me vividly of the pictures of the starved of India, found dead during the famines, with their bones almost protruding through their skin. The woman seemed literally to have wasted away to skin and bones. The body bore marks of brutal treatment. There was a gash in the abdomen, and a broad path across it showed where a hobnailed boot had torn its way. The bosom was bruised as if it had been beaten with a hammer. On the temples were black and blue marks. Drs. Jones, McDonald, and Jarvis noted these wounds. To make sure no poison had been administered I had the viscera examined by Professor Ellis, in Toronto.

"The body was that of Lillian Carpenter, a bride of six months. She was married to James Carpenter, who had a farm in the township of Tuscarora, near Hagersville. I looked up Carpenter. He was a bad lot. His neighbours had no liking for him, and those who knew him best distrusted him most.

"There had been several incendiary fires in that section of the country. Farmers had lost cattle, and flocks of sheep had been broken up in the night and driven to the woods, and many stolen or killed. A midnight marauder seemed to be living a high-handed life in the county. There was an Indian reserve near Carpenter's farm.

"I called on Carpenter. He was a low-browed, sullen-faced, surly bully.

"'How did your wife die?' I asked.

"'None of your —— business,' said he.

"It was a real pleasure to set to work on the case with renewed zeal and determination.

"'Did you see her die, Carpenter?' I asked.'

"'Naw, why should I?' he growled. 'She ought to have been good and glad of a chance to die. She was no good, anyhow.'

"I learned from friends of the dead woman that she was an epileptic. Then I understood why the burly Carpenter regarded her as worthless or worse than worthless.

"It was a difficult case in which to get specific evidence. Carpenter's neighbours were not given to visiting frequently at his house. They told me much about cruel treatment, but I wanted eye-witnesses. At length I went among the Indians on the reserve, and I met an old Indian whom I had known for some years, and he led me aside into the woods, and sat down with me on a log, and, under pledge of secrecy, told me of a haunted house where, in the night, screams had resounded. Some of the Indians had come to look upon the house as under a spell, and were in the habit of going to it under cover of darkness, and sitting in the shadow, waiting to hear the spirit wail.

"'It wails like a woman,' he told me. 'It cries out in long, loud, shrill cries.'

"'Has no one ever seen it?'

"'Oh yes,' said he. 'It takes the shape of a woman. It has been seen various times. My son has seen it rush out of the house all in white, with its long hair streaming down its back, and its feet bare. It ran through the woods, shrieking as it ran, and waving its arms. The man of the haunted house pursued it, beating it, and knocking it down. It begged for mercy, and would clasp the man's legs, and kiss his hand and his feet like a dog. Then it would fall over, and the spirit would work upon it, making it writhe, and jerking its face all out of shape, trying to turn it into a dog or a cow, or a wild beast. For hours in the night it would lie out in the woods, and twice it had not even the white robe on it. Then it would creep back into the house after the man who had kicked it, when it fell over, and had left it lying in the woods.'

"'When was the spirit seen last?'

"'Not for two weeks,' said the old fellow. 'They tell me it is buried away, and that the voice sounds out no more in the haunted house.'

"'Where is the house?' I asked.

"'I will show you myself to-night,' he said.

"That night the old Indian led me in a roundabout way to the house of James Carpenter. I saw some shadowy figures squatting near by.

"'Our people; they are listening for it,' said the old fellow.

"'It will not come again; it is gone for ever,' I said.

"'Not the voice,' said the old fellow. 'Voices never die.'

"'But what is the voice without the spirit?' I asked him.

"'The voice is the spirit,' he answered.

"I kept all this a profound secret as I had promised. But I set to work among the more civilised of the Indians to obtain competent evidence of Carpenter's beating his wife, and driving her out of the house. Meanwhile Carpenter was locked up in gaol. After his arrest a woman in Petrolea wrote a letter saying she was the lawful wife of Carpenter, and that they had one child, then with her. She added that

Carpenter nearly starved her to death, and that she still bore upon her body the marks of his brutality, and that she would carry them with her to the grave. She gave the year of their wedding as 1888, and the place as Waterford.

"Carpenter was tried in Brantford on December 10th, 1896, for murder. He was defended by Lewis Hyde, who made a strong fight to save him. But the evidence could not be upset as to his brutality. My search among the intelligent Indians was not fruitless. Carpenter was found guilty of manslaughter, and was sent to Kingston Penitentiary for a long term of years. The Indians listened in vain thereafter for the voice of the wailing spirit of the haunted house."

29

SIMPERING JIM ALLISON

OVER the hill from Galt, in the county of Waterloo, lies North Dumfries. The road that climbs the hill sweeps round in a big curve on the other side, as it enters the valley. Up a lane, leading from this valley road, stood a little white farmhouse, with a big, unpainted barn near by. It was screened from the main road by a clump of trees, although the house stood in open ground with its door fronting on an orchard, its kitchen window opening on a cornfield. The woodpile loomed up at the end of the house nearest the barn. Rain-barrels stood in a row against the house. Milking pans shone in the sunlight. A dog dozed in the lane. Chickens scratched and pecked, and lazily fluffed their feathers and settled in the dust. It was a hot morning—August 9th, 1897. Out of the house stepped a woman. She was a beauty. The freshness of girlhood had been supplanted by the charm of full womanhood. Her complexion was pale pink and white. Her big eyes were laughing and merry. A tot toddled after her, yawning drowsily, then turned back indoors. The woman shaded her eyes and looked toward the barn.

The shrill squeals of an angry pig rang out. A man's gruff voice sounded, and then around the corner of the barn came Anthony Orr, the farmer, with a big sow in his waggon.

"Going, Tony?" called the woman.

"Yep!" shouted Tony Orr. "Back in a couple of hours."

He drove away with his nine-year-old son, Norman. A moment later the hired boy, Jim Allison, appeared with two cows, and started them down the lane. They were to go to the Barrie farm near by. The woman watched her husband until the bend in the road hid him from view. She saw the Allison boy in the lane with the cows. She began to sing softly, so as not to disturb her two children—Maggie, aged ten, and a-year-old baby, still asleep upstairs. Half an hour passed.

Two days before, a buggy, with an easy-going horse, had come up the lane. A stout, jolly-faced man had alighted, and had hitched his horse and had sat chatting and laughing with the handsome woman. They seemed to know and understand one another well. The man had entered his buggy and gone away, as he had come, alone. He was nowhere in sight on this morning, although he was half expected. The woman had been sitting with dreamy eyes and gentle smile, her hands clasped and lying idly in her lap. She was a pretty picture in the sunlight. Tony Orr had reason to be proud of his wife. There had been gossip of her fondness for travel and for clever companions. There even had been a tale of an elopement and a penitent return to Tony's arms and forgiveness. Neighbours had known of men callers at the white farmhouse. But Tony said all was well, and on the Orr farm that meant all was well. The woman sat still in the sunlight.

Two hours later Tony Orr returned. The farm boy, Jim Allison, was standing at the side gate of the house fence, laughing.

"What's the matter?" asked Orr.

"Oh, nothing," said Allison, laughing all the louder.

"What's the matter?" demanded Orr.

"Oh, nothing," laughed Allison.

"What's up?" roared Orr.

"Your wife's gone," said Allison.

The baby was lying on the front steps. The little girl, Maggie, was sitting on the porch. Orr hurried to the kitchen. The breakfast dishes had not been touched. Orr ran out of the house, and saw Harry Blair, an agricultural implement dealer from Galt, just getting out of his buggy. Harry Blair was stout and jolly faced.

"My wife's gone!" shouted Orr.

"Gone! Gone where?" exclaimed the disappointed Blair.

Orr and Blair searched for her, and then got into Blair's buggy and drove to Galt, thinking she might have gone with

Weldon Sidney Trevelyan, a medical student who was spending the summer in Galt, and who had been calling on her. They found Trevelyan, and he knew nothing of the woman. Orr returned home, and organised a search for his wife. The authorities were notified.

"Many believed there had been an elopement," says Murray. "Mrs. Orr was good-looking, a great favourite with men, but had a reputation. Her maiden name was Emma Borland. Her parents were well-to-do and lived at Bright. She was thirty-seven years old, and was born in Innerkip. She was first married to John Arnott, of Innerkip, who died when she was twenty-two, and three years later she married Anthony Orr, to whom she bore three children. To her children she was a loving, careful mother. To her husband she was said to be an indifferent wife. About two years previous to this she had run away with a hired man named Mulholland, but her husband caught her and her two children at Niagara Falls, and took them home again. Tony Orr was a nervous, excitable man, who had trouble with other men on account of their frequent calls on his wife. A week passed, with no trace of the wife's whereabouts.

"At first, before traces of blood were found, the elopement theory vied with the suicide theory. On the day before Mrs. Orr disappeared, Tony Orr's father was buried. Mrs. Orr attended the funeral, and some of the Orr family treated her coldly. The Orrs were an old family of good standing. On the way home from the funeral Mrs. Orr remarked that 'she was no use and guessed she'd get out of here.' This remark was the basis for the suicide talk.

"I went to the Orr farm. The boy Allison and the medical student Trevelyan had been held in Galt, and Harry Blair, the agricultural implement agent, was under surveillance. I looked the house over, a one and a half story white brick house with a frame kitchen. It was situated in a tract of country that, owing to the swamps and marshes in which it abounds, is most desolate. About two hundred yards from the house was a swamp or marsh of about one hundred acres, and above the wet and rank grass and weeds and thick soil grew almost impenetrable shrubs and trees. In this swamp was an excavation eighteen inches wide and six feet long and eighteen inches deep. It was newly dug, and clearly was an unfinished grave. I visited it in the night, and carefully took from the upturned surface the print of a man's foot, a precise clue to the digger of the grave. In order to get this, I turned back the overturned earth after digging under it so as not to break its surface and destroy the footprint I knew must be there. I took this to my hotel in Galt, unknown to anyone in the affair.

"I returned to the Orr house. A picket fence separated the patch of garden from the corn patch adjoining the house. One of the pickets of this fence was gone. The paling mark was not of long exposure. I saw this was on a line between the house and the swamp, with the corn patch lying between. One of the furrows in this corn patch was raised slightly. John Orr, Tony's brother, poked it with his stick. Six inches beneath the surface lay Mrs. Orr, face down, buried amid the corn within thirty feet of her house. That put an end to elopement or suicide theories. When I saw the half-dug grave in the swamp I knew there had been murder. The grave in the corn patch was but temporary. The murderer intended to hide the body for ever in the swamp.

"Back to Galt I went. Trevelyan proved an absolute alibi. Harry Blair, agitated over the whole affair, was not at the farmhouse when the deed was done, and had nothing to do with it. Tony Orr was five miles away at a neighbour's, with his son and the sow. Allison—I went to see this boy. I had his old shoe, and it fitted the footprint by the grave in the swamp. He looked almost a freak. He was about seventeen years old, big for his age, and tremendously stocky in his build. His bow legs were big and muscular. His hands and feet were enormous. His shoulders were broad, his neck was thick, his arms were long and powerful. His features reminded me of the features of a frog. The forehead was low and retreating, and the face was very full at the sides. The hair was brown, cut close, and the eyes were a greenish brown—large, watery eyes, uneasy, shifting, catlike. The mouth was very large, and the lips were full and seemed to simper, giving the face a cat's expression. He walked with a peculiar, rolling motion, as if he would have preferred to be on all fours. He wore heavy, clod shoes, blue jeans, a calico shirt, and a faded, slouch hat pulled well over his eyes.

"I sat down and faced this boy.

"'What do you know of this murder?' I said.

"'Nothing,' he answered, with a grin.

"'Tell me where you were on that morning,' said I.

"'I left Orr's, with two cows, about 7.20,' he said. 'I got to Barrie's farm about eight o'clock, and I left there about 8.50 and got back to Orr's about 9.40. When I got back Mrs. Orr was gone.'

"'How did you know she was gone?'

"'She was not anywhere around,' said the boy.

"'Where is your shot gun?' I asked.

"'Just before I left with the cows, Mrs. Orr asked me to show her the gun, and she asked me how it was used, and I explained it, and then put it back and went on with the cows,' he lied glibly.

"His gun, which always was kept in the house, was found hidden in the hay-mow in the barn. It had been discharged. There were blood-stains on it.

"'Allison,' I said slowly, 'you killed Mrs. Orr.'

"He started up, white as flour, shaking like a man with ague. I waited for his confession. He mumbled, hesitated, and—sat down and grinned. For four hours I worked with him. He grinned and lied.

"An idea previously had occurred to me. Allison's father, Alex Allison, was city scavenger of Galt. The father had seen the boy alone. That night the father was followed. It was before the finding of the body was generally known. The father had gone to the swamp to finish, for his son, the half-dug grave. The boy had told him of it.

"'Allison,' I said to the boy, 'your father says you dropped your knife at the grave in the swamp.'

"'No I didn't, for I left it when I went——'

"He stopped. It was on the tip of his tongue trembling, quivering, almost out.

"'That's enough,' I said.

"Some newspapers declaimed against my examination of

this boy, and talked of a sweat-box system, and asserted the boy's innocence. In due time their mistake was revealed.

"The evidence was overwhelming when it all was collected. There was no need to use the footprint by the grave. Allison was proved by neighbours and folk on the road to have the exclusive opportunity to do the deed. His blood-stained gun had been fired, and the empty cartridge found in it was one he had taken from a box in the house. John Orr and his family on the next farm had heard a gunshot after Tony left with the sow. Allison had called out Mrs. Orr from the house, shot at her, clubbed her to death, then buried her temporarily in the corn-field, and at night dug the grave in the swamp. He had importuned her, and she refused him, and the murder followed.

"The grand jury found a true bill on November 29th, and Allison's trial followed at once. Chief Justice Meredith presided. H. P. O'Connor, K.C., prosecuted, and J. R. Blake and J. J. H. Weir defended. On Friday, December 3rd, 1897, this seventeen-year-old murderer was found guilty, and was sentenced to be hanged in Berlin gaolyard on Friday, February 4th, 1898. His father fell in an epileptic fit when he heard the verdict.

"Smiling serenely, Jim Allison went up to his death. He mounted the scaffold unaided at eight o'clock on a raw, snowy morning. He shook hands politely with the guards, the hangman, and the minister, waited quietly while the black cap and noose were adjusted, stepped on to the trap at 8. 1, and dropped into eternity.

"Allison had learned to read and write a little in his six months in a cell, and he had scrawled laboriously the following on a piece of paper:

"'I am sorry for my crime. I did it out of ill-will. I hope those whom I wronged will forgive me, and that no one will turn this up to my people. My sentence is just, and I hope God will have mercy on me.'

"He signed this, and read it to them when they came to take him out and hang him."

30

THE TURNIP PIT TRAGEDY

BOYS were the bane of Ephraim Convay's life. He detested them as a nuisance, a pest, a plague. He had a long nose, and when he passed a boy he turned up this great nose, wrinkled his forehead, and made a wry face, as if he had been taking castor oil. The boys for miles around knew of his dislike, and they seized every opportunity to torment him. Naturally this increased his ire against all youth. He owned two big farms near Princeton, in the county of Oxford, within a few miles of the Blenheim Swamp, where Birchall murdered Benwell. Ephraim warned all boys to keep off his land. He vowed that any boy caught trespassing would be dragged to one of his barns and chastised until he tingled.

"This amounted to nothing more or less than a challenge to all the boys around to make life miserable for old Ephraim," says Murray. "They teased him in a thousand ways. At night, when he was asleep, a fiery face suddenly would loom up at his bedroom window—a face with eyes like balls of fire, and a voracious mouth extending from ear to ear, and grinning hideously. A gentle tapping would begin on the window, made by clackers, otherwise a bunch of nails tied to a nail previously driven in the window-frame, and swayed to and fro by means of a long string. Ephraim would rise up in wrath or terror and gaze on this ghastly face. He would make for his gun and blaze away at the apparition, only to discover it was a jack-o'-lantern perched on a tall bean-pole. At other times his door would refuse to open, and he would find it nailed shut. His chimney would refuse to draw, and would smoke him out of his house, investigation revealing a bag of wheat stuck in the flue. One evening, when he went home, he found his house dark and his doors fastened. He climbed in through a window, and found himself in pitch darkness, with myriad screeching, scratching figures that darted about and leaped over chairs and tables in wild flight, and dealt him stinging blows. He lighted a candle, and found the room filled with cats collected from the entire countryside. When he got into bed he alighted on something cold and clammy. It was a turtle lying in state amid a nest of eggs.

"In the early evenings resounding knocks would thunder on Ephraim's front door. At length he began to hide inside the door with a long club, waiting to hear the knockers approach, when he planned to leap out and belabour them. They heard him in the hall, and withdrew to deliberate. In the meantime a frail and very respectable friend, going to call on Ephraim, walked up to the door and knocked. The door flew open ; out sprang Ephraim, and began to smite the knocker with the club. It was so dark Ephraim could not see who his captive was, and the old man went to work as if with a flail. There were shouts and shrieks of 'Murder!' and 'Help!' The victim rolled over on the ground, beseeching Ephraim for mercy.

"'I'll show you!' roared the excited Ephraim. 'I'll teach you ever to dare to pester me again!'

"The friend thought Ephraim had gone crazy. When the old man finally paused, exhausted, and discovered the identity of his visitor, he was beside himself with shame, and grief, and anger. He vowed deep vengeance on his tormentors.

"'Hi, Ephraim!' they would yell. 'You were a boy yourself once, weren't you?'

"'If I was, I've spent over half a century trying to live it down and atone for it!' roared Ephraim. 'No one ought to be born into this world under thirty. So long as the Lord could fix it for us to be born at all, He might as well have made the minimum entry age at least twenty-five. I'd rather have erysipelas all my life than have a boy around for half a day. You know where to look for St. Anthony's fire, but a boy is nowhere when you want him, and everywhere when you don't want him.'

"'How about girls?'

"'They are what boys might have been,' said the old man, with a soft smile. 'My mother was a girl once.'

"'Wasn't your father a boy?'

"'Yes; but he got over it as quick as he could,' snapped Ephraim.

"Ephraim's big farm was worked on shares by Russell Grover. Ephraim and Grover did not get along well. Grover had a young fellow working for him named George Frost. Like others, Frost teased Ephraim. On the afternoon of March 26th, 1897, the boy was found dead on the barn floor, with a bullet hole in his body. The Department was notified and I went to the farm. Ephraim had denied any knowledge of the shooting. So did Grover. Ephraim said he was not about when it happened and threw suspicion on Grover. Grover said he was away at the time and he threw suspicion on Ephraim. I learned from others that Grover was not near the barn on that afternoon. There was a turnip pit beneath the barn. To get to it several boards in the barn floor had to be raised. This trap had been moved recently and not replaced evenly. I raised it and went down into the pit. I saw the turnips, and we rolled them back from one corner and there discovered recently turned earth. We dug it up and there lay a revolver. It was a new one. I went to Princeton and to Woodstock, and finally found in Woodstock the store where Ephraim had bought it. I learned from some of his neighbours that he had said he bought it for Grover, and to William Kip he had said: 'There will be murder down at the farm before April 1st.' I learned also that Ephraim had told Harvey Grover, Russell Grover's brother, that 'Frost and I have had a little *fracas*, and he has fainted on the barn floor.'

"I went to Ephraim again, and this time he confessed. He said he had gone down into his turnip pit to shovel up some turnips. He noticed that as fast as he shovelled them up and turned for another shovelful the turnips rolled back into the pit from the floor of the barn. Then he heard a spitting noise, as if a cat was facing a dog. He looked up and saw the boy Frost on his hands and knees peering into the pit and spitting at him and rolling the turnips back on him. Ephraim said he grabbed his shovel by the handle end, and gave Frost a pat with it. His story was that Frost then seized a plank and shoved it down into the pit at him, and seemed to be preparing to send another after it when Ephraim whipped out the revolver, fired, and Frost fell. At first the old man thought to bury him in the turnip pit, but the barn floor already was dyed crimson, so he left the body to lie where it fell. 'Before he fell he staggered over by the door,' said Ephraim. 'I stuck my head out of the pit, and he turned and looked at me—looked, looked, looked at me, and then he fell. I dodged back into the pit, and then crept out and stepped over the body, and later went to Harvey Grover and told him I thought Frost must have fainted. I felt very sorry as I sat in the pit and thought of the boy lying on the barn floor.'

"Ephraim was tried at Woodstock in September 1897. He insisted on taking the stand and he fretted and fumed until his counsel, Wallace Nesbit and A. S. Ball, called him to testify. He began slowly and calmly, but when he came to the story of the tragedy he grew very much excited and gasped for breath, swayed to and fro, thumped on the floor with his foot, got down on his hands, and graphically portrayed the scene in the turnip pit, and finally wept frenziedly. The defence showed that a brother of the prisoner had been in an insane asylum at Toronto, and swore witnesses to prove another brother was light-headed. The jury found Ephraim guilty of manslaughter, and Justice Meredith sent him to Kingston Penitentiary for seven years.

"'I hope there are no boys there,' said Ephraim. 'I'd be tempted to try to escape on the way if there were.'

"I advised him not to try it, and told him of what happened to Frank Osier a month before."

31

WHY HUMPHREY WENT BACK TO PRISON

In the parlance of rogues, a fence is a person or place where disposition may be made of stolen goods with no questions asked. Fences usually are in cities, although occasionally in the country there are receivers of stolen property, who, in turn, transmit it at a profit to city buyers. In the end, stuff stolen in the country finds its market in the city. Most of the fences are known to detectives, and some of them occasionally are sources of valuable information. In Canada there are comparatively few fences. Property stolen in Canada by professional crooks usually is smuggled into the United States and disposed of in the larger cities of the Continent.

"But there was one crook who beat the world in his method of disposing of stolen stuff," says Murray. "It puzzled me for quite a while. The robberies began in September 1899. Various burglaries were committed in the counties of Dufferin, Halton, and Grey. Horses were stolen, a buggy was stolen, a load of sheep was stolen, hogs were stolen, household utensils were stolen, and to cap the climax came highway robbery and attempted murder. Then came burglaries in Georgetown, Cooksville, and other towns.

"Early in September a minister in Whitby tied his horse in front of a house, and when he came out horse and buggy were gone. Shortly thereafter a team of horses and waggon, standing in Orangeville, eighty miles from the scene of the stealing of the minister's horse and buggy, were stolen, and vanished as if driven up into the clouds. Then three cows were stolen out of a field and driven across fields and into the woods, and there they vanished. A farmer driving along with a load of hogs stopped his team by the roadside to go up a lane and talk with a neighbour. When he returned his hogs were gone as if they had melted away, without leaving a grease-spot to tell what became of them.

"A Catholic church at Dixie was entered in the night and the chalice and other valuables were stolen by this mysterious hand, and were powdered up before being taken out of the church. A farmer named Brunskill was driving to Toronto, with his boy, to see the Exposition. At half-past four in the morning, at a lonely spot on the road, two men jumped out and hoarsely ordered him to halt. The farmer whipped up his horses. One of the men grabbed the horses by their heads as they sprang into a gallop, clung to them and brought them to a standstill, while the other man leaped into the waggon and struck the farmer over the head with a sandbag. The boy had jumped out and fled. The highwayman was rifling the pockets of the farmer, and was preparing to beat him into utter unconsciousness, when two men with a team drove along. The two robbers fled. The timely arrival of the team saved the farmer's life, for the highwaymen were wrathful over his whipping up his horses to escape.

"What was puzzling me most of all was how the robbers were secreting their plunder. They must have a hiding-place somewhere, for it was impossible to smuggle horses, waggons, buggies, hogs, and other bulky things away and out of the country without some trace of them appearing. Finally a farmer lost a load of sheep, and soon thereafter some sheep were sold by a stranger to a butcher in Barrie. From this butcher I obtained a description of the stranger, and I knew him at once for Charles Humphrey, a desperate crook, who had got out of Kingston the day before the first robbery occurred. He had stolen the minister's horse and buggy, and had driven on from Whitby to the county of Dufferin. After the assault on the farmer on the road to Toronto, Humphrey appeared with the minister's horse and buggy, and tried to sell them, three counties away from where they were stolen. I had arranged for prompt notification if any strangers appeared with any horses, buggies, waggons, hogs, sheep, or household utensils to sell, and when I received word of this offer I immediately started to run down the mystery of the hiding-place of all this booty.

"I traced the stranger along the roads he had taken, and

up in the mountains of the county of Dufferin I came upon a farm, an isolated, lonely place. It had been rented by a stranger, and it was none other than the rendezvous of Charles Humphrey. He would sally forth from it into adjacent counties and steal right and left, from sneak thieving to bold burglaries or desperate hold-ups on the highway. Then back he would travel, under cover of darkness, and hide his plunder. He was stocking the farm by stealing.

"'I was going to land a threshing machine next week,' he said to me after his arrest, and when he was about to return to Kingston.

"'It would have left its tracks in the road,' said I.

"'Oh no,' said he. 'I had that fixed.'

"So he had. After selecting the machine he intended to steal, he had measured its wheels and prepared big leather casings to which he had fastened tyres the width of ordinary tyres. He intended to fit these casings over the wheels, and thus leave only a waggon track in the road.

"Humphrey went back to Kingston Penitentiary for robbery. His pal disappeared, and was none other than his brother. When Humphrey got out recently I had him tried for robbing the church, and he is back in Kingston Penitentiary again, with seven years to serve. When he gets out he can answer for one of the other crimes and go back again. He is too hopelessly clever and irresponsible to be at large."

32

LAING OF LAWRASON'S, THRIFTY THIEF

FEW thieves are thrifty. Most crooks are improvident. Many of them, after realising on their plunder, by its sale at a fence or by the division of stolen money, make a bee line for a gambling house, or fritter it away on wine and women, or spend it in high living on a tour around the country. There are some who save the revenue from their booty, regarding the proceeds of their crimes as their income, and living not only within their means, but putting by a great part of it for a rainy day or old age. Not one in ten thousand, however, gets rich at the business. They earn a living at it, and their earnings go far easier than they come.

" A crook, as a rule, has as little sense in the way he gets rid of his money as he has in the way he gets hold of it," says Murray. " There are crooks who make a living by fleecing crooks; they steal the stealings of other crooks, and they say frankly that a crook is the easiest lamb in the human flock to shear, if you know how to go about it. Occasionally, however, you meet a thrifty thief, who is a miser with his stolen money, and who hoards it, and puts it out to enrich him by legitimate return from honest investment.

" J. P. Lawrason was a private banker in the town of St. George, in the county of Brant. In the first days of 1900 Mr. Lawrason came to Toronto, and called at the Department. He said there was a shortage of $8,000 or more in the funds of his bank. He did a large business, and was desirous of having the matter cleared up. I went to St. George, and looked at the ledgers, and suspicion pointed straight at Arthur E. Laing. Laing was a young man of thirty. He was a prominent church member, was married, had a happy home, and two little children, and was held in high esteem in the community. He had worked for Banker Lawrason for about seven years as accountant, and then went into business for himself.

"'What did you pay this man Laing?' I asked Banker Lawrason.

"'I paid him $35 a month.'

"'Your business is large?'

"'About $1,000,000 a year,' said the banker.

"It was the same old story. Some banking institutions put a premium on crime by not paying employees enough to live on. A salary of $420 a year is not princely, and does not leave a surplus when a man tries to raise a family on it. Yet Laing had been raising a family and prospering. He could not do it on $420 a year. In looking over the ledger I found forty-six pages burned and mutilated beyond legibility These pages had contained various accounts. I went to see Laing.

"'Mr. Laing, who mutilated the Lawrason ledger?' I asked.

"'A lamp,' answered Laing, who was pale and trembling.

"'How did a lamp do it?'

"'The lamp was on the wall, and it happened to fall and set fire to the book,' said Laing.

"'But the lamp was not lighted, was it?'

"'Oh yes, it was dark,' said Laing.

"'How came you in the bank after dark?' I asked.

"'I—I—was doing some left-over work,' said Laing.

"I learned, in talk with townspeople of St. George, that Laing was in the habit, for several years, of making frequent trips to Hamilton. I went to Hamilton, and learned from people who knew him that he usually called at the Bank of Montreal when he was in Hamilton. I found Laing had kept a running account at the Hamilton branch of the Bank of Montreal for several years. This $35 a month man had been making deposits regularly of sums vastly in excess of his salary. The books showed, for instance:

"In 1893, September, 9th, $185.50; October 26th, $300; November 9th, $175; December 14th, $130; December 16th, $150.

"The year 1894 ran the same way, the deposits varying from $85 to $400. On May 2nd, 1895, he had drawn out

$2,693, and later deposited $2,400 more, and in December 1896 withdrew $3,020. These represented money stolen from Banker Lawrason. Laing was saving his stealings. He went about it quite deliberately. To have stolen $20,000, or $50,000, or $100 000 at one grab would have meant instant discovery, and would have necessitated immediate flight, and a life in exile, or a surrender and long term of years in the penitentiary. He set out to steal gradually, bit by bit, the largest amounts possible, and still escape detection. He spread his stealings out over a number of years, and when suspicion seemed imminent he burned the pages in the ledger that would have made it difficult for him to assert his innocence. He did not squander his stolen money. He salted it away, put it out at interest, invested it. He robbed Banker Lawrason of about $8,000 in this way.

"'Mr. Laing,' I said, 'you made your $35 a month go a long way in bank deposits.'

"He went to pieces. It was a total loss of self-control. He ranted at himself for being a fool. Then he abused banks. He said they paid their men meagre wages, and left them to handle thousands when they were in actual need of single dollars. There was quite a painful scene with his wife and children. I arrested him on January 24th, and Magistrate Powell remanded him to Brantford gaol. He practically admitted his guilt. When he came up for trial he was sent to the penitentiary for three years.

"'When your family is dependent on you, and a cold winter is staring you in the face, and you are getting only $35 a month, and have nothing for a rainy day, the sight of thousands of dollars lying around loose is a great inducement,' said Laing.

"So it is, so it is, a powerful inducement—although I suppose nothing should induce an honest man to steal."

33

MELVIN HALL, FREEBOOTER

BURLY, brutal, and brigandish, Melvin Hall spread terror and ruled as a despot in a section of Canada for many years. He was like a border robber of old Scottish days, or a freebooter of the lawless times of early England. He plundered the countryside, he preyed on the farmers, he had an organised band of ruffians and villains and desperadoes, he played fast and loose with the law, he cared not for life or property. His name was a token of trouble, and sight of him was regarded as an ill omen. He dared anything, he feared nothing.

"Massive and powerful, a giant even among big men, he towered six feet four inches and weighed two hundred and forty pounds, with a neck like a bull's, a head like a bulldog's, a chest like a baboon's, and a tread like a panther's," says Murray. "He was forty years old. He rode roughshod through the counties of Stormont, Dundas, and Glengarry, and spread fear along both sides of the St. Lawrence River. One night he would make a raid in the United States and escape in boats across the river. The next night he would sally forth into one of the Canada counties, pillage a farm, and ride away to a hiding-place with his plunder. Wherever he went a part of his gang always was within hail. He warned the country folk that those who sought to bring the law upon him would find their barns burned to the ground, their houses tumbled upon their heads, their crops destroyed, and their cattle killed. He had his headquarters on a lonely tract of land near Morrisburg. Here he planned his crimes.

"Among the members of his gang were his nephew, Luther Hall, a medium-sized, stout young fellow of twenty-five; John Stevens, a swarthy-skinned, black-haired, powerful Scotchman, about thirty-seven years old and fairly well educated; Clarence Benstead, a bullet-headed, square-shouldered, lithe fellow, twenty-seven years old, a great runner and walker; and William Markie, a sullen, blunt, gruff man of few words and great daring. Big Melvin was absolutely master of his men. He ruled like an ancient feudal lord. He held trials, meted out punishments, rewarded friends and persecuted foes. What he wanted he took. A Frenchman named Jenack had a beautiful wife. They lived, with their two little children, on a farm. Big Melvin, driving through the country, saw the handsome Frenchwoman with a party of friends. He sent John Stevens to learn her name and where she lived. Three nights later Big Melvin drove up to the house in a sleigh. He sprang out and kicked the door. Jenack opened it.

"'Where is your wife?' demanded Big Melvin.

"The woman appeared in the background.

"'Get your things and come with me,' said Big Melvin.

"Jenack remonstrated. Big Melvin threw him aside.

"'Have I got to go?' said the woman.

"In answer, Big Melvin picked her up and strode out to the sleigh. The two children ran after their mother, barefoot in the snow, and clung to the runners of the sleigh, crying for her not to leave them. Big Melvin lashed his horses and as they galloped away he reached over, tore the sobbing children loose and flung them into a snowdrift, whence their father rescued them. The woman lived with Big Melvin thereafter at his rendezvous near Morrisburg.

"The people feared to incur Big Melvin's enmity. So he went his lawless way. Dwellings were robbed, cellars and granaries were looted, folk were held up on the highways. Finally Clarence Benstead stole some harness and was caught. The Hall gang warned the countryfolk not to testify against Benstead or any of the gang. But among the witnesses subpœnaed were John McPhee and his wife. McPhee was a farmer and a man of courage. He and his wife went to court to appear against the member of the gang. Melvin Hall was there. He never deserted his men, and the clan always turned out in large numbers with an alibi for the accused. Big Melvin accosted McPhee.

"'McPhee,' said Big Melvin, 'if you give evidence against

Benstead, we'll blow you off the earth.'

"'I've stood it long enough, and danged if I don't tell the truth,' said McPhee. 'I might as well be blown off it as buried into it.'

"This was in March 1900. McPhee testified against Benstead and drove home with Mrs. McPhee, arriving between eight and nine o'clock that night. They had supper, McPhee cared for his horses, and he and his wife sat chatting with their daughter, son-in-law, and grandchild, who had come to spend the night with them. About eleven o'clock, as they were going to bed, the daughter looked out of the window. She saw two shadowy figures approaching the house. One of the two was like a phantom giant.

"'Mother, here come two men,' called the daughter.

"Mrs. McPhee looked out of her window.

"'It's Melvin Hall,' said Mrs. McPhee.

"John McPhee sprang for the door, but before he could open it there was an explosion that rocked the house, smashed the windows, shattered the foundations, knocked the inmates heels over head, and stunned the child lying in bed. It was a dynamite cartridge placed to blow up the McPhees in their room, but luckily they were just retiring at the time and had gone to look out of the window where the daughter had seen the two men.

"All was still for an hour after the explosion. McPhee had crawled to his hands and knees and was sitting by one of the smashed windows. He saw the two figures step out of the gloom and approach the house again. One ran to the door of the house and held it while the other entered the milkhouse. McPhee staggered to his feet, seized an axe, smashed his own door, and sprang out into the night, axe in hand, prepared to battle to the death. Big Melvin came out of the milkhouse, his arms full of plunder. Evidently he thought the McPhees were dead or unconscious, for at sight of McPhee, a ghostly figure swinging an axe, Big Melvin sprang to his horses and away he sped, with his companion, in the night.

"'I know you! I know you!' shouted McPhee, resting on his axe as they disappeared.

"Big Melvin answered with oaths, and galloped on. A young man named Link, who was out late that night, heard galloping horses and heavy curses. He surmised it was Big Melvin, and he darted off the road and concealed himself. Presently Big Melvin and Lu Hall went by, full tilt. Link recognised both of them in the bright moonlight. Big Melvin was swearing. Link hastened on to the farm where he worked, and told his employer that the Hall gang was riding the country again. Link's employer was a fearless man He wakened his son, and they started after the two Halls. They came upon them at the place of a Mr. Emphey, and caught the Halls in the act of stealing and loading grain into a waggon. Big Melvin sprang at them. Father and son were armed with bludgeons. Big Melvin struck the father a heavy blow over the head and down he went. But as he fell, the son, who had put Luther Hall to flight with the stolen grain, turned on Big Melvin and smashed him full on the head with the bludgeon. The giant staggered, swayed, grabbed the son, and hurled him ten feet away, then fell. The son scrambled back, his father revived, and they aroused Mr. Emphey, and dragged Big Melvin into the house, where they dressed his wounds. Big Melvin opened his eyes.

"'I advise you not to try to hold me,' he said. 'I will settle for the grain.'

"The father and son favoured holding him, but Emphey had a plan he deemed better.

"'When will you settle for the grain?' he asked.

"'I will go and get the money, and return here with it,' said Big Melvin. 'I keep my word.'

"Emphey said he would be satisfied, if Hall would bring him the money for the grain. Big Melvin strode out. The moment he was gone Emphey arranged to have three constables notified. The three constables hastened to Emphey's house and secreted themselves. At the appointed time Big Melvin returned. He had kept his word. As he faced Emphey the three constables stepped out.

"'You are under arrest,' said one of them.

"'All right,' said Big Melvin, quietly. 'I'll go.'

"He had thrown off his overcoat when he entered. He

finished his business with Emphey, then turned to the constables.

"'I'll be ready in a moment,' he said, and reached for his overcoat. The constables saw him edging over toward a window with the coat in his arms. They moved forward toward him to put on the handcuffs. With a sudden, mighty swoop of his huge arms, Big Melvin gathered the three of them into a bunch, threw his overcoat over their heads, gave them a tremendous shove, then leaped through the window, sash and all, alighted, with the swarthy John Stevens to aid him, and, with a loud guffaw, sped away.

"The people of the township petitioned the Department for protection. I took up the case immediately. I found Big Melvin gone, Luther Hall gone, John Stevens gone, and the whole gang out of the way or under cover. Big Melvin had a brother back in Iroquois. I set a watch on the brother. He secretly sent a letter from Iroquois to be mailed at Waddington. I intercepted the letter, and thereby learned Big Melvin was hiding over in the United States. He had been staying on a farm near Watertown, in Northern New York. He was a saving thief, and had plenty of money. I prepared extradition papers, and crossed the river to New York. I found Big Melvin on the farm, and he made a great fuss, denying his identity, and fighting extradition. I learned he had been stealing in New York as he had done in Canada. His fight was futile. He was handed over to me for trial in Canada. He raged and swore when he learned he had to go back.

"I took Big Melvin back across the river to stand trial. I have seen crowded court-houses in my day, but the court-house at the trial of Big Melvin was packed to its utmost capacity. The country folk attended from all around. The evidence was overwhelming. Big Melvin was convicted, and he went to Kingston Penitentiary for ten years.

"John Stevens, or Stevenson, was caught, convicted, and got seven years. Luther Hall slipped over from the United States on a visit, and we got him. At his trial in October, 1901, he had about fifteen choice witnesses to swear to an alibi. I showed where every one of this choice collection had been charged or convicted of crime at some time. One of them, thirty-four years before, had stolen a bee-hive. There was nothing the Hall gang would not steal. When Clarence Benstead skipped over the river, he stole from a farmer in New York. He sneaked back into Canada, and hid about twenty miles from Ottawa. During the trials of the Halls I got track of him, and communicated with Sheriff Harder across the river. Benstead was taken before Judge McTavish, of Ottawa, and sent to New York, where he got six years. Bill Markie was caught near Morrisburg, and joined Big Melvin, Luther, and John Stevens in Kingston Penitentiary. Big Melvin, in prison garb, saw his men one by one join the marching lines inside the Kingston walls.

"'They follow their leader,' he said grimly."

34

THE MURDER OF JOSEPH SIFTON

EVERYBODY in Canada who knew Joseph Sifton well called him Old Joe. He was only fifty-eight, but he was fond of folk younger than himself, and for a number of years he had been known as Old Joe. Some said that when he was only forty they had heard people speaking of him in this way. He was rich, as riches go in the farming section where he lived. His home was in the township of London, a few miles from the city of London, Ontario. He owned three or four farms. His wife was dead, and he had one child, a son, named Gerald Sifton, who was thirty years old and lived with his wife on one of the farms.

"For some time Old Joe lived with Gerald, but could not get along with Gerald's wife," says Murray. "So he went to keep bachelor's hall on one of his other farms. At Gerald's lived a good-looking hired girl named Mary McFarlane, whose mother lived in the same township. Mary was an intelligent, bright girl, and Old Joe, unknown to Gerald or Gerald's wife, began to court Mary. It developed later that Mary expected to become a mother, and Old Joe was going to marry her before this would come to pass. In fact, they had set the day, without telling the Siftons or the McFarlanes. It was to be July 1st, 1900. On the morning of June 30th, Old Joe was found, with bleeding head, lying on the ground in front of his barn, as if he had fallen out of the hay mow. He died that afternoon. The Attorney-General happened to be in London a few days later, and County Attorney McGee spoke to him about Old Joe's death, as there was a lot of talk. I went to investigate.

"I began the usual round of inquiry among the family and neighbours. I learned that the day before Old Joe's death Gerald Sifton, the son, had been to London, and did not return until nine o'clock in the evening. Old Joe had bought a wedding ring, and while Gerald was away he took Mary McFarlane in a buggy to see her mother and obtain her consent to their marriage. Mrs. McFarlane refused to sanction the match, saying Joe was too old for Mary. Then Mary told her mother that she had to get married, and she and Old Joe drove away. In the meantime Mary's brother, driving home, met a neighbour named John Sinker.

"'Congratulations!' said John Sinker to young McFarlane. 'I hear that Old Joe is going to marry your sister.'

"Young McFarlane turned around, and drove back to Gerald Sifton's. His sister Mary was there, having returned from her mother's. Mary denied it. Her brother hunted up John Sinker, and told him not to spread such stories about his sister. Sinker replied that all he knew about it was that Old Joe had been to him to borrow his best buggy, saying he intended to marry Mary Mcfarlane. Back to Gerald Sifton's went young McFarlane and saw his sister again, and Mary acknowledged it. Mrs. Gerald Sifton heard the talk, and when her husband returned from London she told him that Old Joe and Mary were about to be married. Gerald Sifton started off on his wheel. He rode to the house of James Morden, a neighbour.

"'There is the devil to pay over at our place,' James Morden stated Gerald said to him. 'The old man is going to marry Mary McFarlane. I'll see he never marries her. If you lend me a hand and help me to kill the old —— I'll give you $1000.'

"'Oh no,' said Jim Morden. 'I'll do nothing of that kind.'

"Gerald argued with Jim, but it was useless, so Gerald rode on to the house of Edgar Morden, Jim's cousin, and made the same proposition. Edgar refused. Gerald then asked him where Martin Morden lived in London. Martin was Edgar's cousin, and was engaged to Mary McFarlane, who was about to marry Old Joe. Edgar told Gerald he did not know Martin's address. So Gerald rode back to Jim Morden and got the address, and started for London. After he had gone, Edgar Morden went to look for Old Joe to warn him to look out. The old man was not at home. Edgar started for Gerald's, thinking Old Joe might be there. It was very dark, and as he neared the house he came upon Old Joe and Mary McFarlane sitting in a buggy under a tree. He told them what Gerald was doing.

"'You had better come to my place,' said Edgar.

"Old Joe and Mary accompanied Edgar to his home, and while there Old Joe drew up a will. They sat up at Edgar Morden's talking until almost dawn, when Old Joe drove to his own house, taking Mary with him. They arrived there shortly after five o'clock.

"Gerald Sifton, meanwhile, had gone to London. He arrived there about one o'clock in the morning. He met Policeman Robinson, and asked him to show him the way to Martin Morden's boarding-house. Robinson did so, and Gerald went in and found Martin. He told Martin that Mary had betrayed him, and while engaged to him was planning to marry Old Joe. Martin stated later that Gerald then offered him $1,000 to kill the old man,

"'So long as Mary is doing that, I want nothing to do with her, and I will kill no man,' said Martin.

"Gerald was familiar with medicines and drugs, as he had studied for a horse-doctor. He pulled out a phial before Martin.

"'I'll see he never gets married,' Martin stated Gerald said. 'You know what that is?'

"'Yes, strychnine?'

"'That's it,' said Gerald.

"Martin could not be persuaded. Gerald left him, and at dawn was back home. He had a hired man working for him, a big overgrown boy, twenty years old. Walter Herbert was his name. Gerald called Walter aside, and offered him $1,000 to go over and finish the old man.

"'We'll say he fell out of the barn,' said Gerald to Walter Herbert.

"Herbert refused. Gerald finally agreed to accompany him. About seven o'clock that morning Gerald and Herbert arrived at Old Joe's house. Old Joe and Mary were there, having driven over from Edgar Morden's. Gerald shouted

" 'Come out and show where you want this hay fork put?' he called.

"Mary McFarlane cautioned Old Joe not to go out.

" 'He's come to kill you,' said Mary.

"Old Joe laughed. He was a husky old fellow, and could have walloped his son with ease in a fair fight. So Old Joe went out. When he appeared, Gerald and Walter Herbert went up into the barn. It was a bank barn next the house. There was a ladder leading up through a little trap into the mow.

"Walter Herbert later told what happened then. He said he and Gerald climbed up into the mow. Gerald handed him the axe and said:

" 'When he puts his head up give it to him.'

"They waited, this son and his hired man, for the old father to climb up to his death. They heard him enter the barn, they heard him start up the ladder, climbing rung after rung. The grey head appeared. Walter raised the axe.

" 'I struck him once, then my heart failed me and I dropped the axe and reached down and grabbed him,' he said. 'Gerald, who had been standing back, came and seized the axe and struck his father several hard blows on the head. He fell down. We pulled him up into the hay mow and cracked him again, and then pitched him out of the mow down on to bricks on the ground outside. A couple of boards had been knocked off the side of the barn, and we threw him out through there head first.'

"Gerald then told Herbert to go and tell the neighbours of Old Joe's fall.

"Mary McFarlane came out of the house. She saw Old Joe lying bleeding. Gerald and Herbert were there.

" 'Oh, you done it!' cried Mary.

" 'Don't say that,' answered Herbert.

"The doctor came. Gerald urged that Old Joe be kept from suffering, and told the doctor he had strychnine. The doctor shook his head.

" 'Would money be any consideration?' said this dutiful son.

"Old Joe died that afternoon, and some days later the

matter came to the attention of the Department. No inquest had been held, and Old Joe was underground. But Walter Herbert confessed, and repeated his confession to his uncle and to a constable. On July 26th, 1900, I arrested Gerald Sifton and Walter Herbert, charged with murdering Gerald's father. They were held for trial. Gerald had one set of counsel and Walter Herbert had another set of counsel. When they were brought in for trial, Herbert, to the consternation of Gerald, pleaded guilty. After this plea the counsel for Gerald got a postponement of the trial. In fact they obtained two postponements.

"Finally, in September 1901, over a year after the crime, Gerald Sifton's trial began. The evidence as I have indicated it was presented. Walter Herbert took the stand, and told the whole story of the black deed. Justice McMahon presided at the trial, and the late Judge William Lount prosecuted. I had been away from January to April of 1901, travelling in the West Indies and visiting friends in Jamaica, the Barbadoes, and England, but I was home in ample time for the trial, even if it had come in the Spring instead of the Fall Assizes. To the amazement of those familiar with the case the jury disagreed. It stood ten for conviction and two for acquittal.

"Over a year passed before the second trial began. In November 1902 the second jury came in. Justice B. B Britton presided at the trial, and R. C. Clute prosecuted. The defence sought to discredit the Crown's witnesses, the defence also produced two witnesses who swore they saw Old Joe going to the barn with an axe to put up a hay fork, the defence also alleged Herbert was not telling the truth. Two of the Mordens, James and Martin, had left the country. I saw them in Davenport, Iowa. The jury brought in a verdict of not guilty. Gerald Sifton walked out a free man so far as the law was concerned. There was indignation over the result. The next grand jury condemned the trial.

"I say now that it was a miscarriage of justice and a disgrace to the country."

35

THE CRIME OF CHARLIE KING

IN the county of Elgin, one of the three counties where Acker and Reilly played fast and loose with the farmers, lived Daniel B. Freeman, a well-to-do farmer, whose land was in the township of Oldboro. In 1886 he and his wife adopted a baby boy and raised him as their own and gave him their own name. He turned out to be a good boy, and in 1902, when he was sixteen, he had grown big and strong for his age. The Freemans cherished him as their own child.

"His name was Willie B. Freeman," says Murray. "Ten years after he was adopted by the Freemans, Daniel Freeman went to the Fagan Home in Toronto, and got an eighteen-year-old boy to work on his farm. The Fagan Home imports English waifs to Canada and places them in honest lines of work. The boy taken by Daniel Freeman was named Charlie King. He was ten years older than Willie Freeman. Six years passed. Charlie King lived with the Freemans, Willie as their son and Charlie as the hired man. Charlie never drank, never smoked. He indulged in church freely, and was a leader of the Epworth League in the Methodist Church, and acted as librarian.

"On the morning of September 6th, 1902, King put up a load of peaches for Daniel Freeman to take to the village in the afternoon. Before Mr. Freeman started, Willie went into the tool-house and was making a pin for a gate on a lathe, when his father drove away. His mother called and he answered her through the window of the drive house. Daniel Freeman had not driven far from his house when he heard the report of a gun. Squirrels were thick and annoying, and a gun was kept in the tool-house for shooting them. Freeman thought it was King shooting at squirrels, although he had been forbidden to use the gun, and Willie never used it. A few minutes after the gunshot, King entered the house and went to Mrs. Freeman.

"'Willie has shot himself," said King. "He's lying dead on the shave horse in the drive house.'

"Mrs. Freeman ran out and upstairs in the drive house, and when she saw Willie she fled screaming. Daniel Freeman, on the road to the village, heard his wife scream and turned back. He went up into the drive house with King. Willie was dying from a gunshot wound in the head. Doctors came, but simply were in time to see him die. King told Mr. Freeman that he heard the gunshot, went upstairs in the drive house and found Willie, shot. The inquest was held and King went on the stand and told his straight story. The boy was buried. Then Daniel Freeman thought it all over and he notified me through the County Attorney. On September 11th, 1902, I went to St. Thomas, got Dr. Lawrence and Dr. Duncan, and on September 13th drove to the village of Bismarck and got Dr. Webster, who attended the boy, and then we four drove to the cemetery and had the body exhumed and made a post-mortem. I saw no powder marks on the face. Moreover the shot had scattered over the forehead in a radius of four and a half to five and a half inches. The gun was not fired at close range or the shot would not have scattered. If it was not fired at close range then clearly the boy did not shoot himself. We drove to the Freeman house. I asked for Charlie King. He came out very slowly.

"'I want you to go over the ground with me inch by inch, and tell me just what happened when you found Willie dying,' I said.

"'He—he—was up—he was in the——' began King, who was quite excited, pointing to the drive house.

"'No, come with me,' I said, leading the way to the foot of the stairs in the drive house. 'Now show me where you were standing.'

"'I went upstairs and saw Willie——' began King.

"'Go on up; I will follow,' said I. 'Go up just as you went up when you found Willie.'

" We mounted the stairs, King first, I behind.

"'Where was Willie?' I asked.

"'He was on the lathe,' said King.

"'Show me exactly where he was,' said I. 'You get on the shave horse and show me.'

" King shivered and then dropped limply across the shave horse, with his head hanging down.

"'Keep your head down,' I said. 'Don't move till I tell you.'

" I stood for several minutes in silence. I could hear King breathing hard. I saw that the position of the body on the shave horse was quite possible, provided the boy had not shot himself. A man who shoots himself is apt to go toward the shot. If you shoot a man across the road he will fall toward you.

"'Where was the gun?' I asked.

"'It was beside him,' said King.

" I got a long stick about the length of the gun.

"'Call this the gun,' I said. 'You get on the lathe again and show me how you could shoot yourself with that gun.'

" King tried to do so but it was an awkward and unlikely attempt.

"'Was any one about but you?' I asked.

"'No one,' said King.

"'Are you sure?' I asked.

"'Sure,' answered King. 'Mrs. Freeman was in the house and I was here.'

" I eyed him, eyed him long and steadily, until he flushed and paled and shifted uneasily. We were alone in the loft of the tool-house, he and I. The doctors were waiting outside with the County Attorney. All was still.

"'King,' I said sternly, 'you or Mrs. Freeman shot him.'

"'I didn't! I didn't!' he cried.

"'What did you do with the gun?' I asked. 'What did you do with it after you saw Willie on the lathe, dying?'

"'I—I—took it downstairs,' he said.

"'Why?' I demanded. 'Tell me why you took the gun

dowstairs and left Willie up here to die?'

"'So—so—no blood would get on it,' said King.

"He was shaken. He began to quiver and shift. I stood looking at him, waiting in silence.

"'Well?' I said.

"He started, hesitated, then burst into tears.

"'Oh! oh! Will I be hung? Will I be hung?' he moaned.

"He writhed as if in physical pain. I called out of the window for Mr. Donohue, the County Attorney, to come up. He came at once.

"'Did you shoot Willie Freeman?' I asked King, in his presence.

"'Oh! oh! I did! Oh! oh!' sobbed King.

"I had him take the stick for a gun, and show us how he did it.

"'I went halfway up the stairs to the left,' said King, on the stairs. 'I stood here, and I aimed like this for his eye. His head was bent over, and he had on an old straw hat. I fired. He fell. Then I went down and told Mrs. Freeman.'

"'What motive had you? Why did you do it?' I asked.

"'They always made too much of him, and I had to do the dirty work, and I thought if I shot him I might get his place,' said King.

"I called in the doctors, and made King show them how he killed the boy. I arrested King. He asked if he could go into the house a minute on his way to gaol. I took him in, and he asked the forgiveness of the Freemans.

"'Oh, Charlie, Charlie! Why did you shoot my Willie?' moaned Mrs. Freeman.

"'I thought I'd get his place,' said King.

"I took him away to gaol. He was tried in St. Thomas in April 1903, a few months ago. Justice Street presided. King's confession to me as an officer was ruled out of court. The defence, however, admitted King did the shooting, but alleged it was accidental, and claimed that King was not competent to understand the nature of the case. He was found guilty of manslaughter on April 23rd, 1903, and at the present time is serving his sentence."

36

IN CONCLUSION

"WHEN a man looks back over his life," says Murray, "he smiles at thought of episodes that seemed very solemn and serious in their day. Time mellows his memory. In the recollections of my career as a detective, that I have cited here, I have given simply characteristic cases. I have passed over countless minor cases, and some larger ones that were counterparts of other crimes of which I have spoken. For crime often duplicates itself in monotonous reproduction of details. Death, for instance, comes usually along well-known thoroughfares, in crime. It travels the way of the shot, the knife, the flame, the drowning, the poison, or the strangling. Its means are limited, but the manner of their manifestation is as varied as anything under the sun. There are few criminals of genius, and particularly there are few murderers with a genius for their work.

"Few make a success of crime. Crime is a merciless, miserly taskmaster. It exacts all and gives little. It does not pay. It is a calling for fools. Yet men of intellect enter it deliberately, and here and there one of them may seem to succeed. If they devoted half the thought, energy, skill, and daring to any other line of business they would make a far greater success of life and of work. But they seem destined to pool their existence with the lives of the hunted. The criminal class goes its way, distinct and separate in itself. It has its own ideas of life, its own laws for its lawless business. It defies authority, and authority, in turn, pounces upon it and metes out punishment.

"I suppose I should take the view that this world is a wicked, dangerous place, infested with masked murderers or desperate workers in the darkness, who rob and slay and well-nigh deprive us of the joy of living. But I hold no such opinion. This world is a grand place, life is a glorious thing. Crime increases, but not out of proportion to the increase in the population of our countries and of the whole world. Where men and women are there will be found good and bad. But the bad are a hopeless minority. Our prisons do not hold the bulk or the majority of our population, and yet a fair share of those who ought to be in prison eventually get there.

"As civilisation and science advance, crime also will advance. The detective business of the future will be far ahead of the detective business of the past. I hope that the future will see it raised to the high place of a profession, whose members will have a pride in their calling and a careful preparation for their duties.

"As for me, I often think of the bygone cases, of quaint characters, of puzzling mysteries, of the solutions, and of the aftermath. They are the children of my career, and as I look over my large and flourishing family in the mansion of my memory, I sit back luxuriously and remark to myself:

"'Well, Murray, you've done pretty well, after all.'"